I0793170

IMAGES
of America
PEND OREILLE COUNTY

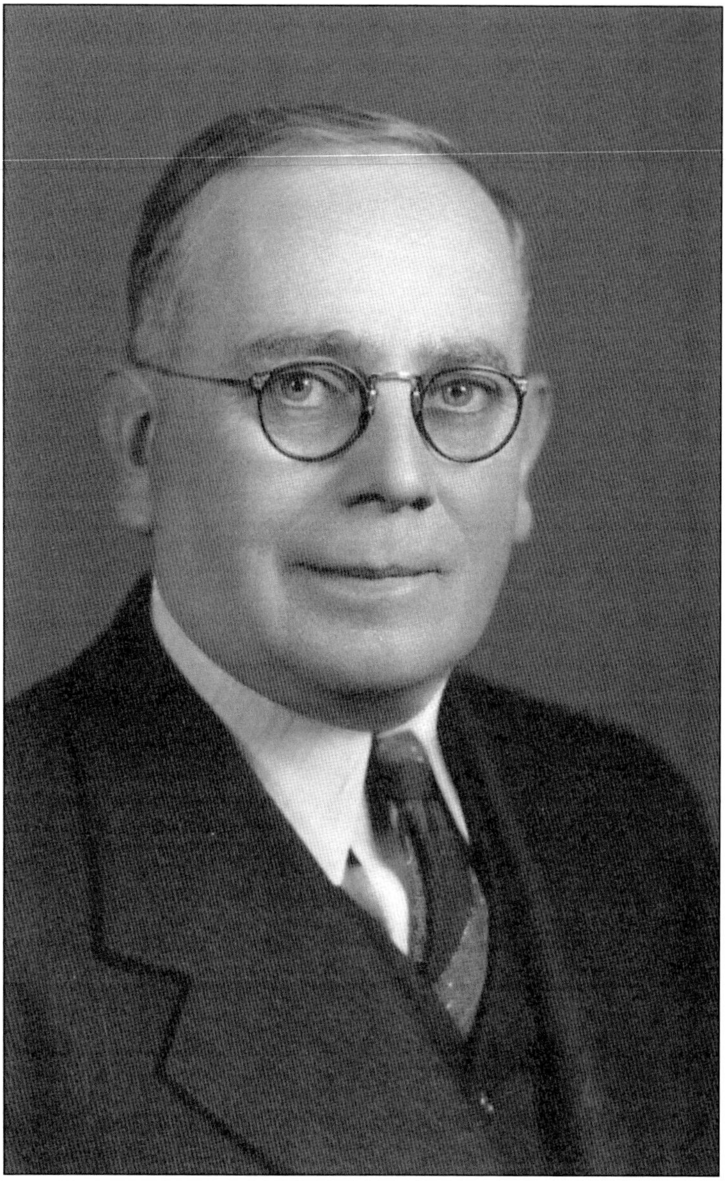

Father of Pend Oreille County. Fred Wolf was born in Elkader, Iowa, on June, 14, 1877. Beginning his newspaper career in the early 1890s, Wolf came to Newport, Washington, in 1907. He bought the *Newport Miner* and published it until 1945. Wolf played an important role in the formation of Pend Oreille County, was elected to the Washington State House of Representatives, and led a successful campaign for the construction of the Interstate Bridge at Newport. He was also president of the Farmers State Bank, a booster of good roads, and a promoter of the county. (Courtesy of the Pend Oreille Historical Society.)

On the Cover: *Elk* Steamboat. Delegates headed for Colville in Stevens County are getting on the *Elk* steamer at the Elk Landing, below Box Canyon, near Metaline, Washington, in the early 1900s. Joe Cusick, the captain, stands at the right of the wheelhouse. (Courtesy of the Pend Oreille Historical Society.)

IMAGES
of America

PEND OREILLE COUNTY

Faith Sheila McClenny

ARCADIA
PUBLISHING

ISBN 978-1-4671-3420-0

Published by Arcadia Publishing
Charleston, South Carolina

Printed in the United States of America

Library of Congress Control Number: 2015936425

For all general information, please contact Arcadia Publishing:
Telephone 843-853-2070
Fax 843-853-0044
E-mail sales@arcadiapublishing.com
For customer service and orders:
Toll-Free 1-888-313-2665

Visit us on the Internet at www.arcadiapublishing.com

To my mother, Julia Anne Clark, who told humorous, tragic, and interesting stories of her family in Ireland, sparking my thirst for history.

Contents

Acknowledgments

Since the early 1900s, people have saved pictures, diaries, and records of the history of Pend Oreille County. Others have sorted, indexed, and cataloged reams of information. It is impossible to list and thank all those who helped to preserve the county's history. As a result of their work, today, the Pend Oreille County Historical Society and Museum is an irreplaceable jewel of the county and the city of Newport. Many thanks to Yvonne Piper, Suzette Keyser, Candace Bradley, Winnie Sundseth, Meg Decker, and Merrill and Muriel Oaks for proofreading; Suzanne and Tony Bamonte for historical information; and Duane Becker and Skip Lightx for computer technical help, support, and encouragement. Thanks to Matt Todd and Arcadia Publishing for preserving history. All photographs not otherwise noted are from the Pend Oreille County Historical Society Museum Collection.

INTRODUCTION

All the people who have stepped into this region have contributed to its history. They have in some way changed it, for good or for bad. Enterprising French Canadian fur traders were among the first white men to come into the Pend Oreille area. They called the local Indians "Pend d'Oreille" (pond-a-RAY), meaning "dangling earrings." Historians believe the Pend d'Oreille and Kalispel tribes wore shell earrings obtained in trade with coastal Indians.

Scenic Pend Oreille County is located in the northeast corner of Washington State. It is 67 miles long and 22 miles wide. The county has a total of 1,400 square miles of land and 25 square miles of water in the river, lakes, streams, and wetlands.

The interesting geography of the county was formed during prehistoric ages. Massive earth movements resulted in the formation of the rugged Selkirk Mountains. Ice-age glaciers and catastrophic floods formed the Calispel Valley and some of the lakes and forced the south-flowing river to turn north. The mountain range and river are the prominent natural features that have shaped the history and development of the county.

The tree-covered Selkirk Mountains cover southeastern British Columbia, the Idaho Panhandle, and the northeast corner of Washington. They were named after Canadian philanthropist Sir Thomas Selkirk. Gypsy Peak (7,325 feet) has the highest elevation in Eastern Washington. The north end of the county had abundant resources of lead, zinc, limestone, and quartzite, which fueled the mining and cement industries for scores of years. The virgin forests kept sawmills running until the 1970s.

The beautiful Pend Oreille River runs through a trench valley between the Selkirk Mountains. It flows for 130 miles out of Lake Pend Oreille, Idaho. At the Idaho and Washington border, it turns north into Canada and joins the mighty Columbia River.

According to ongoing archaeological work, people have inhabited the region for between 5,000 to 10,000 years. In the late 1700s, various Indian tribes, including the Kalispel Indians, claimed as their territory what is now Western Montana, the Idaho Panhandle, a sliver of British Columbia, and northeastern Washington. Eventually, the Kalispel tribe home base was established along the Pend Oreille River. Semi-nomadic hunters and gatherers, their life revolved around the seasons and their environment. In the 1800s, Kalispel life and culture started to change with the appearance of horses and white people. David Thompson, a Canadian fur trader, explorer, and cartographer, made three trips into the region, in 1809, 1810, and 1811, to search for furs and to look for the source of the Columbia River. The first white man to visit the area, he made detailed journals of flora, fauna, and resources, and mapped the area. In the mid-1800s, other white people started to venture into Kalispel territory. Prospectors trudged over the Indian trails, dreaming of another California gold rush. Around the same time, Protestant and Catholic missionaries entered the region.

In 1844, Father Jean Pierre DeSmet and Father Adrian Hoecken, with the help of Indian converts, established the St. Ignatius Mission along the Pend Oreille River. The mission was destroyed by a flood in 1954. A small group of Kalispel Indians moved to Montana and established a new St. Ignatius Mission. The traditional life of the Kalispel continued to change with the influx of setters into the region. For years, the tribe was transitioning from the old ways of living to the white man's ways. On March 24, 1914, an executive order established a 4,629-acre reservation across the Pend Oreille River from Usk, Washington.

The rugged terrain and the thick forests delayed the permanent settlement of the Pend Oreille region. However, with the incentive of the Homestead Act of 1862 and reports of rich resources that began to trickle into other areas, people became interested. Pioneers, packing their belongings on their backs, trudged over the Indian trails into the wilderness. The first white people settled in the Calispel Valley and raised cattle. Others settled along the Pend Oreille River and in the mountain areas. Family members often had to find jobs, such as logging, mining, or harvesting, in the Palouse region or in Spokane in order to survive.

In the late 1800s, a number of small trading posts sprang up wherever people gathered to pick up supplies, mail, and to catch up on news. Primitive mines were worked in the northern part of the region, and small sawmills started to supply the needs of nearby settlers. As the population increased, steamboats were used for transportation of people, mail, and freight. In 1892, the Great Northern Railroad was built to Newport, and in 1908, the Idaho & Washington Northern Railroad reached Newport and continued on to Metaline Falls. Changes in the region accelerated with the arrival of improved and dependable transportation. The era of large steamboats faded away.

The Pend Oreille Valley region was part of Stevens County. A mountain range separated the Colville Valley from the Pend Oreille Valley region. Between the late 1800s and 1910, many changes took place in the eastern part of Stevens County. Population was increasing, transportation was improving, and mining, logging, and agriculture businesses were growing. The future was looking bright for the Pend Oreille region. Homesteaders and settlers were thinking about separating from Stevens County. As feelings grew stronger, Fred Wolf, owner and publisher of the *Newport Miner*, and Fred Trumbull, an Ione attorney, formed a committee to consider the issue. Wolf was sent to the state legislature as a lobbyist. The Washington State legislature passed a bill in March 1911 to create the new county. Gov. Marion E. Hay signed it into law in June 1911. Wolf suggested the new county be named Pend Oreille, after the original inhabitants. Newport, gateway to the region, had the largest population and became the county seat.

Lewis Larsen and Fredrick Blackwell were the leaders in the mining and lumbering industries. Gold-hungry prospectors scoured creeks for gold in the Pend Oreille Valley in the 1850s. Miners staked claims for lead and zinc. However, primitive transportation presented obstacles to getting the ore out of the area. F.G. Jordan and Lewis Larsen both discovered mountains of limestone and quartzite, ores that are necessary for manufacturing cement. In 1901, Jordan set up the Pacific Cement Company, and the community of Cement grew up around the plant. Almost from the start, Jordan was dogged by financial difficulties; the plant and the community began to disappear by 1907.

Lewis Larsen, founder of Metaline Falls, was able to secure financial help and established the Inland Portland Cement Company. In 1914, the Lehigh Portland Cement Company of Allentown, Pennsylvania, purchased Larsen's firm. Cement manufacturing was the backbone business of Metaline Falls for over 60 years. Larsen and others established the Metaline Mining District, which became the leading producer of lead and zinc until strikes and financial problems hit the district in the early 1950s. Teck American Company is reopening the mines at the present time.

The first pioneers started logging and lumbering businesses. Edwin Winchester ran the first sawmill in order to meet settlers' needs. It was followed by other small mills cutting ties for the railroads. The Panhandle Lumber Company, owned and operated by Fredrick Blackwell, and the Diamond Match Lumber Company dominated the logging and lumber industry for many years. The Panhandle sawmill was the backbone in Ione for years. Diamond Match Lumber had several sawmills in the county and produced stock for making wooden matches. The large sawmill at Diamond City had a three-and-a-half-mile tram that carried lumber across the Pend Oreille River. In the busy years of the lumber industry, there were hundreds of large and small sawmills producing lumber for the Inland Empire. In addition to lumber, the industry was producing cedar poles, railroad ties, and posts. The cedar poles were needed for the burgeoning electric, telephone, and telegraph systems throughout the country.

Pend Oreille County also had a healthy agriculture business, which supplied hay and grain for thousands of horses and food for hundreds of loggers, sawmill workers, and miners.

As a result of these flourishing industries, dozens of booming communities sprouted up around sawmills or mines throughout the county. Alas, when the main resources were exhausted, some of the communities struggled to survive, and others became ghost towns. Communities at better locations, with more resources and supporting businesses, survived. Over the years, Newport, Cusick, Ione, Metaline, and Metaline Falls were incorporated, and they continue at the present time.

Today, Pend Oreille County continues to make changes as it moves into the future. Ponderay Newsprint, near Usk, has replaced the mills. Teck America Corporation is renewing the mining industry in the north end of the county. People are drawn to the area by the top-notch entertainment at the Cutter Theatre in Metaline Falls, the friendly County Fair at Cusick, rodeo at Newport, art groups, water sports, and outdoor activities. The mountains, lakes, and river lure tourists, businesses, and those who appreciate quiet rural living to Pend Oreille County.

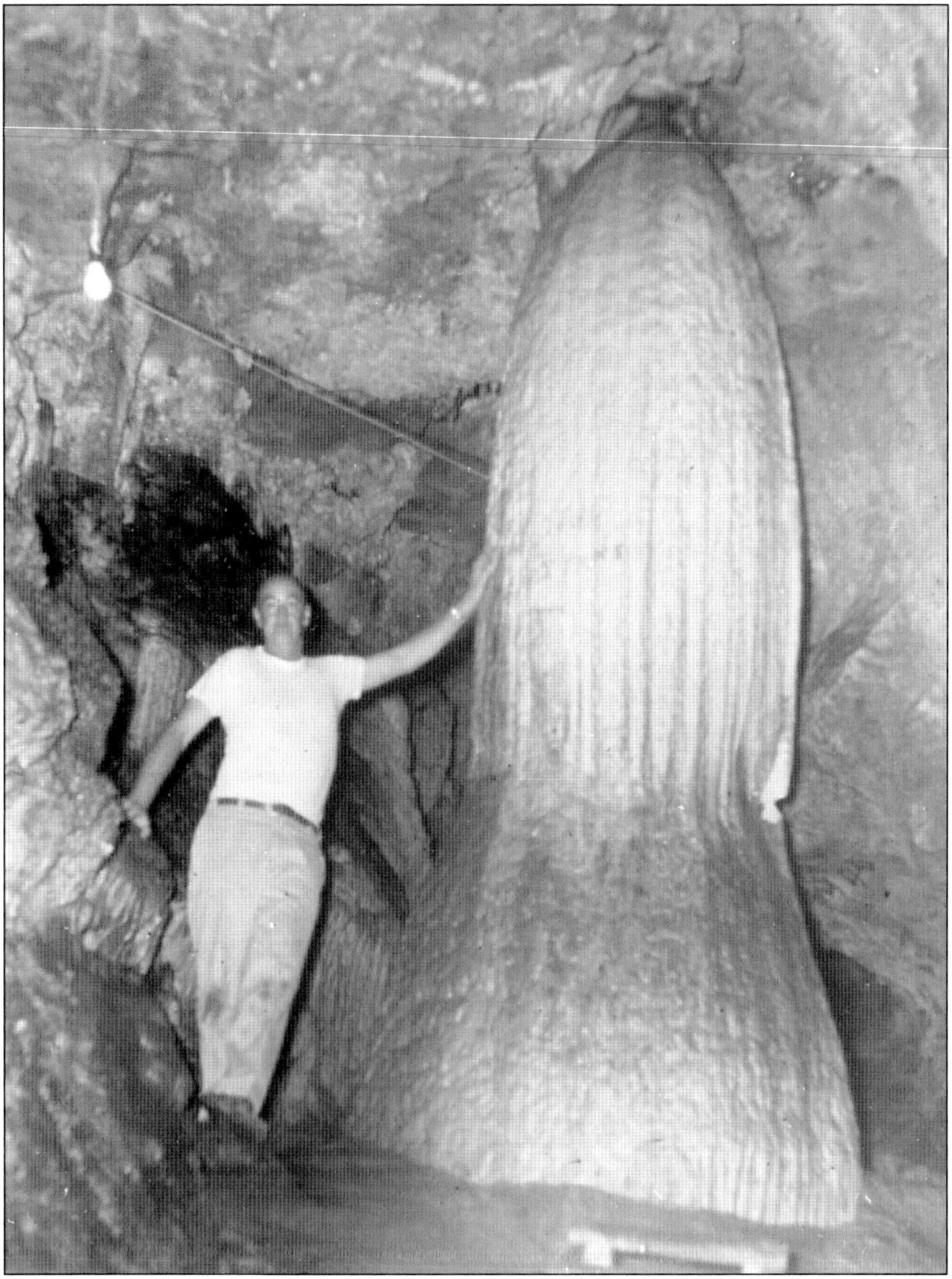

Gardner Cave. The second-largest limestone cave in Washington State, Gardner Cave is located in Crawford State Park, about 11 miles northeast of Metaline. It was discovered in 1899 by Ed Gardner and bears his name. Folk stories claim that Gardner, a bootlegger who had a moonshine still nearby, often kept his liquor in the cool cave. Today, only occasional packrats and bats occupy the cave. In 1921, W.H. Crawford, a Metaline Falls merchant, acquired 40 acres of land around the cave and deeded it to the State of Washington for use as a park. The interesting cave has stalactites and stalagmites, which are formed by weak acid water that seeps through the ground. Rimstone pools are formed in shallow basins in the floor. Visitors are asked to stop at the local US Forest Service ranger station for information.

One

Selkirk Mountains and Pend Oreille River

The rugged terrain of the Selkirk Mountains and the treacherous Pend Oreille River delayed the settlement of the area. The mountains cover most of Pend Oreille County. Geologists consider the range to be part of the Cabinet Mountains and the western edge of the Rocky Mountains. Gypsy Peak (7,325 feet), the highest point in the county, is located in the Selmo-Priest Wilderness area in the Selkirk Mountains, in the northern part of the county. Monumental Mountain (5,669 feet) and Calispel Peak (6,855 feet) are located in about the middle of the county.

The rich ore resources kept the mines, quarries, and the cement business periodically active since 1910 in the Metaline region. Logging camps and sawmills were running until the late 1970s. The mountains abound with wildlife, including grizzly bears, deer, lynx, wolves, and other animals. The wilderness is considered ideal for those interested in birds, plants, and butterflies, and is a rock hound's paradise.

The Pend Oreille River, a major tributary of the Columbia River, flows through a narrow valley in the middle of the county. The river flows for over 60 miles from Newport to just over the Canadian border, where it joins the Columbia River. Prior to the construction of three hydroelectric dams in the 1950s and 1960s, the turbulent river flowed past forested mountains and roared over Box Canyon Falls, went through Grandview Canyon, and squeezed through the 18-foot-wide Z Canyon, where the river turned on its edge between 200- and 500-foot rocky cliffs.

Pend Oreille County has several unusual and interesting geographic features, such as the limestone Gardner Cave system in Crawford State Park, the Manresa Grotto (Indian Caves) on the Kalispel Indian Reservation, and the rather mysterious Devil's Well, a 50-foot-wide hole filled with water year-round.

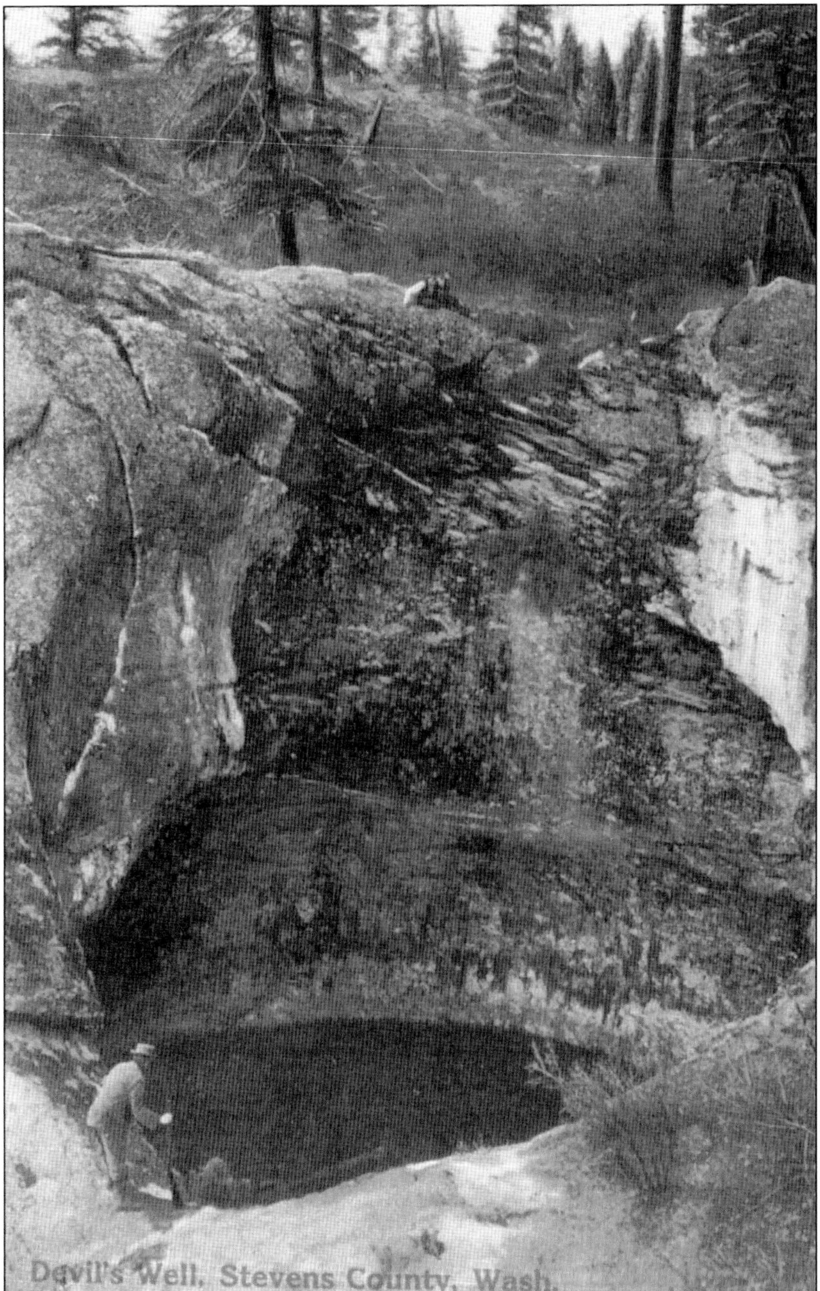

DEVIL'S WELL. Located on a cliff overlooking Horseshoe Lake in the southern end of the county is a geological oddity, Devil's Well. It is a large, vertical hole about 50 feet across with smooth granite walls. The hole is filled with water of an indefinite depth. It is kept full of water, which seeps through the ground or comes from rainfall. During the spring runoff, the water rapidly swirls in a circular motion as it exits through cracks in the wall. Pend Oreille County is a fascinating region for rock hounds and geologists interested in ores, gems, fossils, and geological oddities. Newport lies at the tip of the horseshoe-shaped Newport fault, one of the stranger geologic structures in Washington. The Tiger geographic area contains sandstone and pebble conglomerates.

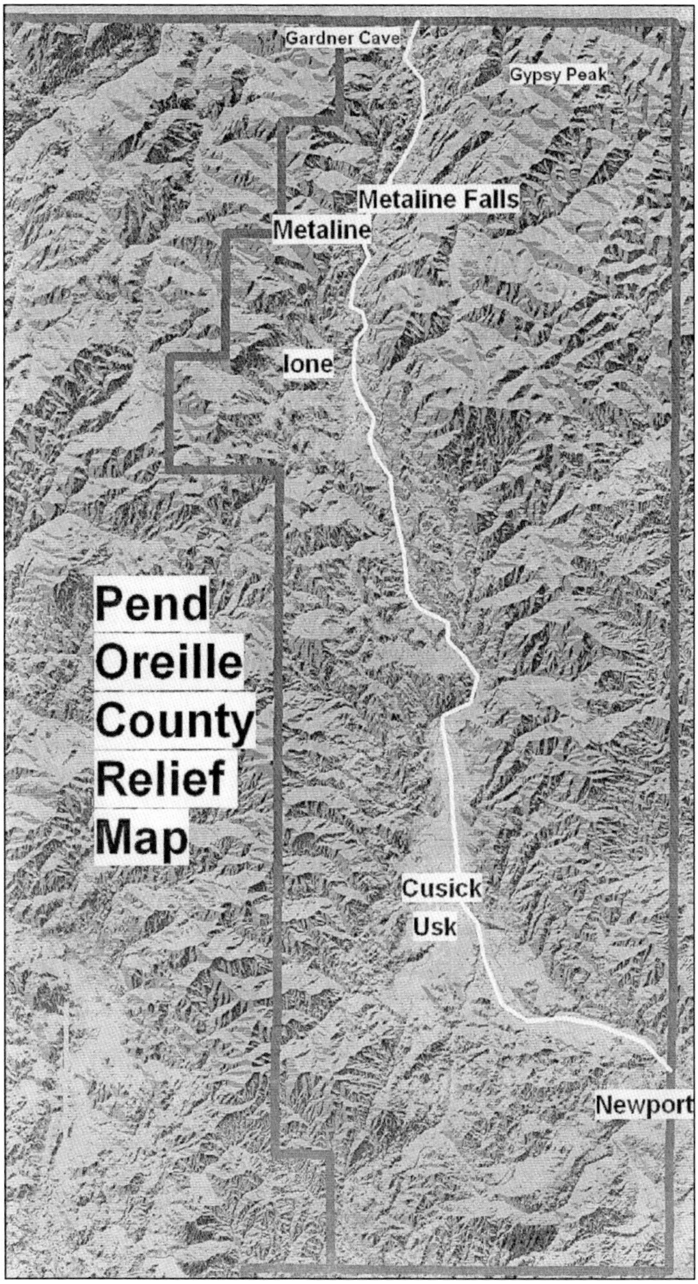

County Relief Map. This relief map of Pend Oreille County shows the geographic features of the Selkirk Mountains, Pend Oreille River, and five principal towns. Prior to the coming of white people in the late 1800s, the mountains were covered with thick virgin forests. As the Pend Oreille River flows north, it gradually falls deeper and deeper into the trench valley running through the middle of the mountains. From Newport to Jared, Washington, it falls about 10 feet; from Jared to Metaline Falls, it drops almost 30 feet; and, as the river flows farther north, it drops 210 feet through Z Canyon and Grandview Canyon to the Canadian border. Hydroelectric dams at Albeni Falls, Box Canyon, and Z Canyon constructed in the 1950s and 1960s have tamed the river. (Courtesy of Meg Decker.)

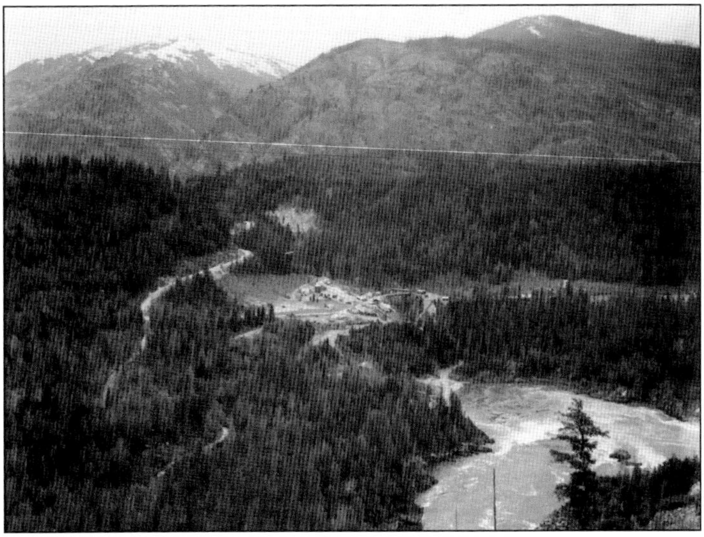

Selkirk Mountains. The Selkirk Mountains border the Pend Oreille River and cover most of Pend Oreille County. The mountain range covers parts of British Columbia, Idaho, Washington, and Montana, and is named after Thomas Douglas, Fifth Earl of Selkirk, philanthropic sponsor of Canadian settlements. This photograph shows part of the snow-capped range, thick forests, Pend Oreille River, and a mine facility.

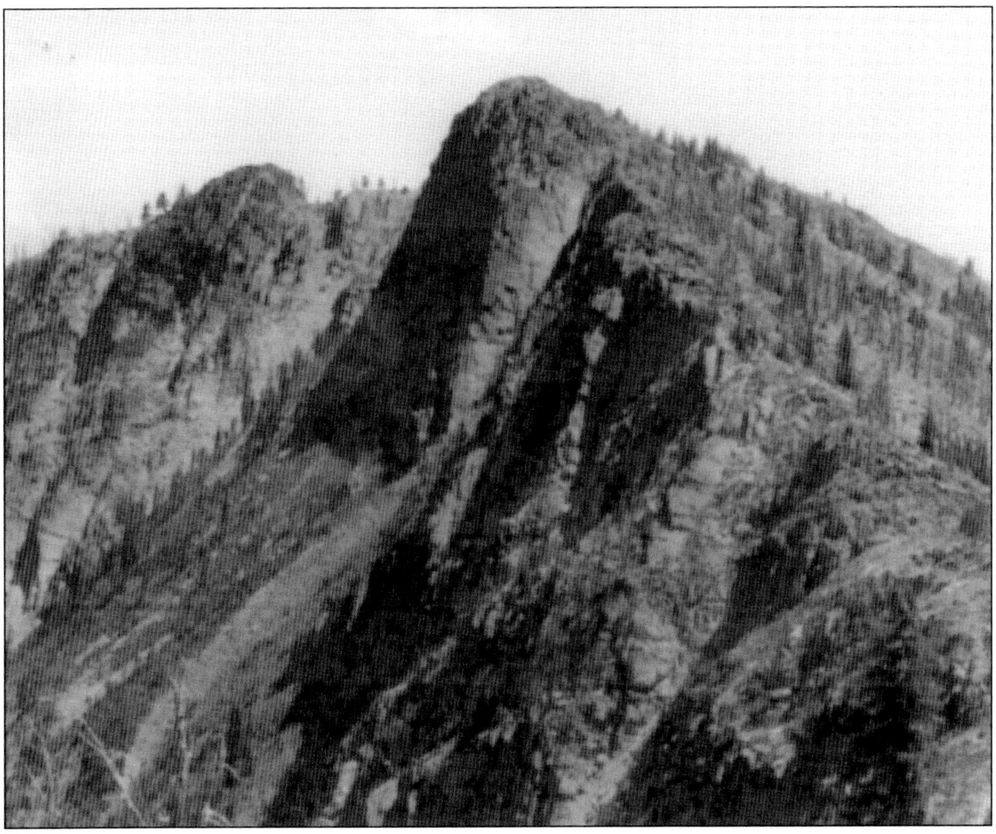

Gypsy Mountain. Rising 7,325 feet, this peak is located in the Colville National Forest in the northern part of the county. The mountain tempts hikers to climb its forested footings and rocky cliffs. The Prouty family, part-time prospectors and ranchers in the Colville area, lived like gypsies during the summer. They named the mountain, a ridge, a meadow, and several other places in the county. (Courtesy of John Ogmundson.)

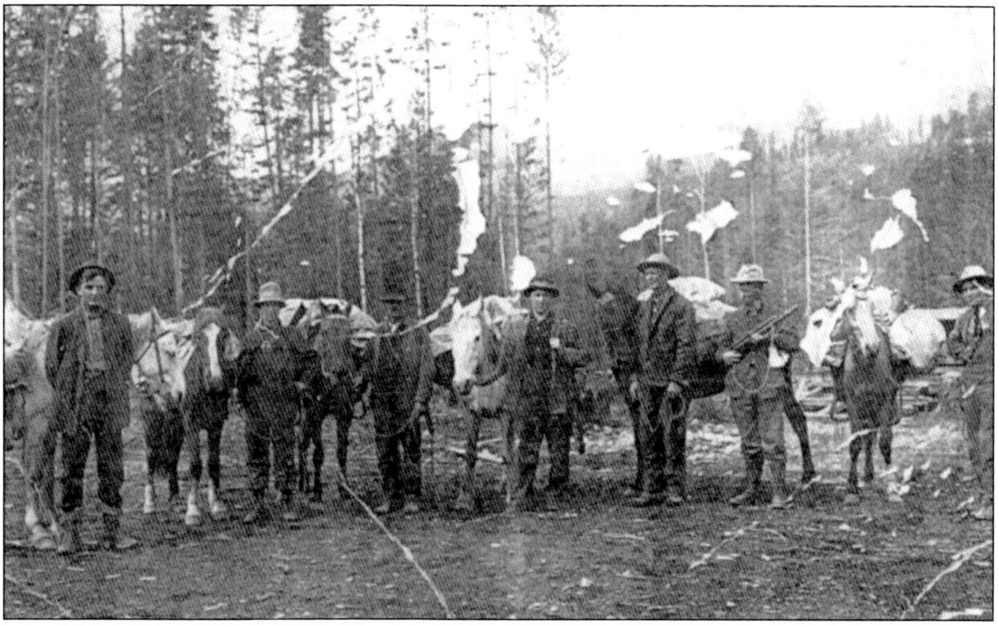

PACK TRAIN. In this photograph, the Prouty brothers and others are on their way to their Gypsy Copper Mine in the Selkirk Mountains on May 15, 1912. Their pack horses are loaded with gear and supplies. From left to right are George Austin Theis, Guy Deemer, Charles Henry Prouty, Frank Shoemaker, Jessie Bert Prouty, Jim Deemer, and Ralph Prouty. The mine was unproductive.

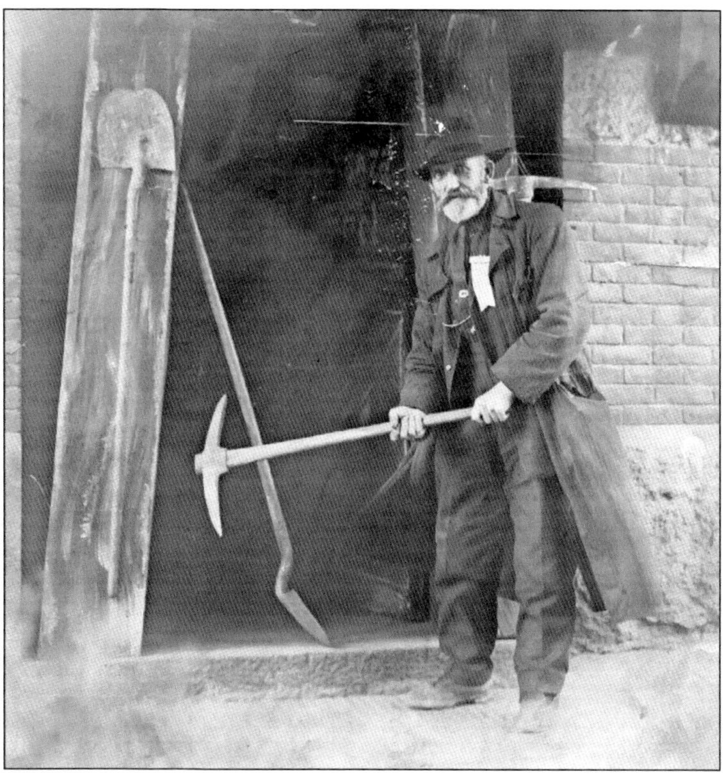

PROSPECTOR. Mr. Hudson, an early prospector, shows off his primitive equipment. He and others dreamed of a gold rush. They used the old Indian trails to get into Pend Oreille Valley regions. They hiked through thick brush, climbed mountains, and scoured the banks of streams and the river to pan for gold.

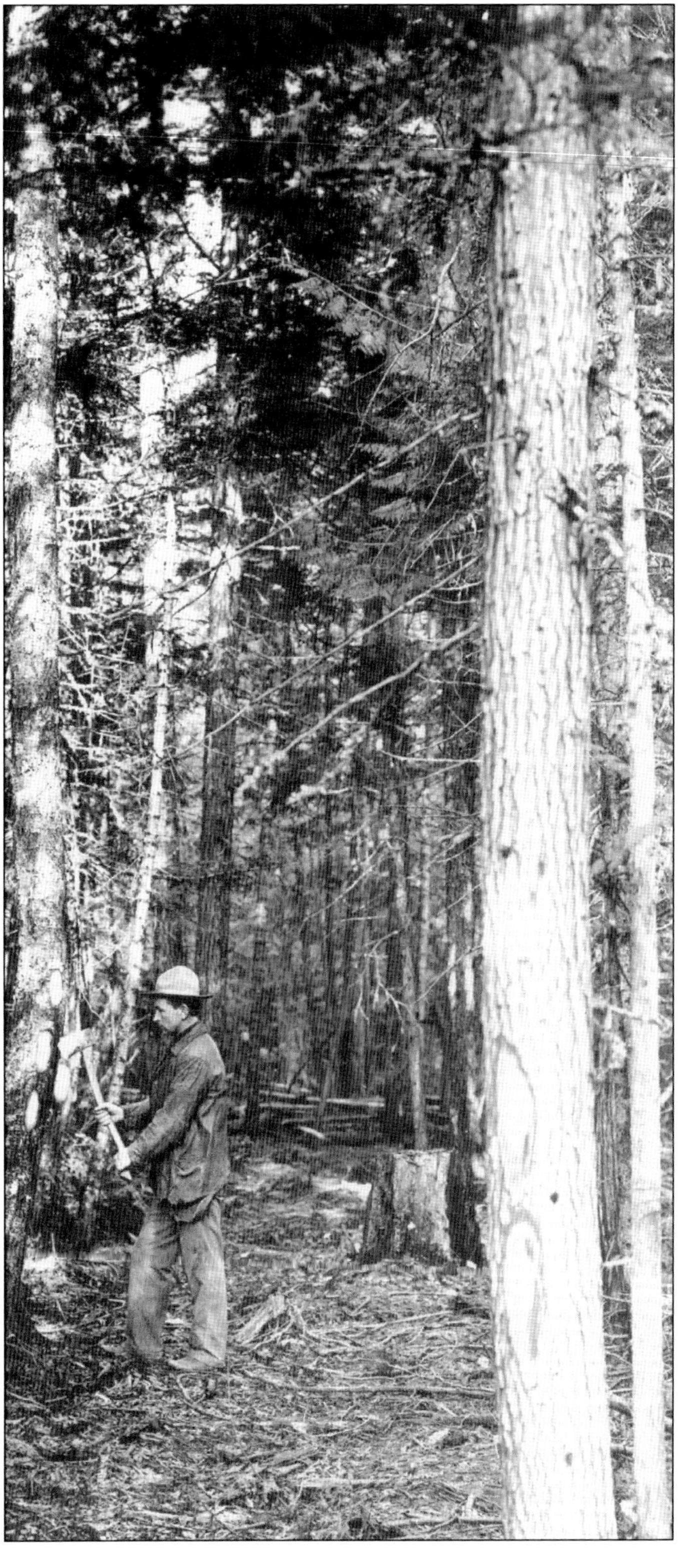

FOREST. Pend Oreille County was once covered with dense forests. Here, Lewis P. Larsen is checking out the site of the future Mill Pond, which would become part of his hydroelectric project. The trees were cut down and Sullivan Creek was dammed to create a reservoir for a power house in 1909. The project provided electricity for the large cement plant and the town of Metaline Falls.

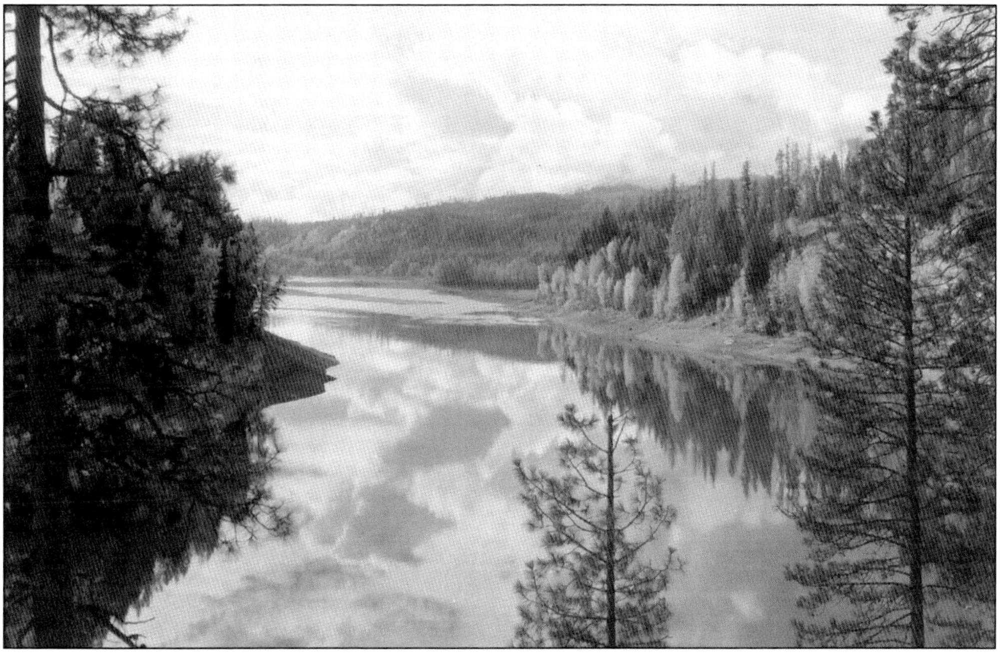

Pend Oreille River. The river flows out of Lake Pend Oreille and is joined by Priest River and Cocolalla Creek in Idaho. At Newport, it turns north and becomes increasingly turbulent as it flows for over 60 miles into Canada, where it joins the Columbia River. Today, paddlers can go online and learn about the Pend Oreille Water Trails before exploring the river.

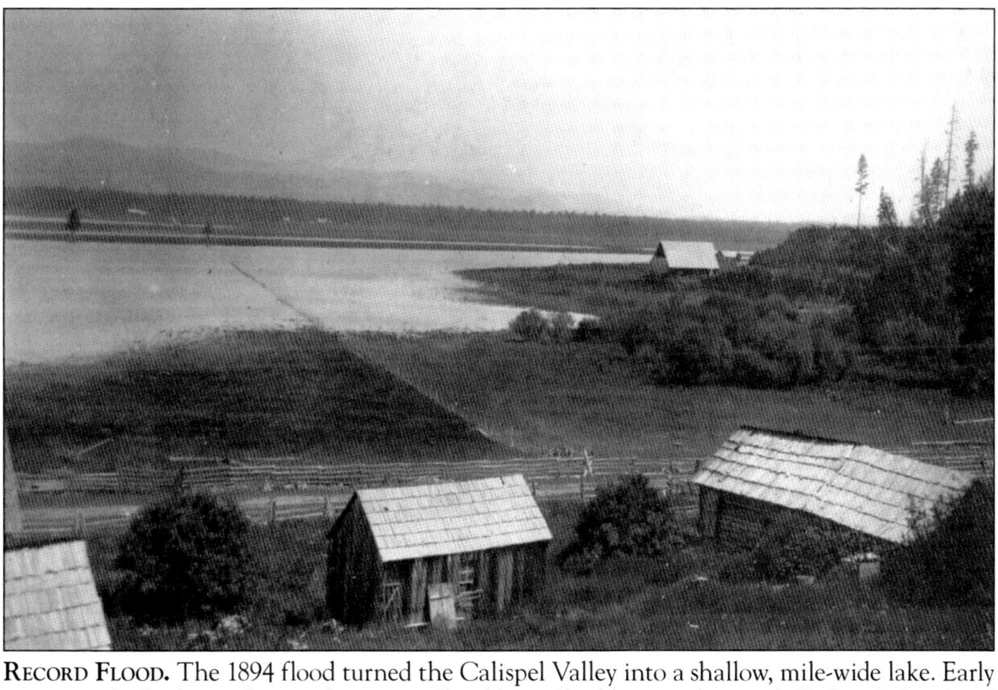

Record Flood. The 1894 flood turned the Calispel Valley into a shallow, mile-wide lake. Early pioneers who built too close to the river suffered loss of buildings and animals. Robert P. Jared and the Gregg family were among those affected by the record high water. Prior to the construction of three dams on the Pend Oreille River, floods occurred almost every spring.

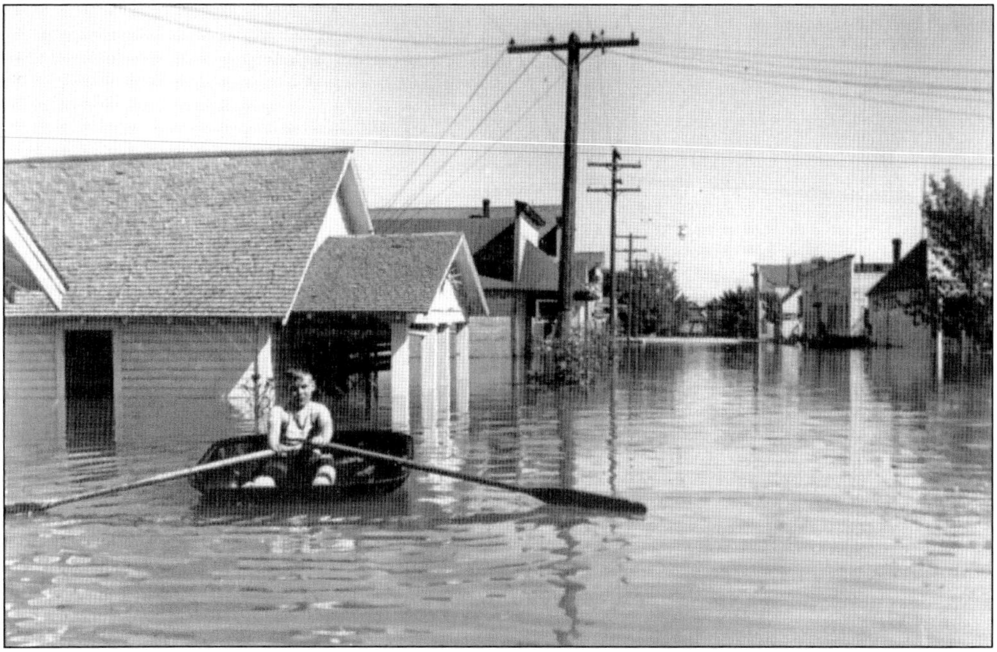

1948 Flood. The 1948 flood was the second record flood in the Calispel Valley. At that time, the valley was settled with communities, farms, sawmills, and businesses. The cost of repairing dikes, cleaning up, and restoration ran into the millions of dollars. It was years before the region was back to normal. Here, an unknown young man rows his boat between houses in Cusick.

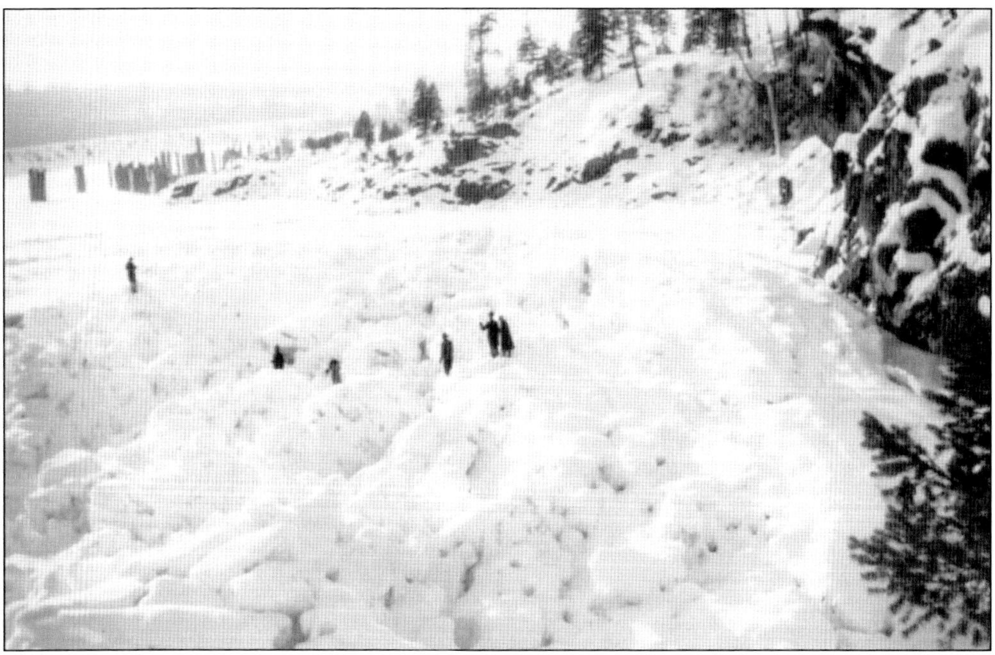

Albeni Falls. In 1929, Albeni Falls near Newport, was frozen over during the severe winter. People were able to walk or drive horses and sleighs across the river. Prior to the construction of Albeni Falls Dam in the 1950s, the falls roared past two small rocky islands and over and around several outcroppings. The falls were named for the early homesteader Albeni Poirier.

Peewee Falls. This beautiful waterfall is located in the northern part of the county, just south of present-day Boundary Dam. Prior to the building of the dam in the 1960s, the falls flowed over a 200-foot cliff into the Pend Oreille River. Today, it is a much lower waterfall, but it continues to be a beautiful sight for those who paddle their canoes on the river.

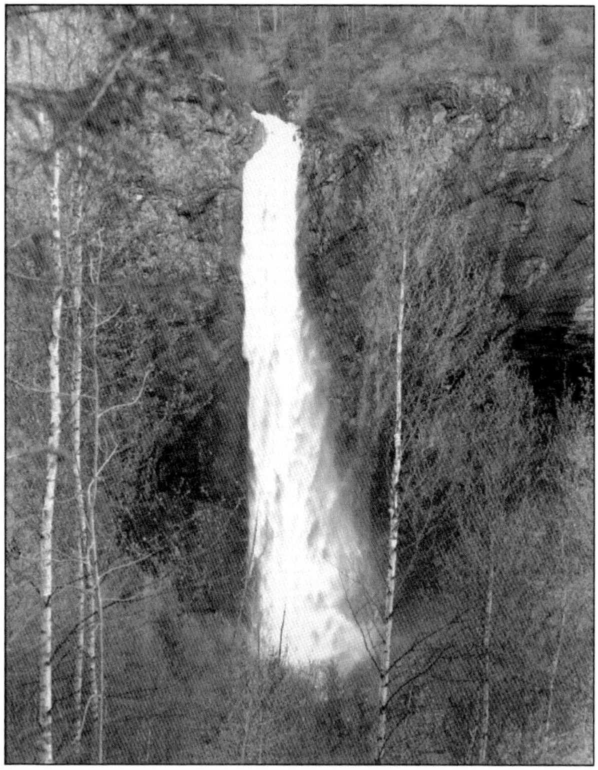

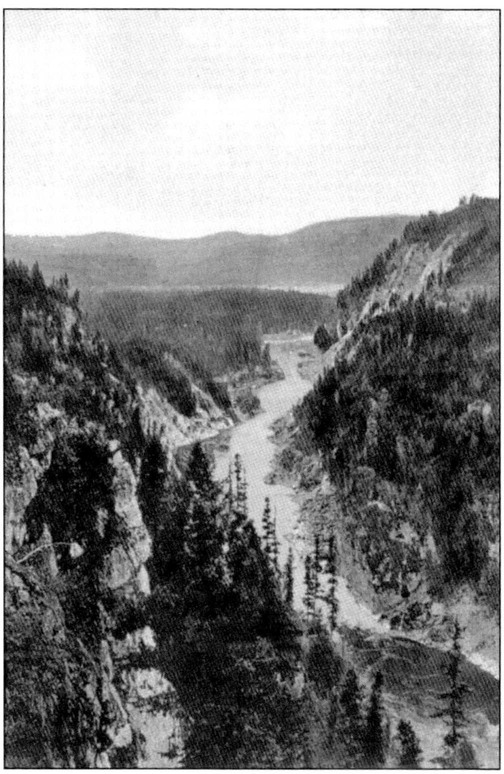

Grandview Canyon. This canyon cuts through the forest-covered Selkirk Mountains north of Ione. It presented a challenge to the pilots and a thrilling ride for the passengers riding the *Metaline* and *Nancy* launch steamboats. Today, the canyon is hidden from the highway and so can only be appreciated by boaters.

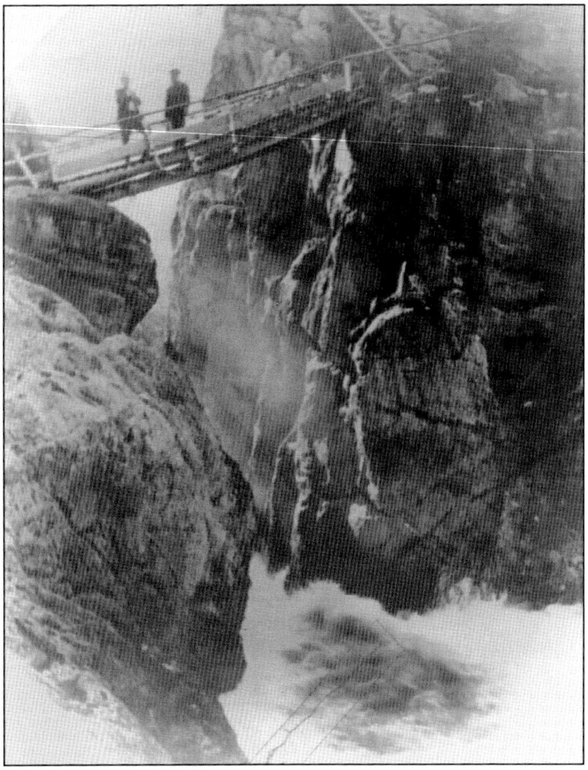

Z Canyon. This two-mile-long canyon was located seven miles north of Metaline Falls. It is where the Pend Oreille River turned on its edge and roared through a narrow zigzag canyon between 500-foot rock walls. Here, early pioneers gingerly walk along an 18-foot plank bridge across the canyon. Today, most of the canyon is under water behind Boundary Dam.

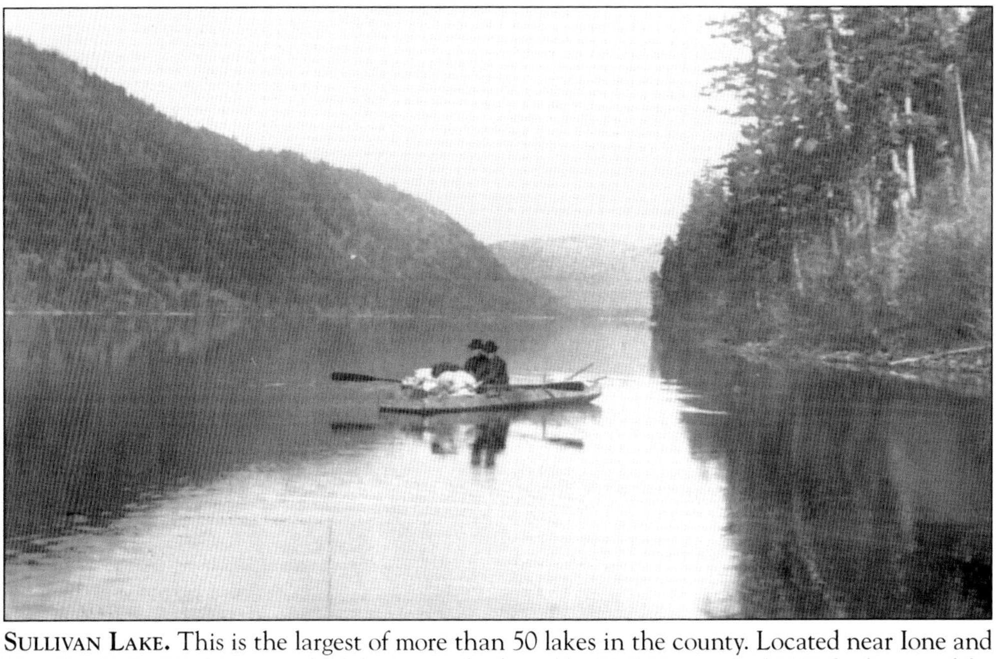

Sullivan Lake. This is the largest of more than 50 lakes in the county. Located near Ione and Metaline Falls, Washington, the lake is overshadowed by Hall Mountain (6,332 feet), named for Elmer Hall, one of the founders of Ione. The lake's rich history included Caribou Lodge, built in 1902, and a 1930s Civilian Conservation Corps (CCC) camp. Today, the lake has the Sullivan Lake Forest Ranger Station. Visitors can enjoy camping and hiking trails.

William H. Wright. A naturalist, Wright was owner and promoter of the Marshall Lake Power & Land Company at Marshall Lake, Washington. He hunted, studied, and wrote two books about bears, *The Grizzly Bear* and *The Black Bear.* During pioneer days, wildlife abounded in the wilderness areas of Pend Oreille County. Bears were among the dangerous predatory animals that preyed on the pioneers' livestock.

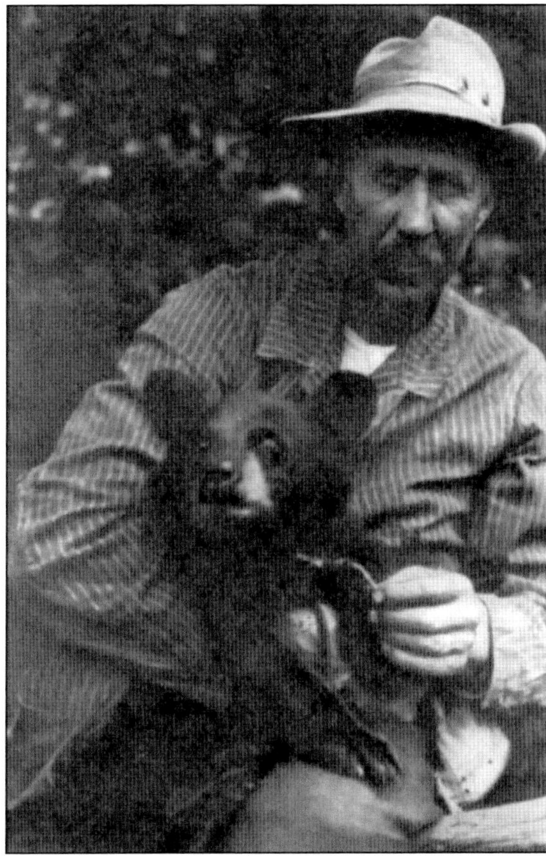

Bears. Many species of bears are found throughout North America. William Wright hunted and wrote about grizzly bears. They are a subgroup of brown bears that were found in the Selkirk Mountains in the early 1900s. Grizzlies are large mammals that can weigh between 400 and 800 pounds. They are omnivores and often prey on other large mammals, such as moose and deer, as well as cattle and horses.

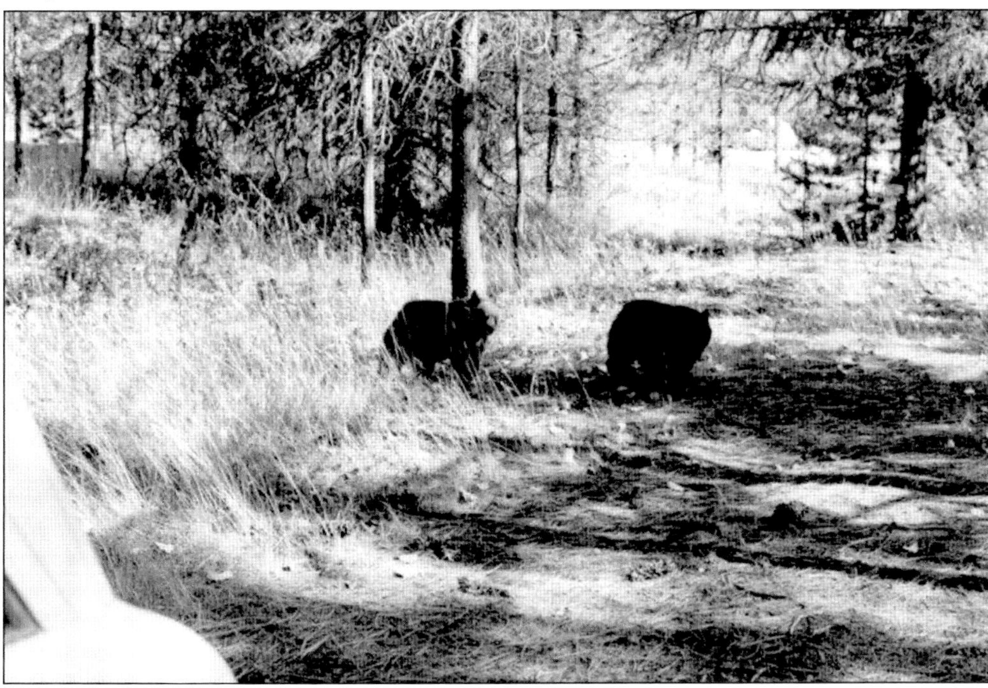

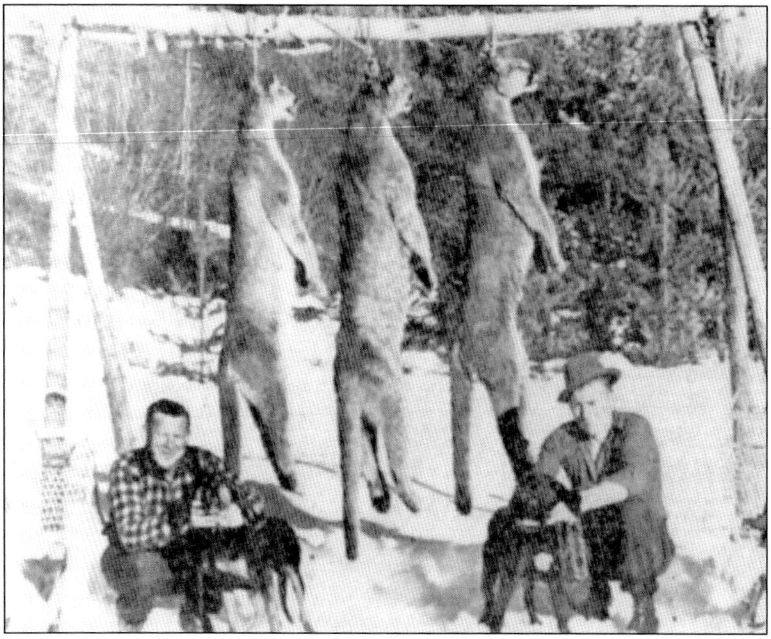

Cougars. Bud Moon was a well-known cougar hunter in Pend Oreille County, the Idaho Panhandle, and Western Montana. In those early years, cougars kept isolated pioneers on alert, watching family members and livestock. Even today, there are occasional reports of cougar sightings in the more remote areas of the county.

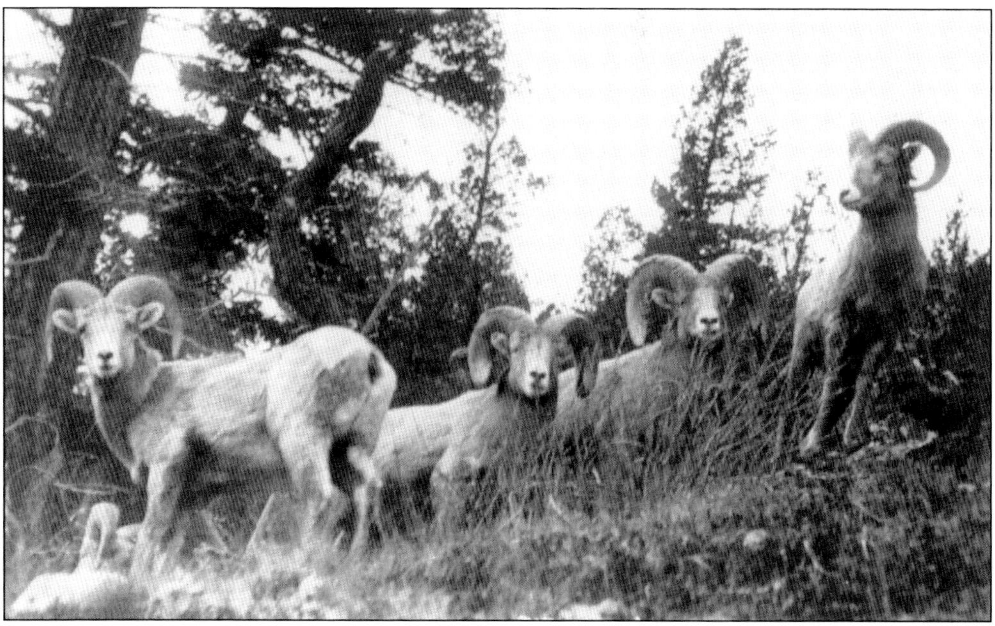

Bighorn Sheep. In earlier years, there was a large herd of bighorn sheep in the wilderness region in the county. The present-day small herd was started in 1972 with sheep from the Canadian Waterton National Park and several from the Thompson Falls, Montana, area. Today, the small herd numbers about 20. They are a local tourist attraction in the Halls Mountain and Sullivan Lake area.

Two

The Kalispel Indian Tribe

The Kalispel tribe is a subgroup of Pend Oreille Indians, who spoke the Salish language and lived a similar lifestyle. Prior to the 1800s, the various tribes lived in southern British Columbia and slowly immigrated into their present location. The Kalispel Indians settled along the Pend Oreille River. They were primitive, semi-nomadic hunters and gatherers who roamed over a large territory and lived according to the seasons and their environment. They skillfully used natural materials to make tepees, lodges, canoes, tools, and weapons; collected wild medicinal herbs; gathered and preserved camas roots and berries; and fished and hunted. The Kalispel were known as the "camas people." In the summer season, they traveled to the Kettle Falls, Washington, area and joined other Indians in fishing and drying salmon or crossed the Rocky Mountains for buffalo hunts. They got along well with other tribes and were seldom involved in inter-tribal frictions and wars.

Kalispel life and culture dramatically changed with the appearance of horses in the mid-1700s, which gave them greater mobility, and the encroachment of white people, who introduced infectious diseases, liquor, and guns. In 1809, the famed explorer, cartographer, and fur trader David Thompson visited and kept the first written record of the Pend Oreille region. He returned in 1809, 1810, and 1811 to search for the Columbia River. Gold-hungry prospectors followed the fur traders.

Father Jean Pierre DeSmet and Father Adrian Hoecken established the St. Ignatius Mission along the Pend Oreille River in 1844. The Catholic missionaries hoped the Kalispel Indians would become farmers and lead a settled life. The 1854 flood ended the mission. Some of the Kalispel moved to Montana to establish a new St. Ignatius Mission. The life of the Kalispel Indians continued to change as more settlers poured into the area. After years of struggle, the Kalispel Indians were granted a reservation by Pres. Woodrow Wilson in 1914. Their 10-mile-long reservation runs along the Pend Oreille River, 16 miles from Newport.

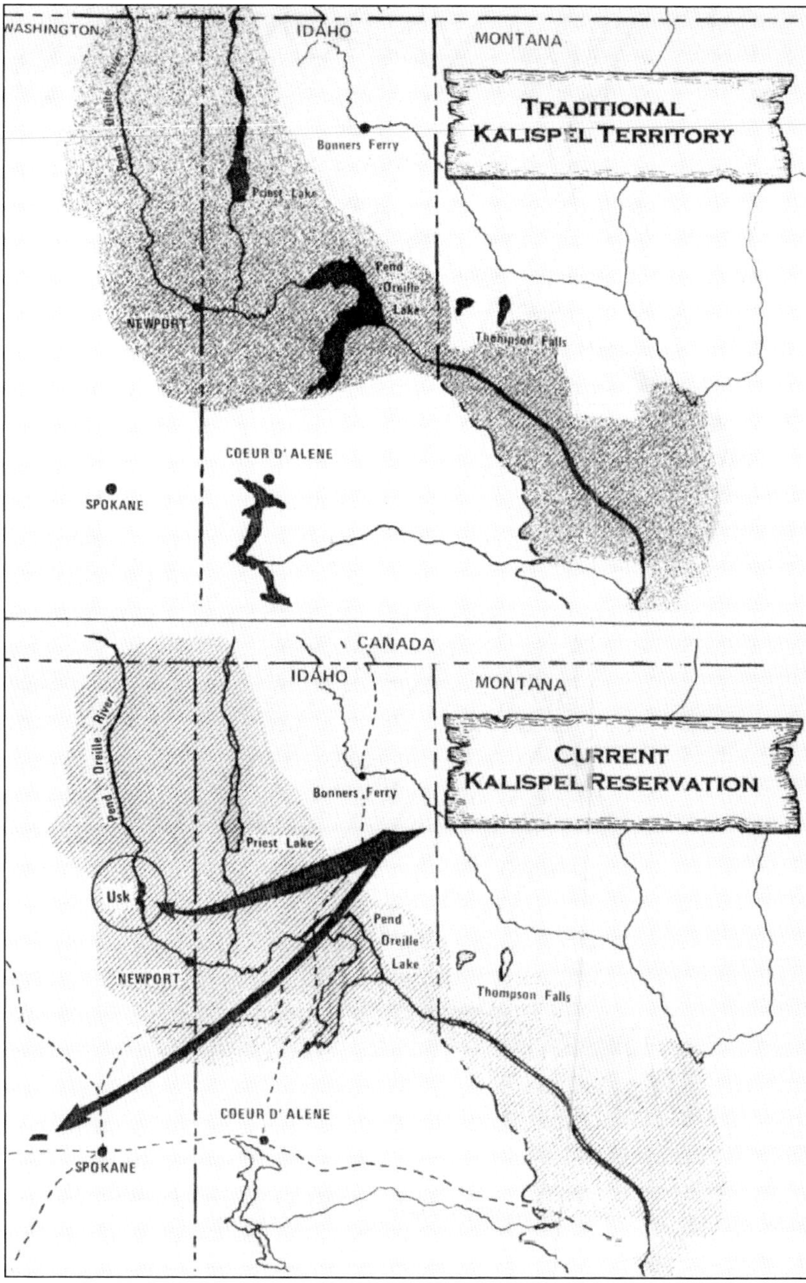

KALISPEL TERRITORY MAP. The traditional territory of the Pend d'Oreille Indians and the Kalispel tribe stretched from Plains, Montana, along the Clark Fork River, through Northern Idaho, along the Priest Lake, and along the Priest and Pend Oreille Rivers. The rivers served as water highways, connecting the Kalispel to food sources, other tribes, and social gatherings. At present, their 4,557-acre reservation is located along the Pend Oreille River and is the smallest reservation in the State of Washington. Today, the Kalispel tribe owns and operates the Northern Quest Resort and Casino near Spokane. They recently constructed the Camas Center complex on the reservation. The center provides educational classes, a medical center, a recreational swimming pool, and other facilities, which the tribe generously shares with the greater community.

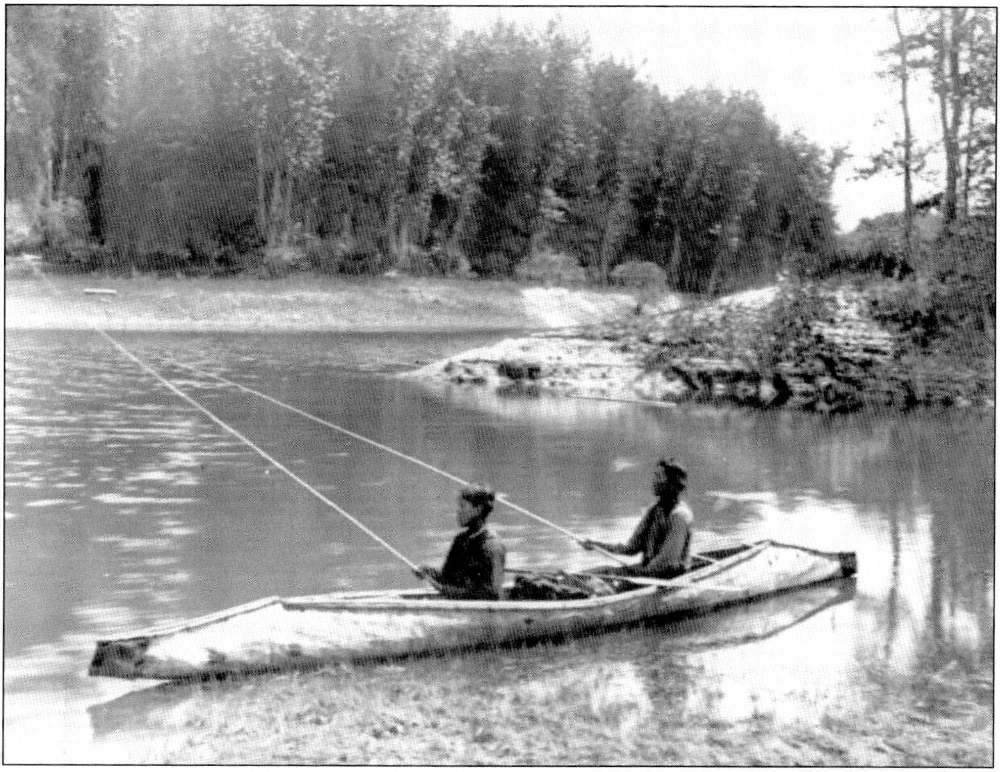

KALISPEL CANOE. The sturgeon-nosed bark canoe was a treasured possession of Kalispel families. Skilled tribesmen used simple tools to build the canoes out of the inner bark of pine trees, cedar-ribbed slats, and pitch tar. The maneuverable canoes were able to slide through thick cattails and swamp grass along the banks and glide in the turbulent current of the Pend Oreille River.

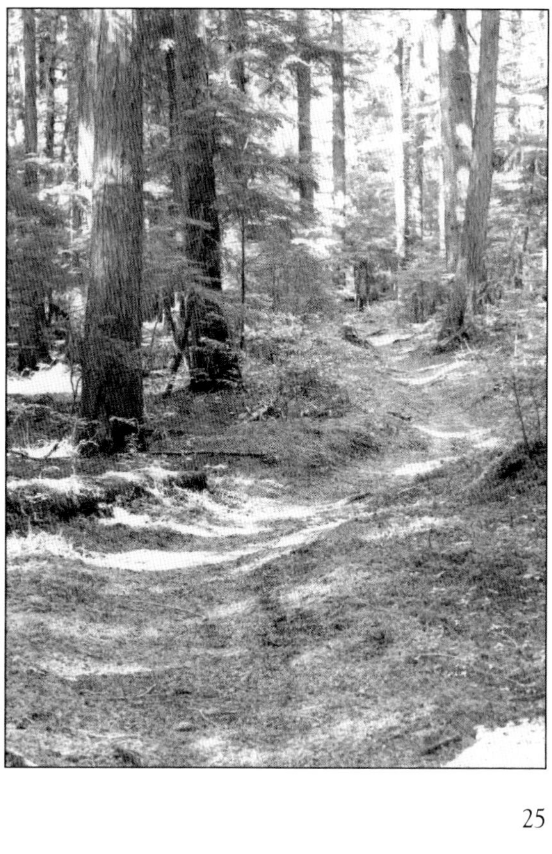

KALISPEL INDIAN TRAIL. The Kalispel Indians used a network of trails through the mountains and forests to connect with food sources and other tribes. There were trails that wandered north to Kettle Falls, Washington, where the Indians fished for salmon. The well-used Kalispel Trail (kullspel) went through the camas meadows at Cusick, Washington, skirted Sacheen and Fan Lakes, and joined trails in the Spokane region. Later, that trail was used by the pioneers.

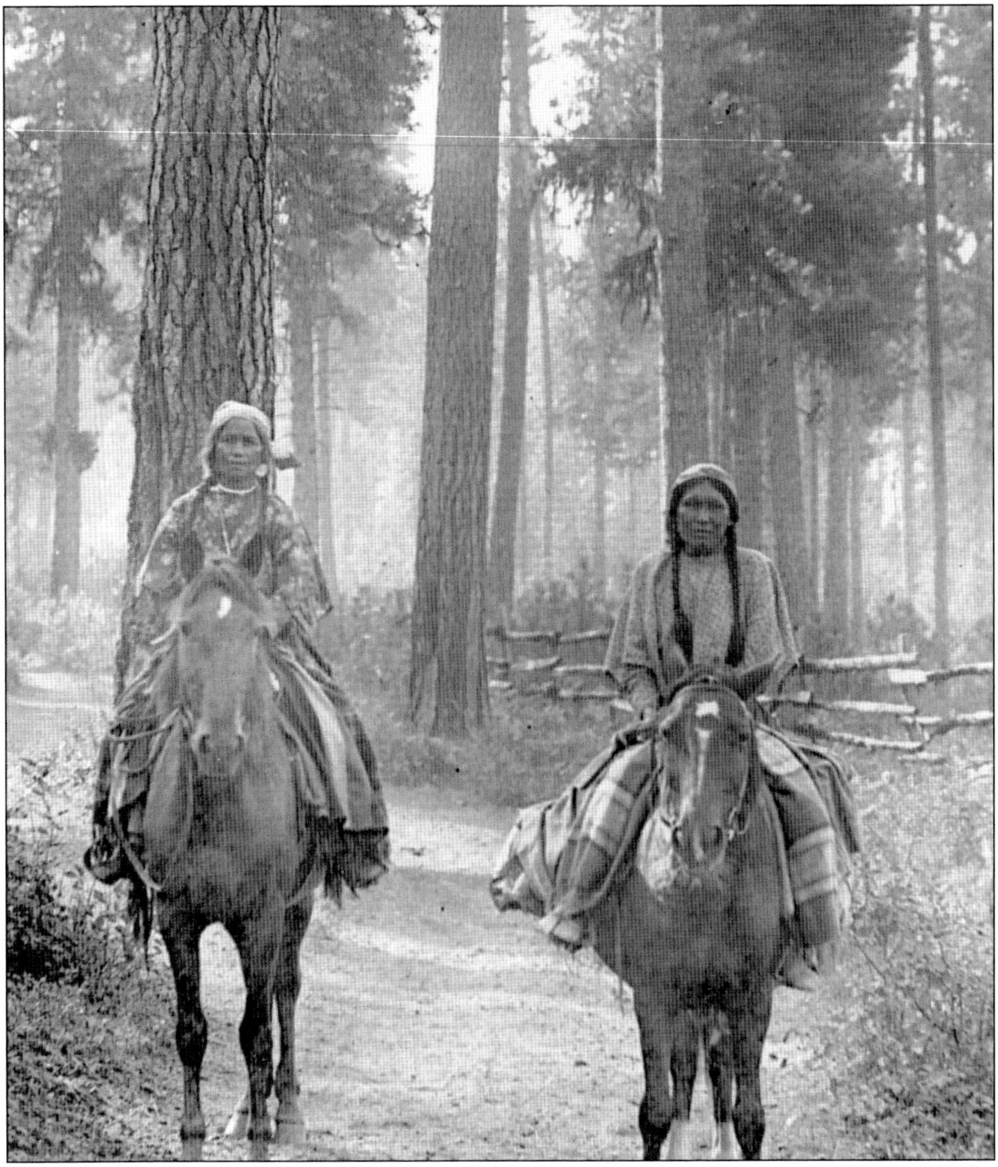

KALISPEL WOMEN ON HORSEBACK. Louise Andrews (left) and Lucy Seymour ride through the forests in 1907. The first horses arrived in North America during the days of Spanish conquest. Indian slaves of the Spaniards were not allowed to have horses, but they learned to work with them. Eventually, some of the horses were captured by the Indians and began to spread across the country. By the 1700s, horses arrived in the West. The Nez Perce, Crow, and Blackfeet Indians began to acquire the animals. The Cayuse and Nez Perce developed the spotted Appaloosa. The animals made traveling faster and easier, and could carry heavy loads. Horses brought changes to the traditional life of the Kalispel Indians.

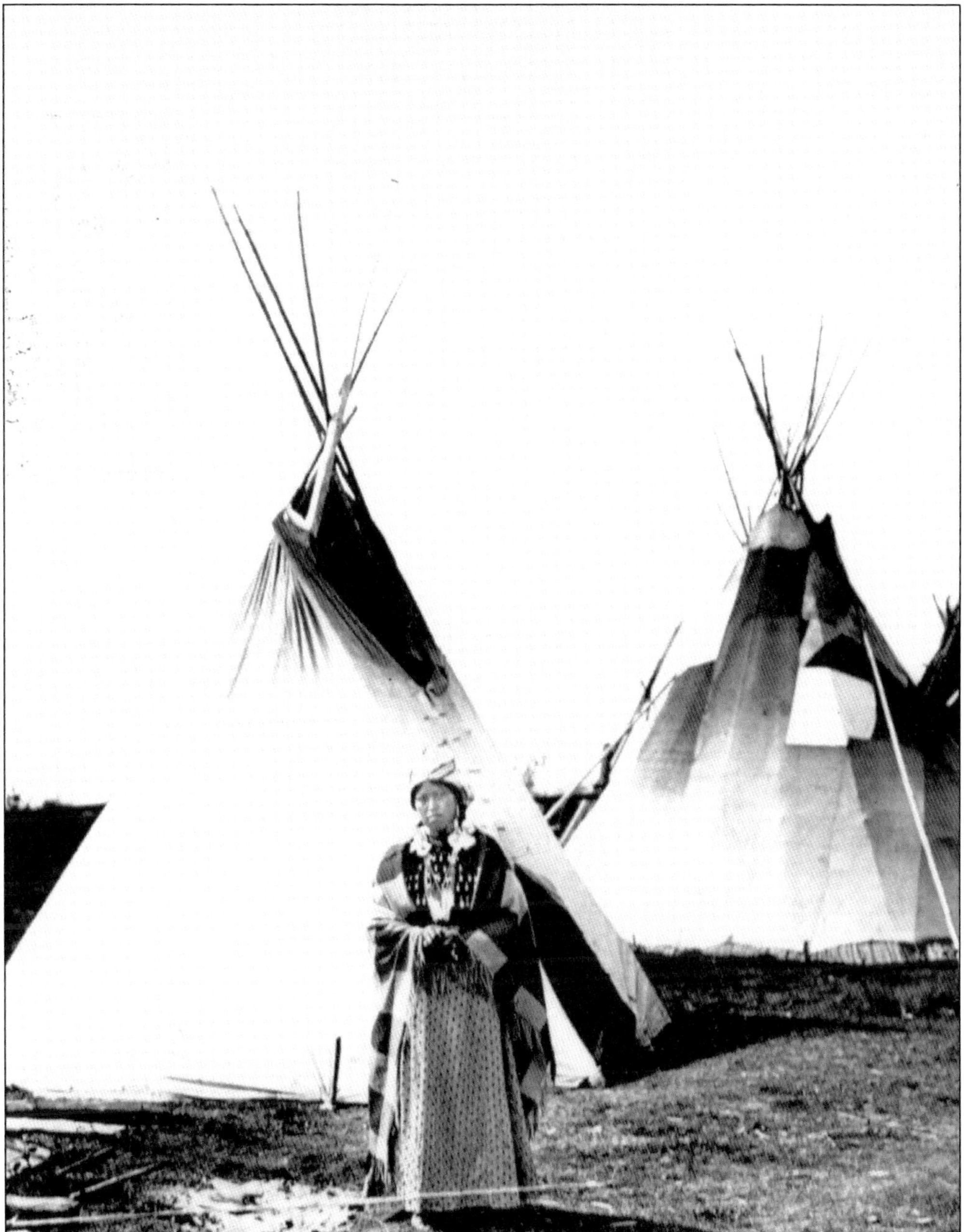

TEPEES. Tepees were lightweight, portable, and easily assembled or disassembled shelters for the ever-moving Indians in their search for food. Indian women were in charge of acquiring the materials needed to built a tepee, put them up, and take them down. Kalispel women used either tule mats (tule grass) or hides to cover their tepees. Large tepees had space for sleeping, cooking, and storage.

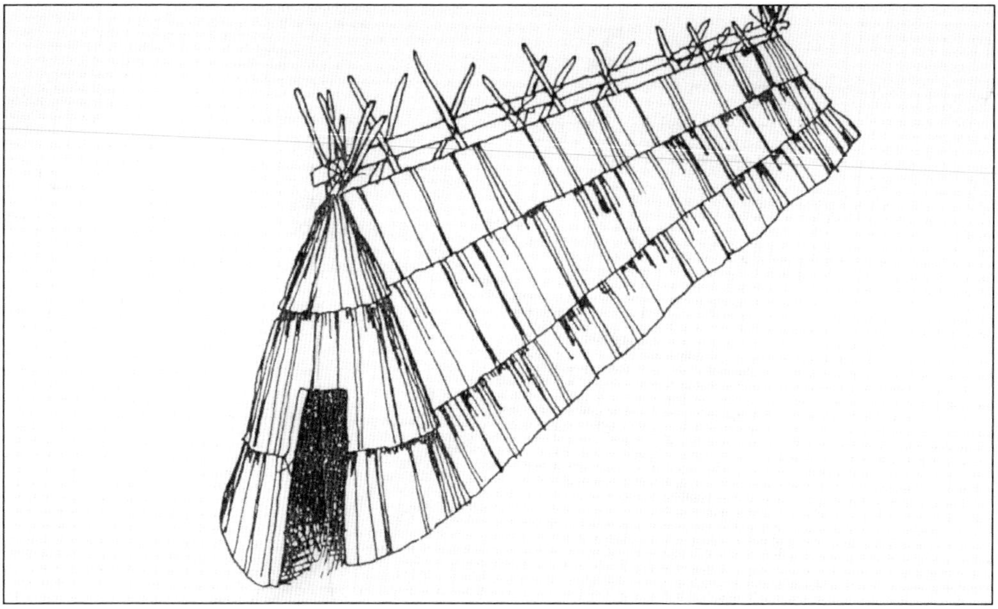

Kalispel Lodge. Winter lodges were multi-family shelters. A lodge could be 12 feet wide, and the length depended on the number of people living in them. The Indians in the early fall would scout around for locations that were dry, out of the wind, and protected from heavy snow. Strong, slender poles were used for the framework, which would be covered by either tule mats or hides. In a lodge, two or more families might live together, sharing sleeping and cooking spaces.

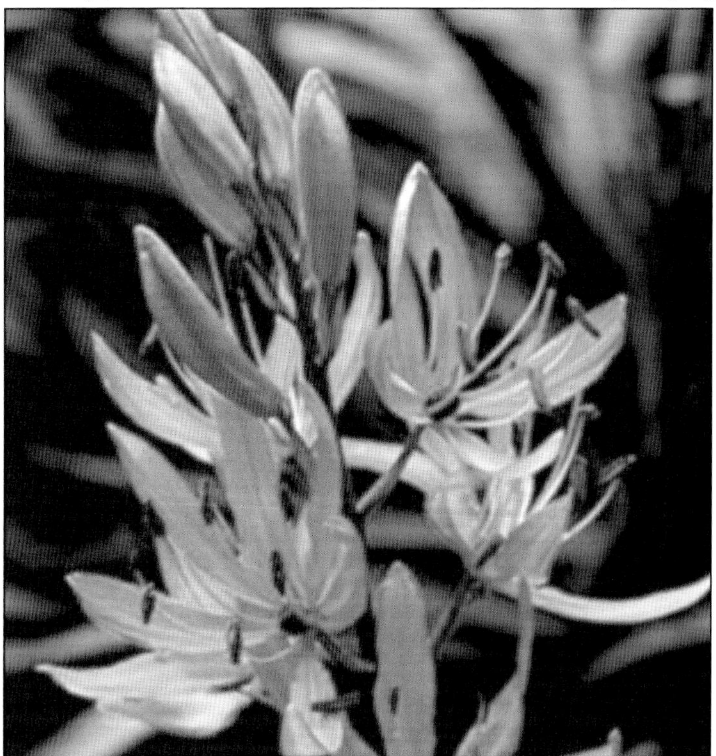

Camas Plant. The Camas root was a very nutritious source of food for Indians. In the spring, the blue flowers filled the Calispel Valley; from a distance, the valley looked like a lake. In the summer, Kalispel women used a sharpened stick or deer horn to dig the camas roots. The camas would be steamed in underground ovens, dried, ground up, and formed into patties.

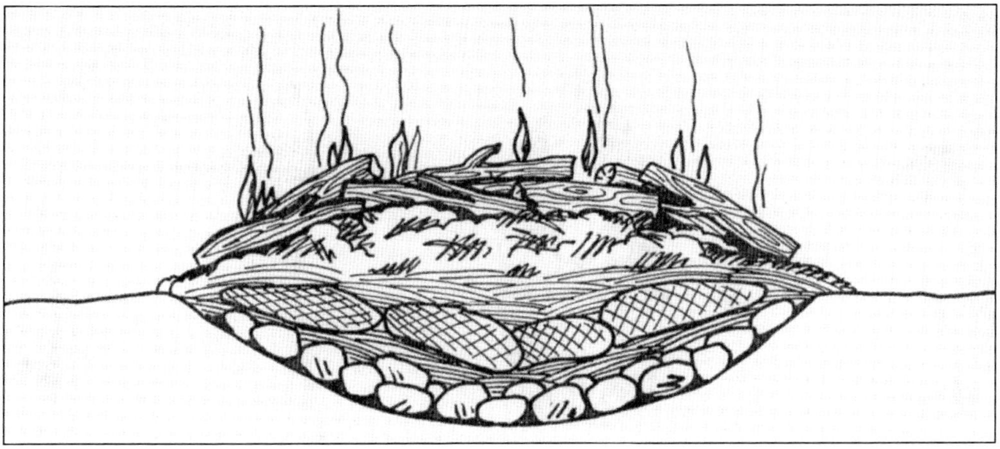

KALISPEL OVEN. Earthen basins were filled with firewood and rocks and burned until the rocks were red hot. Cedar-bark bags would be filled with camas roots and layered between skunk-cabbage leaves and covered with soil. Another fire would be started on top of the oven and burned for several days. The sacks of camas would then be removed and prepared for winter food.

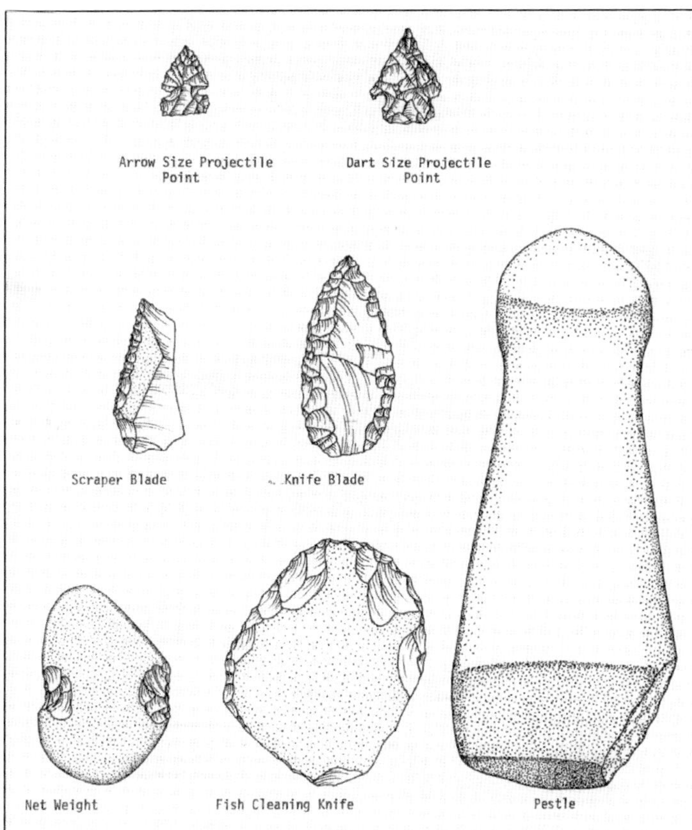

KALISPEL STONE TOOLS. These are depictions of stone tools that the early Kalispel Indians used in daily life. Included here are stone arrowheads, meat scrapers, knife blades, fish-cleaning tools, and pestles for grinding grains and roots. After fur traders arrived, Indians were happy to trade beaver hides for manufactured arrowheads, axes, knives, pots and pans, and anything else that would make their life easier.

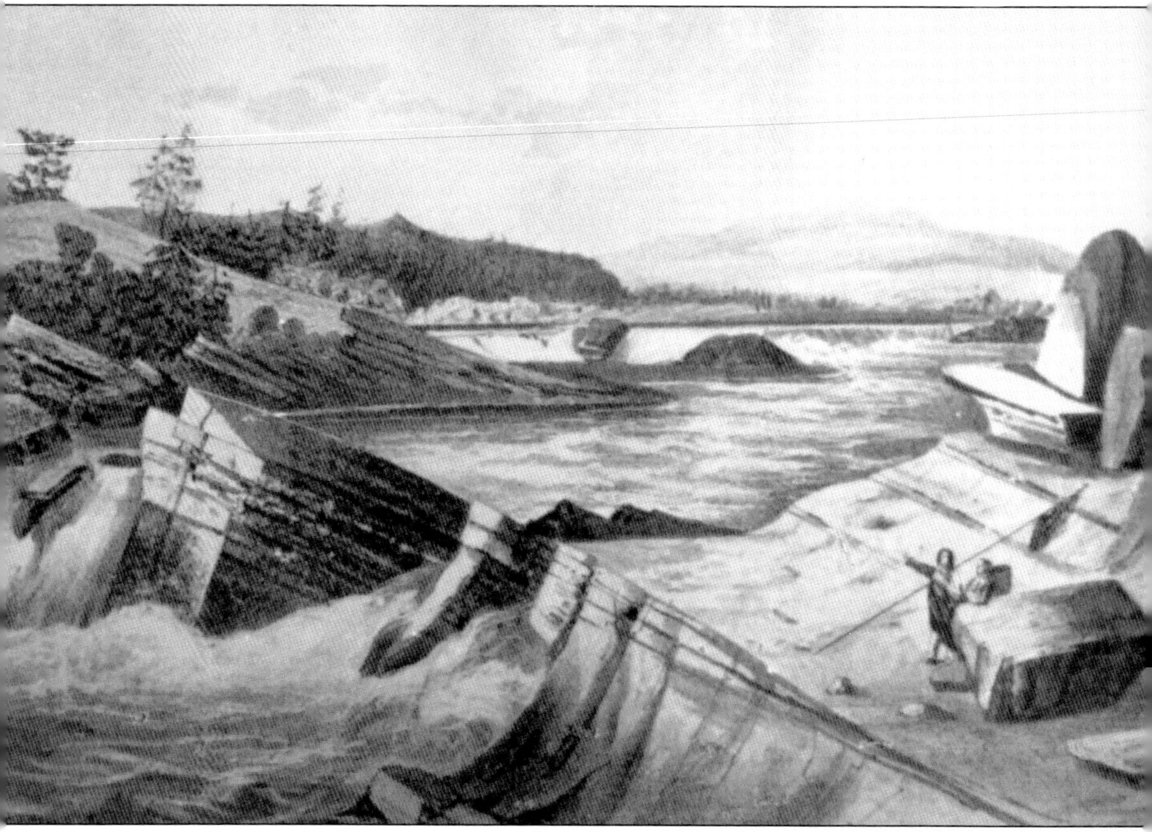

SALMON FISHING. Each summer, when the salmon were running in the Columbia River, the Kalispel Indians would join other tribes at Kettle Falls, Washington. After ceremonial prayers, they followed traditional methods of fishing using spears, nets, and woven baskets. Using primitive stone tools, Indian women carefully prepared the fish and dried them for winter food. John Mix Stanley, an artist, engraved this picture of an Indian man and woman with a spear, net, and basket beside early Kettle Falls. Stanley was employed to assist Gov. Isaac Stevens on the railroad survey in 1853. His drawing shows the rushing water pouring over jagged rocks.

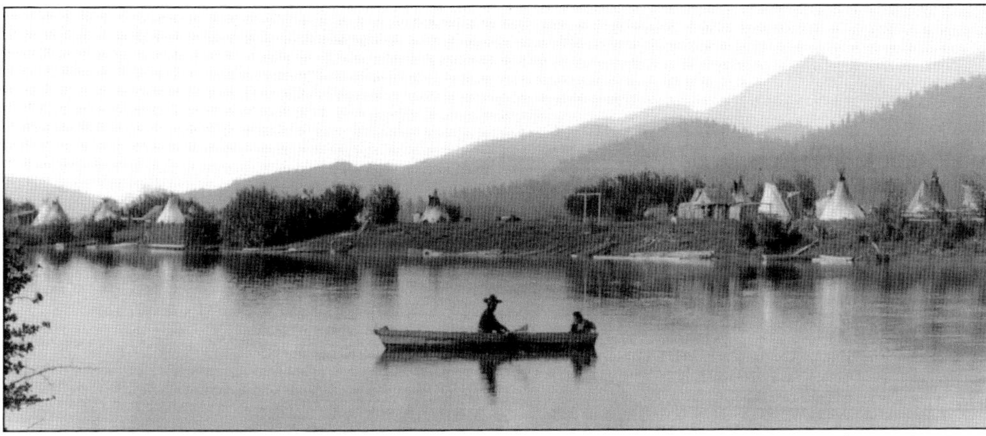

Two Indians in Canoe. Katherine Frye (right) and Alexander Revasis canoe down the Pend Oreille River. It has been estimated that, at one time, several thousand Kalispel Indians lived in the area. The mountains protected them from enemies, there was fishing in the river, hunting in the mountains, and plenty of roots and berries for food.

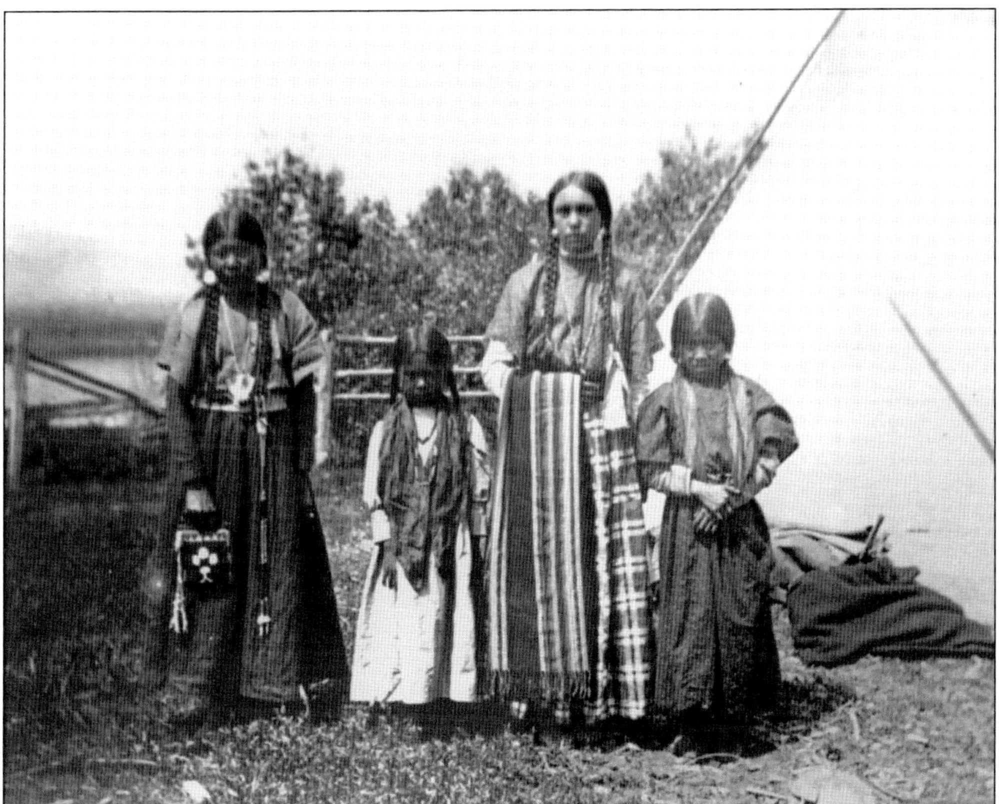

Indian Girls. These four attractive girls show off their best dresses and braided hair. The Pend Oreille River and a tepee are in the background.

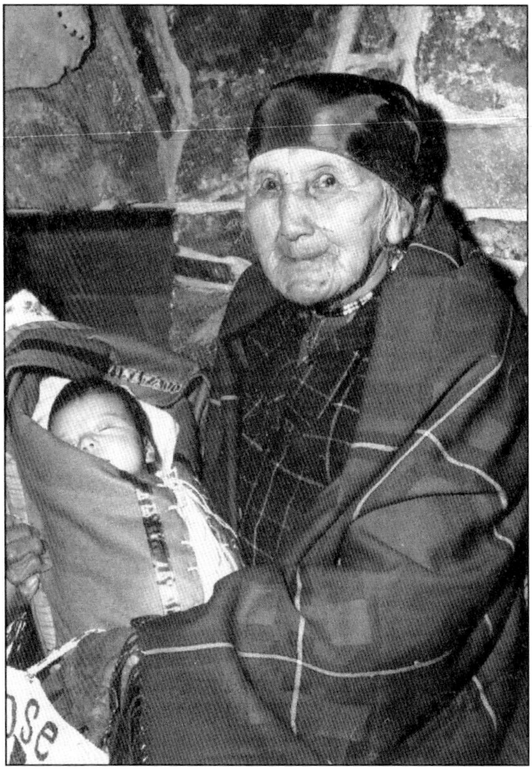

Kalispel Family. Katherine Frye, 91, shows off her great-granddaughter, Tina Marie Nenema. Frye and other Kalispel women lived during a time when the tribe was in a period of transition from the traditional Indian ways into the white people's culture and life.

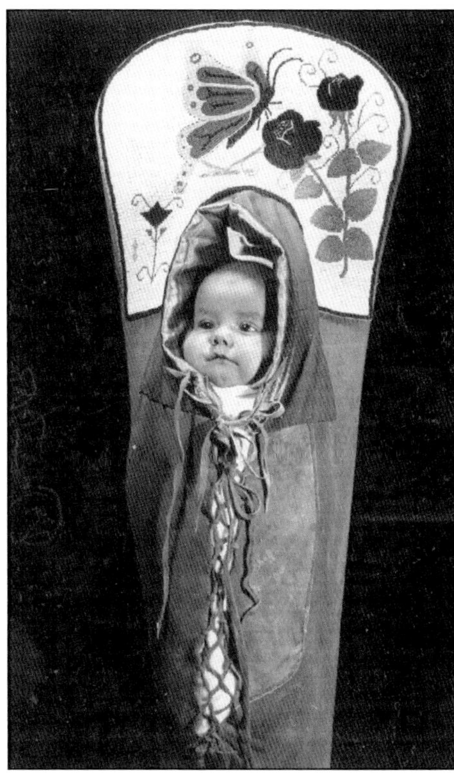

Baby's Beaded Board. A Kalispel Indian baby, Christina Bowman (Smiling Child), is shown on a traditional beaded board. Each seed glass bead is sewn individually onto the backing. It is very complicated, time-consuming and delicate work and takes years of practice to perfect. Originally, beads were carved from natural materials, such as horns, bones, and shells. Glass beads appeared during Colonial days and spread across the country.

CHIEF BASIL ANDREWS. In the early years, the Kalispel tribe was led by chiefs and subchiefs. Chief Andrews was one of the Kalispel leaders. The tribe struggled through many years of changes in its traditional way of life. Various Indian chiefs, US and state government officials, Jesuit Catholic Church leaders, and others tried to assist them.

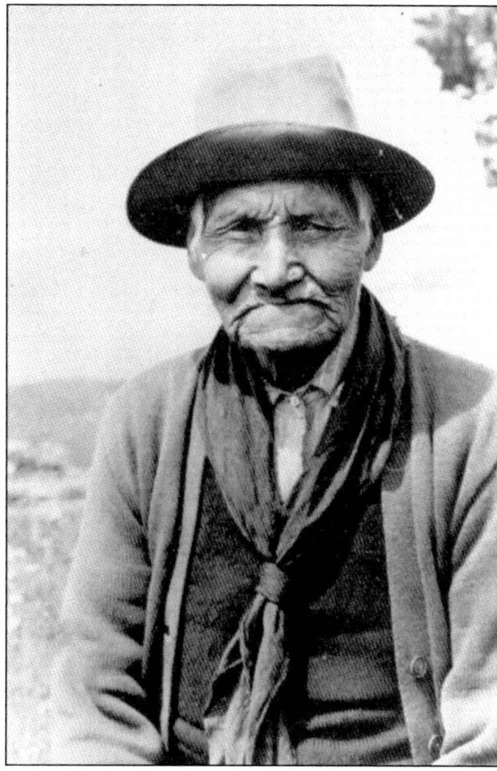

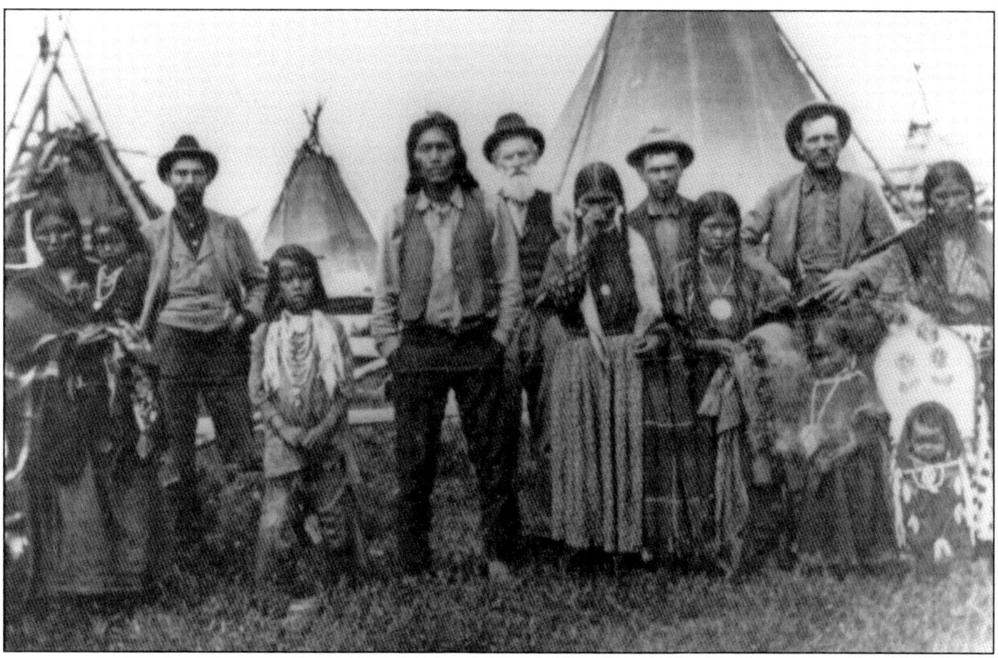

CHIEF BIG SMOKE. Big Smoke (center) was the last official chief of the Kalispel Indians. He is pictured with members of the Kalispel tribe and a group of white people. Shown in the background are three tepees. Today, the tribe has a general council with representatives of all the members of the tribe. The elders of the tribe have an unofficial leadership role.

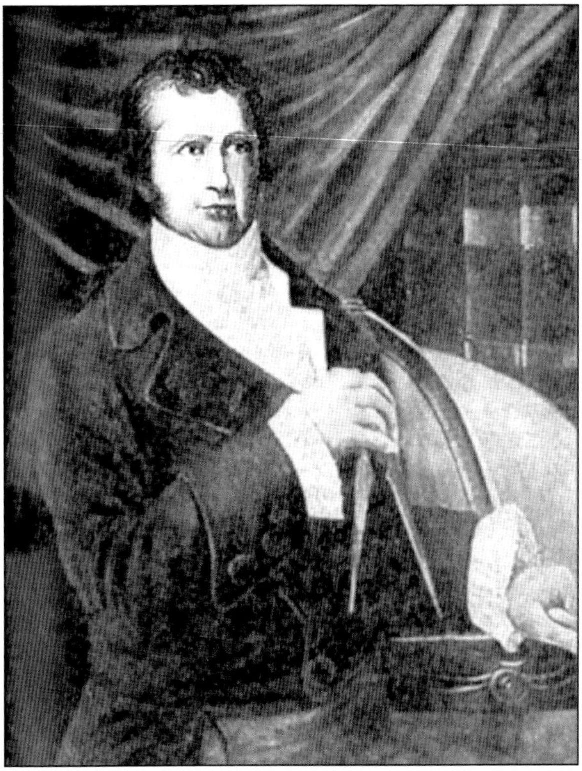

DAVID THOMPSON. Born in 1770 in England, Thompson became an apprentice to the Hudson Bay Company. He was a fur trader and surveyor and became a world-famous cartographer. In 1809, he was the first white man to visit the Pend Oreille region and the Kalispel tribe. His extensive journals give a glimpse into the early days of the area and the inhabitants before the coming of white people.

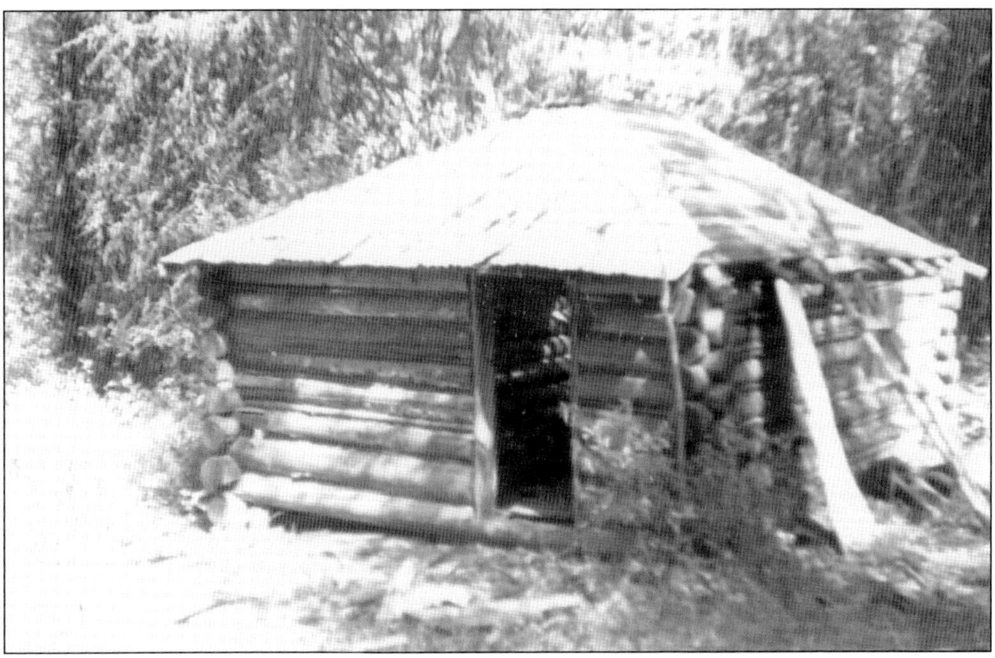

HUDSON BAY COMPANY CABIN. This is a remnant of an early Hudson Bay Company cabin near Davis Lake, Washington. It was used in the early 1800s, when the Kalispel Indians traded beaver hides for manufactured arrowheads, axes, wool fabric, guns, tobacco, and other items. The worldwide fur-trading business resulted in many changes in the lifestyle of all the Indians in the country.

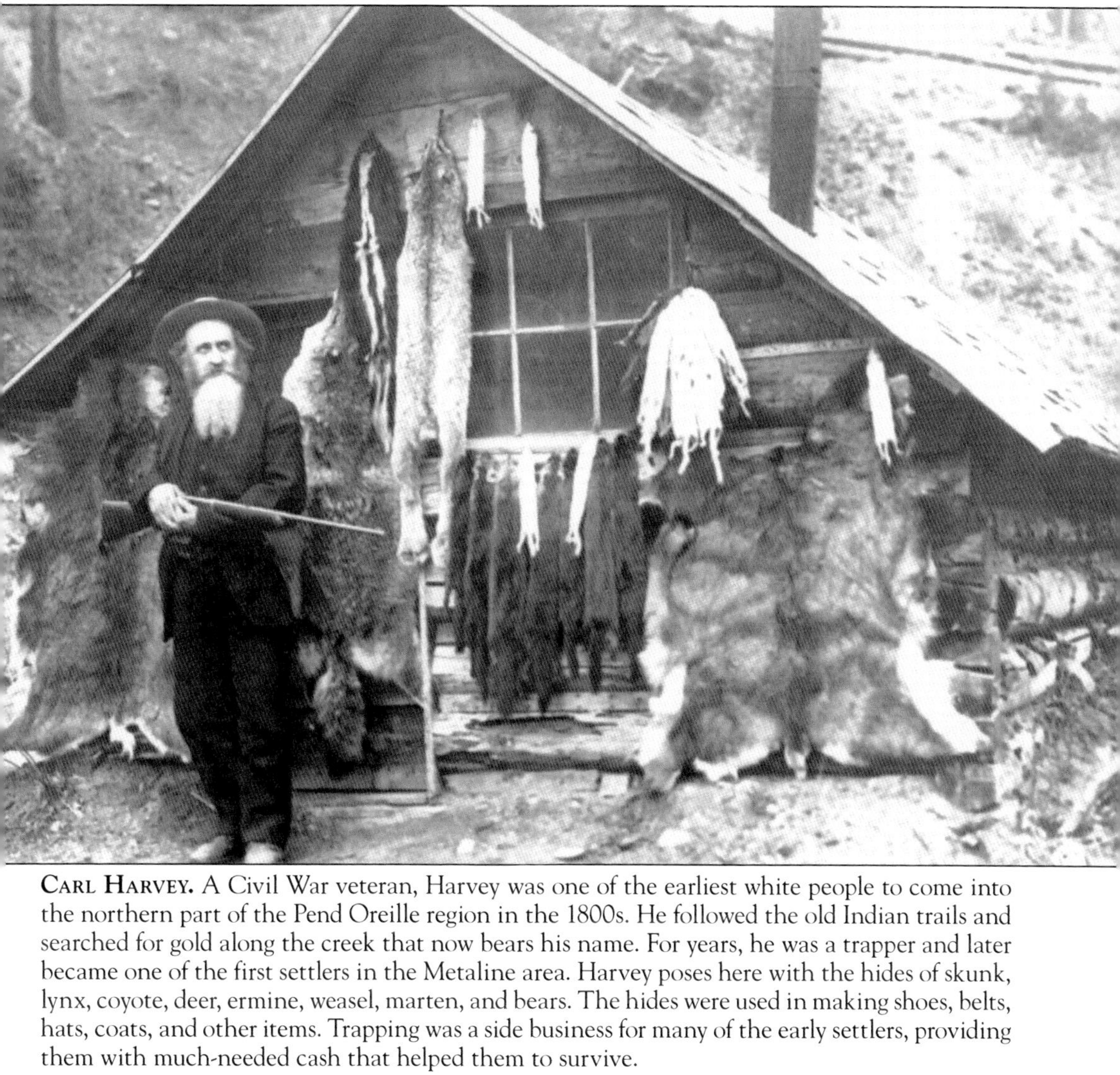

Carl Harvey. A Civil War veteran, Harvey was one of the earliest white people to come into the northern part of the Pend Oreille region in the 1800s. He followed the old Indian trails and searched for gold along the creek that now bears his name. For years, he was a trapper and later became one of the first settlers in the Metaline area. Harvey poses here with the hides of skunk, lynx, coyote, deer, ermine, weasel, marten, and bears. The hides were used in making shoes, belts, hats, coats, and other items. Trapping was a side business for many of the early settlers, providing them with much-needed cash that helped them to survive.

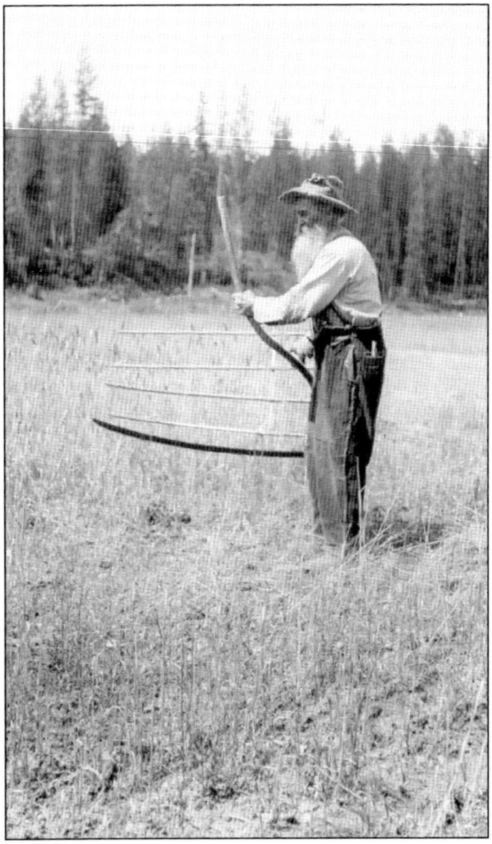

Carl Harvey Harvesting. After years of prospecting and mining, Harvey settled down, cleared land, and built a cabin in the Metaline area. He is shown harvesting his rye crop. He is buried not far from his cabin. Years later, Harvey's neighbors got together and, after a brief ceremony that included Boy Scouts, Girl Scouts, veterans, and friends, honored him as a Civil War veteran and early settler in Pend Oreille County.

Catholic Fathers. Father Pierre Jean DeSmet (right) was a Jesuit Catholic missionary to the Indians in North America. He was born at Termonde, Belgium, on January 30, 1801. He attended preparatory seminary at Mechelen, Belgium, and entered the Jesuit novitiate in 1821. Father DeSmet died at St. Louis, Missouri, on May 23, 1873. He established many missions in the West and crossed the United States and Europe to raise money for the missions. The Flatheads had heard stories of the "Black Robes" and the "Book" and wanted to learn more about Christianity. In 1844, DeSmet and Hoecken (left) were missionaries to the Kalispel Indians.

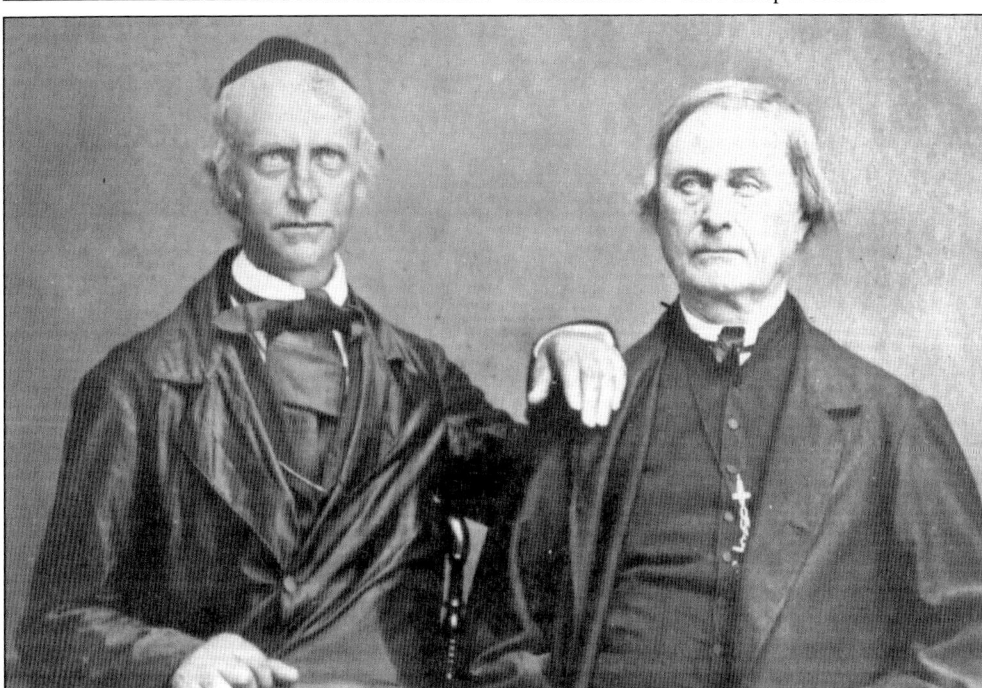

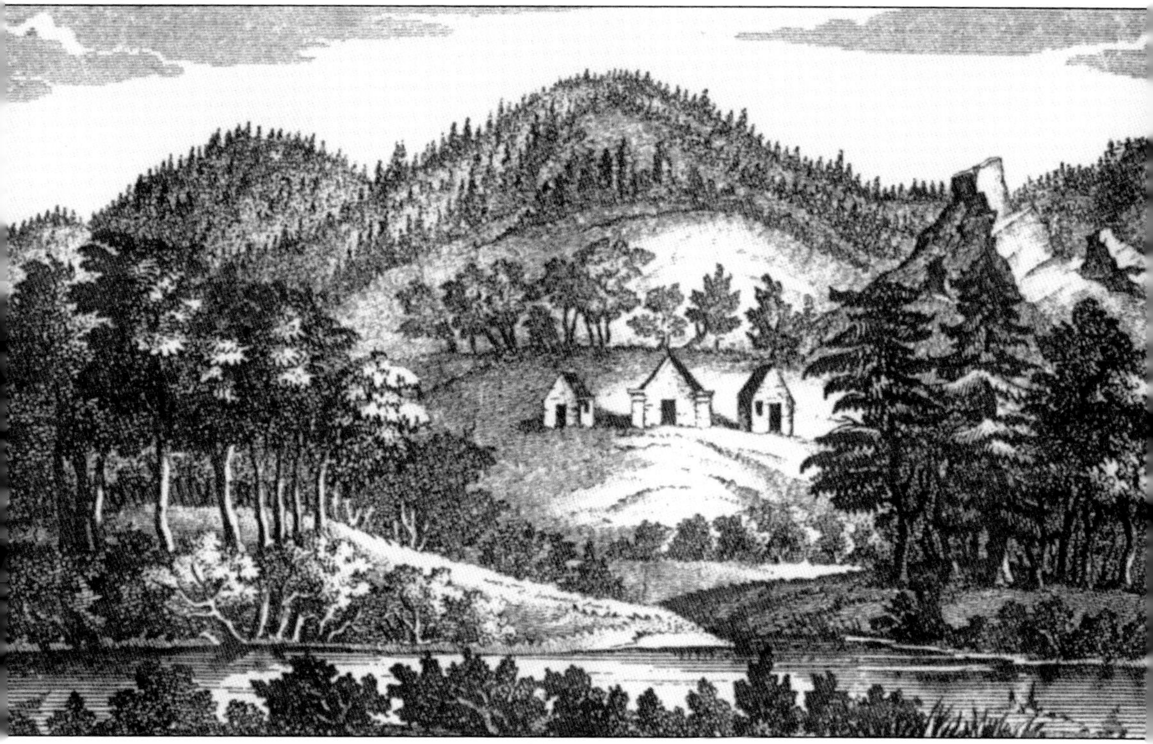

St. Ignatius Mission. This mission was established by Father DeSmet, Father Hoecken, and Brother John McGean. It was located close to the grotto, across the Pend Oreille River from Usk. The missionaries helped the Kalispel Indians clear land, plant crops, and construct buildings. Their goal was that the Indians would lead settled lives. The mission was successful for several years. However, it was located on clay-type soil and on a flood plain. In 1854, a severe flood washed away most of the buildings and ruined the fields. The Kalispel Indians were encouraged to move to Montana and start a new St. Ignatius Mission. There were mixed feelings about leaving their home along the Pend Oreille River, and many drifted back home. In 1914, the Kalispel were granted a reservation along the river.

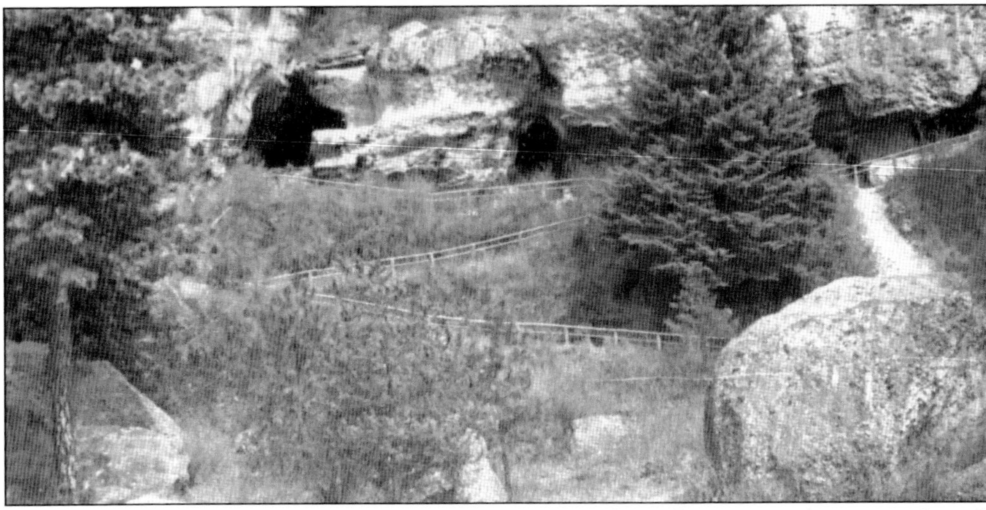

Manresa Grotto. The Manresa Grotto is a large natural conglomerate rock cave on the side of a cliff located on the Kalispel Indian Reservation. The cave had a stone altar and flat rock slabs that were used as seats. It was part of the St. Ignatius Mission, which operated from 1844 to 1854 by Father Jean DeSmet and Father Adrian Hoecken. The grotto continues to be used for special church ceremonies.

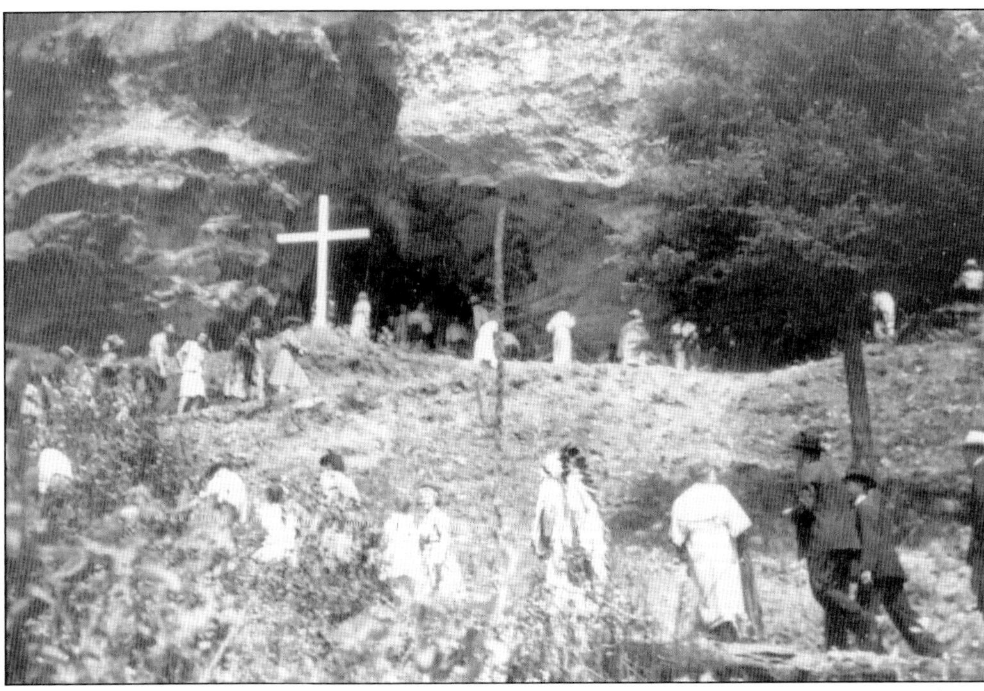

Mission Centennial Celebration. On July 2 and 3, 1944, Kalispel Indians and visitors gathered at the Manresa Grotto for a centennial celebration of the St. Ignatius Mission. Since then, there have been a number of positive changes in housing, erection of major buildings, and improvements in the lives of the members of the tribe.

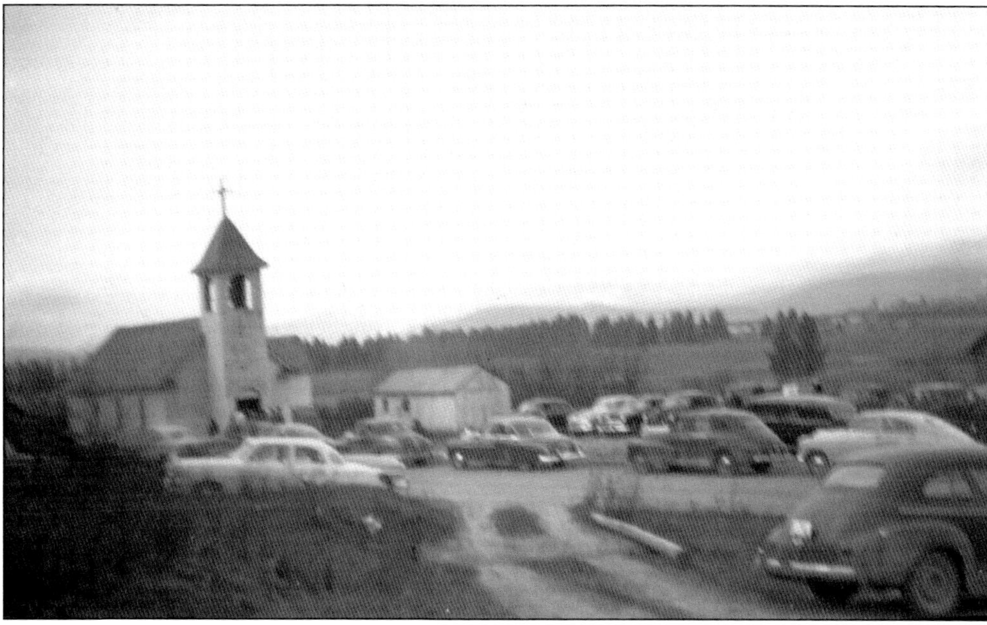

Kalispel Catholic Church. The small Our Lady of Sorrows Catholic Church is located on the Kalispel Indian Reservation. The priest from Newport, serves mass several times during the month.

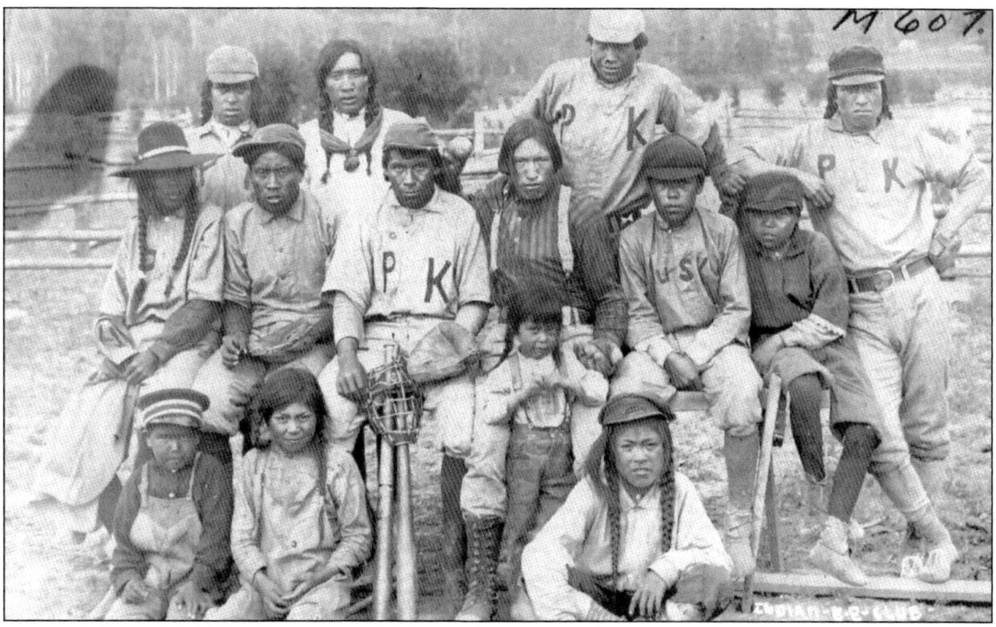

Kalispel Baseball Team. Baseball games were a big attraction for the communities in the early days of the county. The Kalispel Usk team included adults and children. Shown here are, from left to right, (first row) Abraham Nick, Helen Nick, unidentified, and Mildred Nick; (second row) Willy Tom, Mose Nick, Alice Ignace, Willy Sam, Frank Nick, and Ignace Nick Back; (third row) ? Andrews, Antoine Peuse, Leo Peuse, and Ray Pierre.

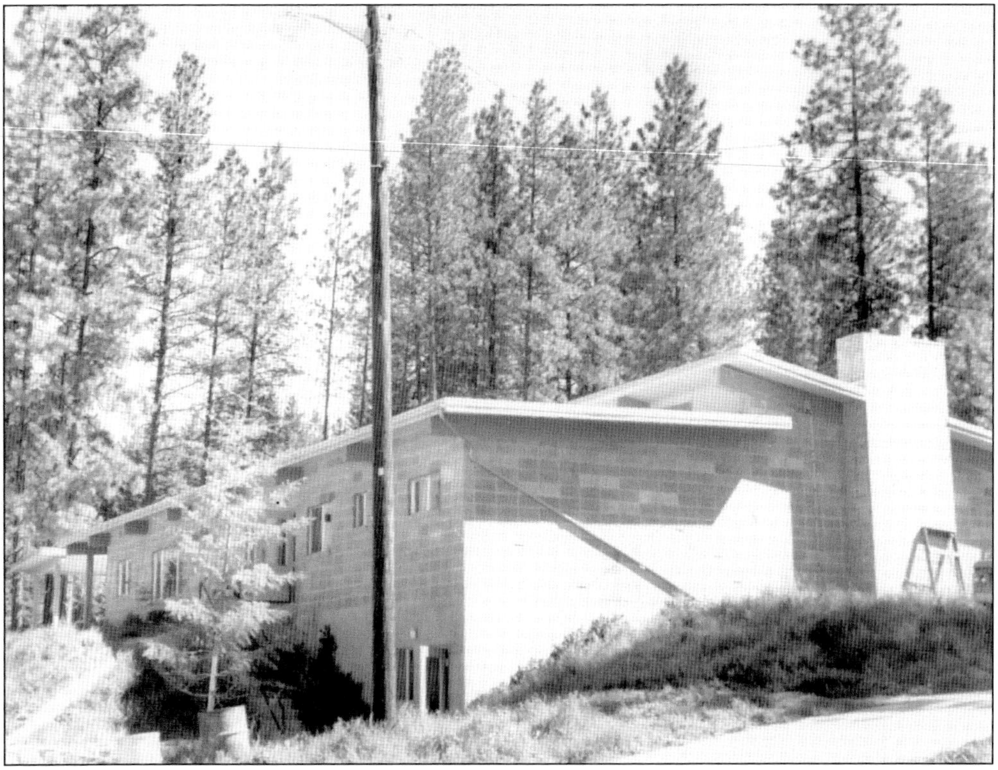

KALISPEL RESERVATION BUILDING. This is one of the buildings that have been added to the Kalispel complex on the reservation in recent years. The tribe has made many changes to improve living conditions for all of its members. Its future lies in the young people.

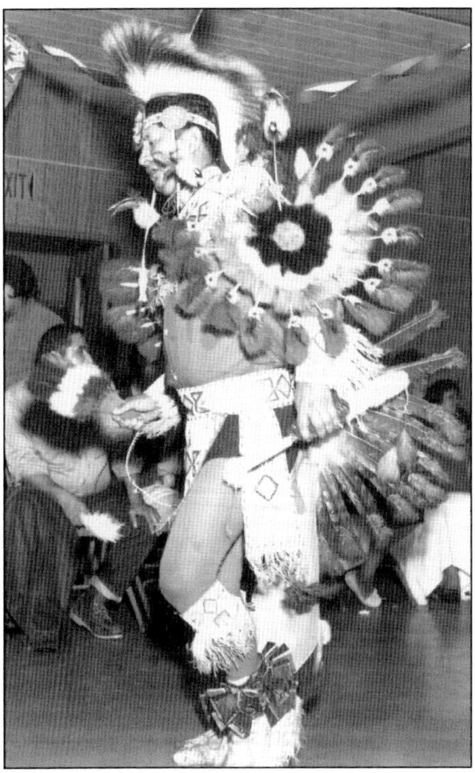

KALISPEL POWWOW. Every summer, the Kalispel tribe invites other tribes and visitors to its annual powwow at the Ceremonial Park on the reservation. The tribe members, old and young, are encouraged to wear beautiful costumes and compete in intricate traditional dances, stick games, and races. There is also a buffalo barbecue and other activities. Visitors are encouraged to observe and take photographs of the large buffalo herd.

Three

A New County

The 1862 Homestead Act lured thousands of people to the western United States, drawn by the promise of land ownership and adventures. Free land was available to anyone who filed for it, improved it, and lived on it for five years. The Northern Pacific Railroad and real-estate businesses advertised for pioneers.

By the mid-1800s, land-hungry pioneers began to migrate into the Pend Oreille Valley, which was then part of Stevens County. The first pioneers settled in the open meadows, such as Calispel Valley, and started farming and ranching. Others homesteaded in the mountains and valleys. Pioneer life was not for the faint of heart—for most, it was a daily struggle just to survive.

The Great Northern Railroad reached Newport in 1892, and settlers began to pour into the region. By 1911, the population had increased, industries and businesses were starting to flourish, trains were running through the region, and roads were improving. The region had a healthy-looking future. For years, there had been idle talk around pot-bellied stoves and spittoons about separating from Stevens County. People often grumbled about the long trip to the Stevens County courthouse in Colville. Businesspeople were unhappy about representation and the use of tax money. When residents of the area began to agitate for a county of their own, Fred L. Wolf, owner and publisher of the *Newport Miner*, and Fred Trumbull, an Ione attorney, blanketed the county with petitions and lobbied legislators. Sen. Oliver Hall of Colfax, brother to Elmer Hall, founder of Ione, was very sympathetic to the proposal for a new county. The legislature passed a bill creating Pend Oreille County, and Gov. Marion E. Hay signed it into law. It went into effect on June 10, 1911. The new county was named after the Pend d' Oreille tribe, which had inhabited the region for years. The enthusiastic governor joined the celebration by taking a train trip the length of the county, from Newport to Metaline Falls.

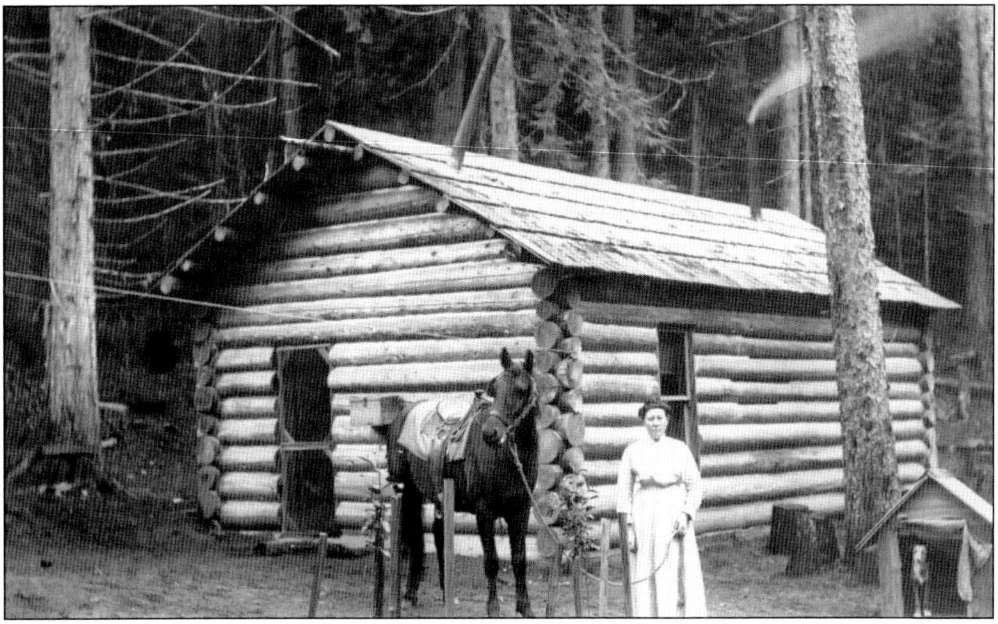

Mrs. Olson. This woman, identified as Mrs. Olson, is standing in front of her log house with her pony and dog. Pioneers who settled in forest areas had to cut down the trees and select dry, straight pine or spruce logs of approximately the same size. They carefully notched each log and fit them tightly together. Moss or clay was used to seal the cracks. Shakes were used as roofing. The small cabins usually had one or two rooms.

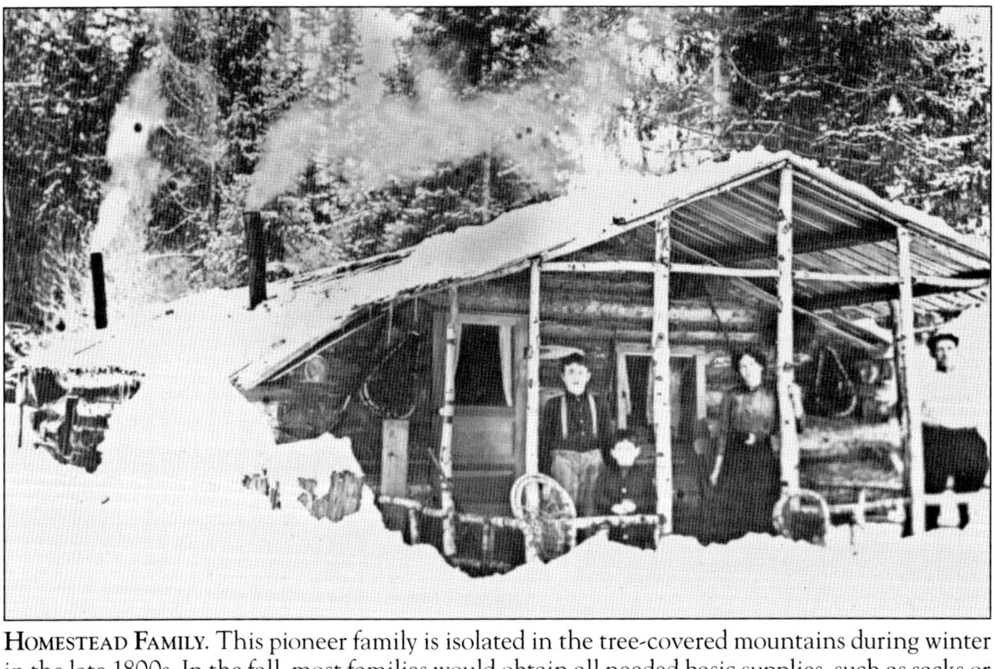

Homestead Family. This pioneer family is isolated in the tree-covered mountains during winter in the late 1800s. In the fall, most families would obtain all needed basic supplies, such as sacks or barrels of flour, sugar, salt, and maybe some canned food for the long winter months. Snowshoes were necessary to travel trails in order to hunt or perhaps get to a trading post for mail or to visit neighbors.

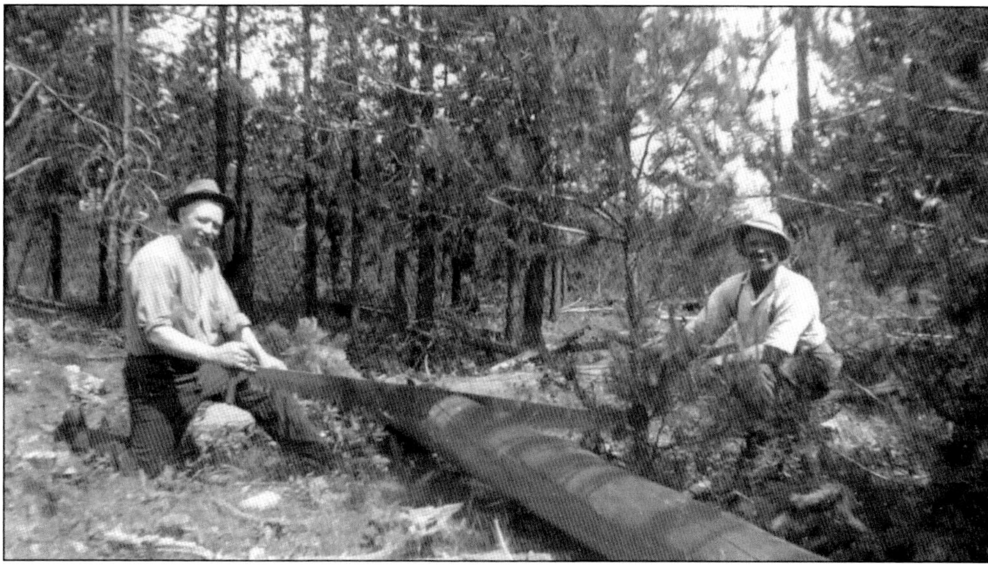

CROSSCUT SAW. Ernest (left) and Ed Sherman are shown using a crosscut saw to cut a log. Early homesteaders who moved into wooded areas used a few basic tools, such as axes, wedges, and crosscut saws, to cut down trees before they could plant gardens and crops or build log houses and other buildings.

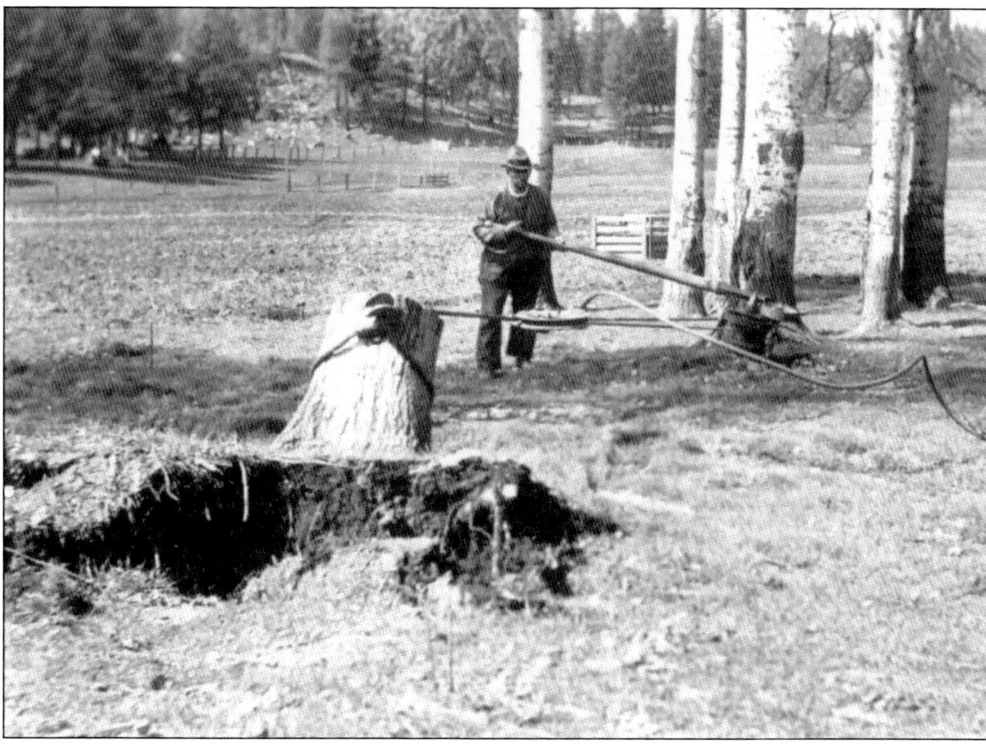

STUMP PULLER. Shown here is an early stump puller. Before the soil could be worked for a garden or crops, stumps had to be pulled, dug, blasted, or burned out. It was backbreaking and time-consuming work for the pioneer farmers. This farmer uses cables and slowly pulls out the stump. Some farmers used horses.

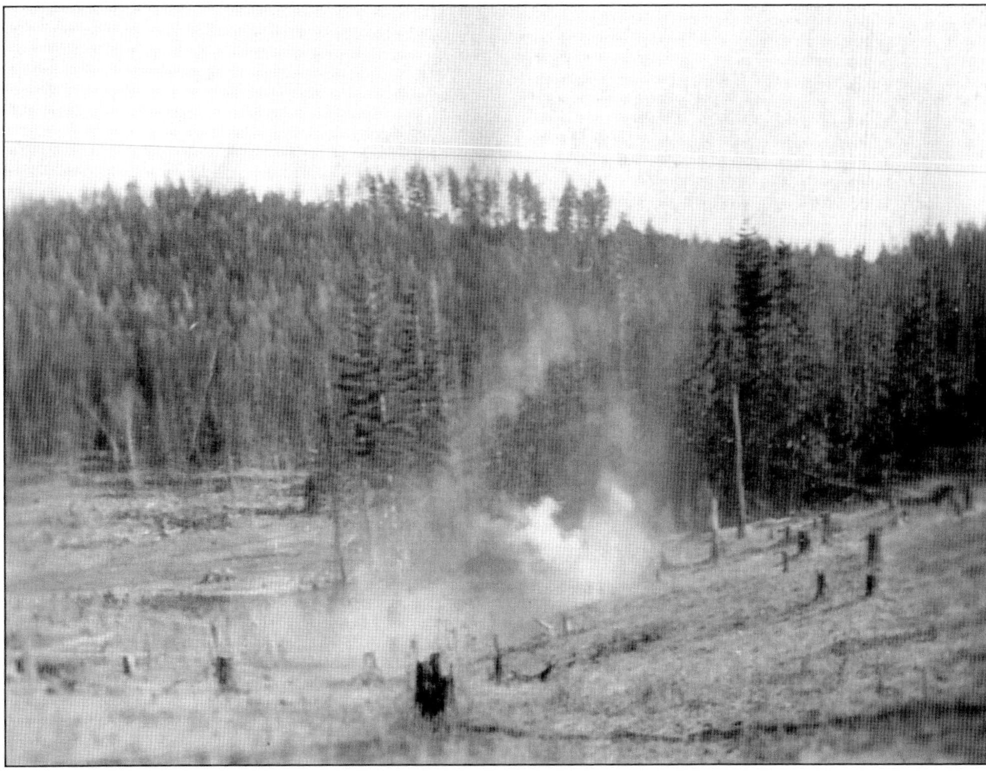

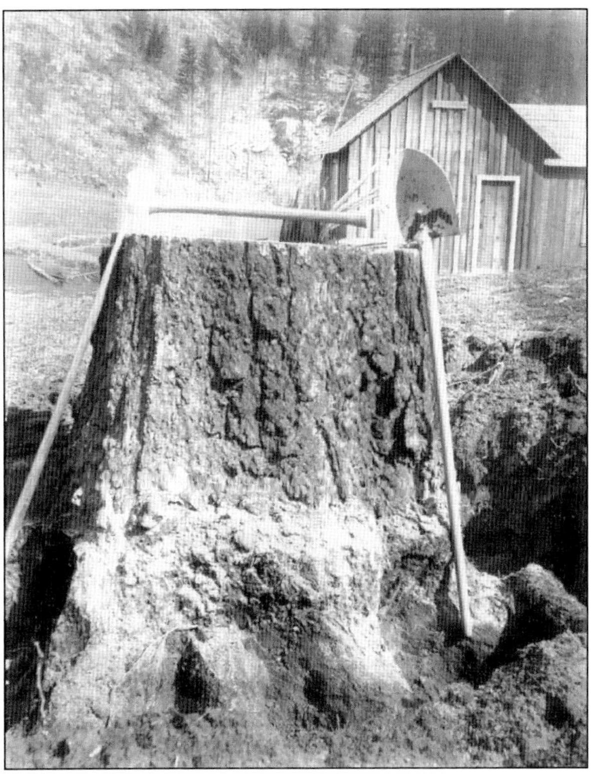

Blasting Stumps. Many farmers used dynamite to blast out stumps. It required putting blasting powder under the stump and lighting a fuse. In the 1920s, Earl Hupp, Pend Oreille County extension agent, obtained cheap government blasting power for farmers. When Gov. Marion Hay toured the new county in June 1911, at his stop at Cusick, the welcoming committee surprised him by blasting stumps for a new park.

Pioneer Tools. A basic shovel, an axe, and a pick were often used by early farmers to dig out stumps in order to clear land for planting crops. Such tools were priceless possessions for young farmers in a time when money was scarce. In some cases, a wilderness was cleared and tamed with fewer tools than what the average person has on his garage shelf today.

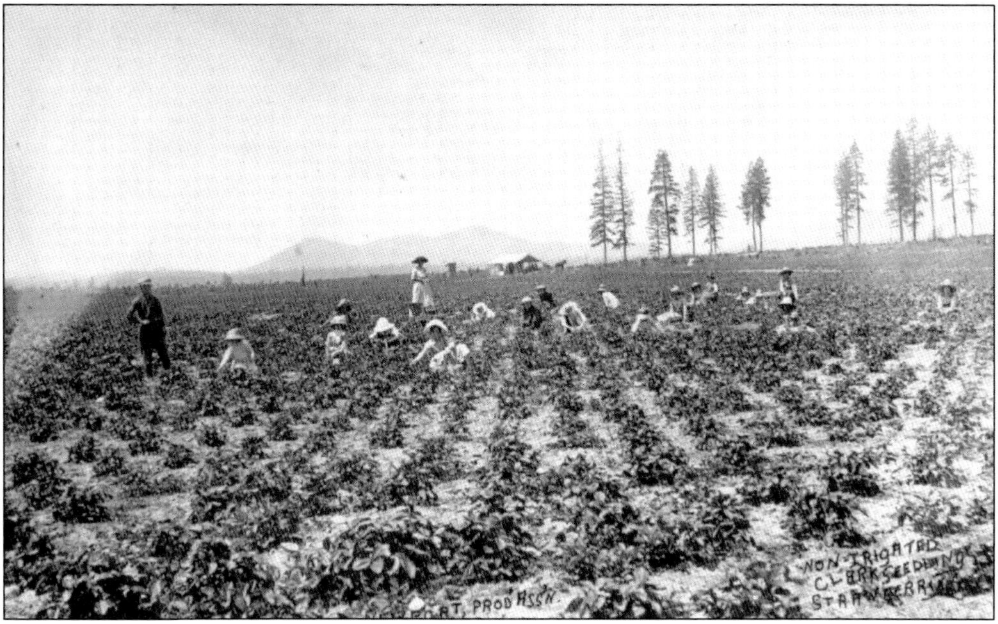

STRAWBERRY FIELD AT SILVER BIRCH. The Silver Birch strawberry farm was located on a bench outside of Newport. Charles Talmadge owned and operated the farm. He raised prize-winning hogs and cows. In 1895, he and his brother Warren acquired 40 acres of land and platted the townsite of Newport. They formed the Newport Washington Land Company.

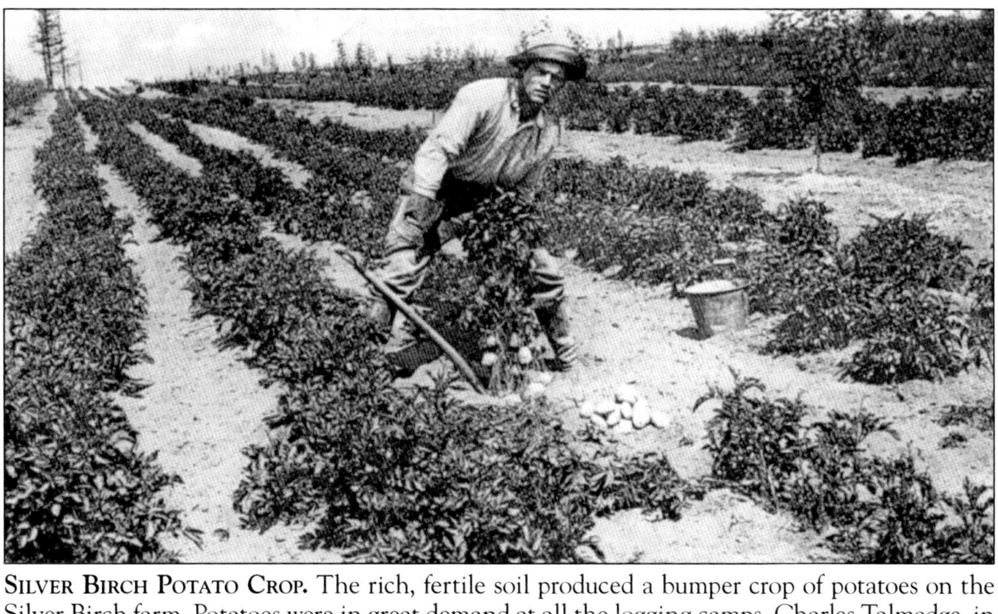

SILVER BIRCH POTATO CROP. The rich, fertile soil produced a bumper crop of potatoes on the Silver Birch farm. Potatoes were in great demand at all the logging camps. Charles Talmadge, in addition to running his farm and prize-winning stock, was manager of the opera house and vice president of the Pend d'Oreille State Bank.

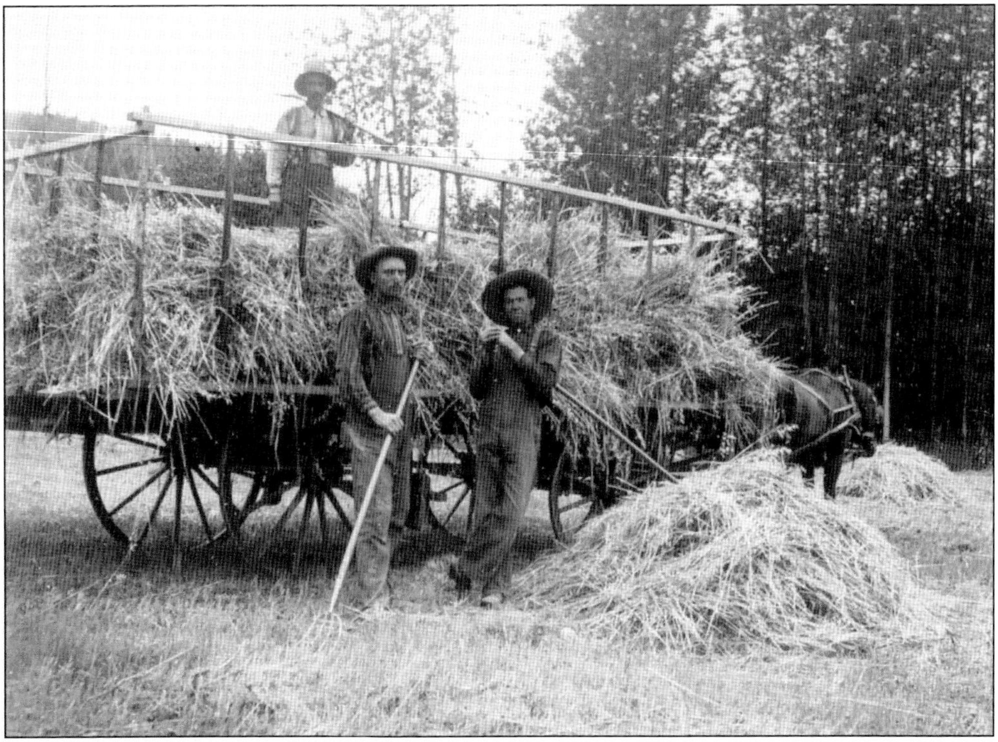

Harvesting Hay. Men harvest hay at the Sky Ranch in Spring Valley, near Newport. In the early years, the rich soil produced outstanding hay crops. Sky Ranch was one of the largest and most-productive ranches in the area. Harvesting required many workers and horses. Often, neighbors helped each other to harvest.

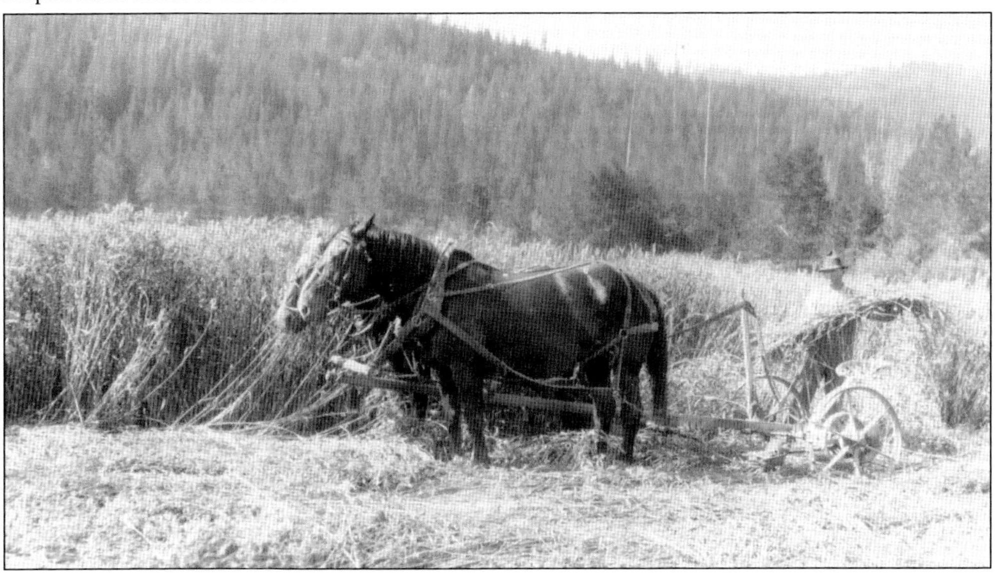

Fred Johnston Cutting Wheat. Johnston, an early homesteader in Spring Valley, is cutting wheat by hand. It will be put into shocks, dried in the sun, and then threshed at a stationary threshing machine. In his spare time, Johnston enjoyed taking photographs of daily life at his farm. Albums of his photographs were donated to the Pend Oreille County Historical Society.

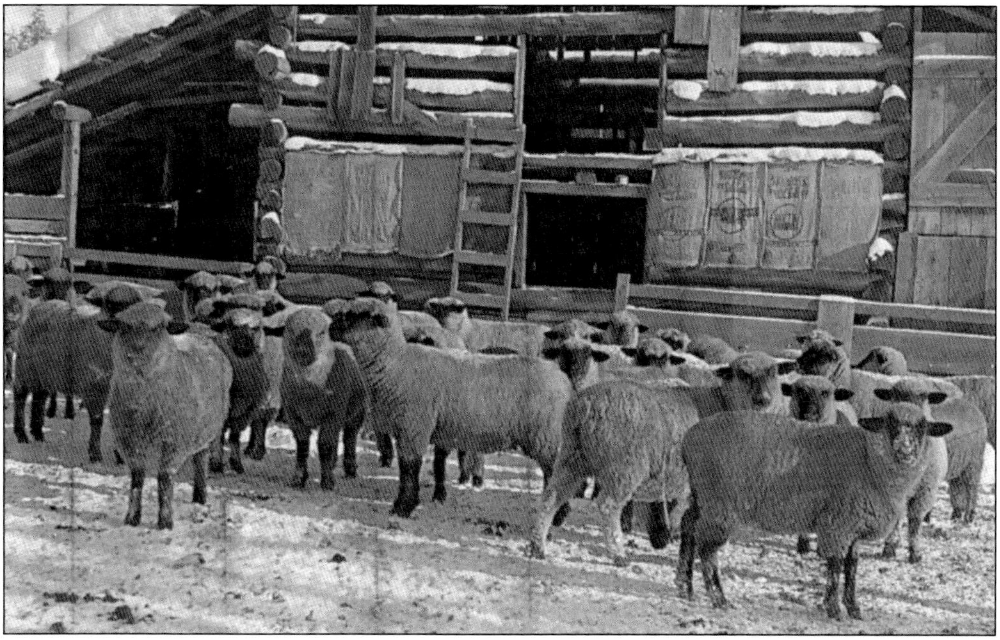

Sheep. Raising sheep was a good cash crop for many farmers. Here, a flock of sheep moves around the Sky Ranch barn in Spring Valley. Successful farmers in the area raised cattle, sheep, and other animals.

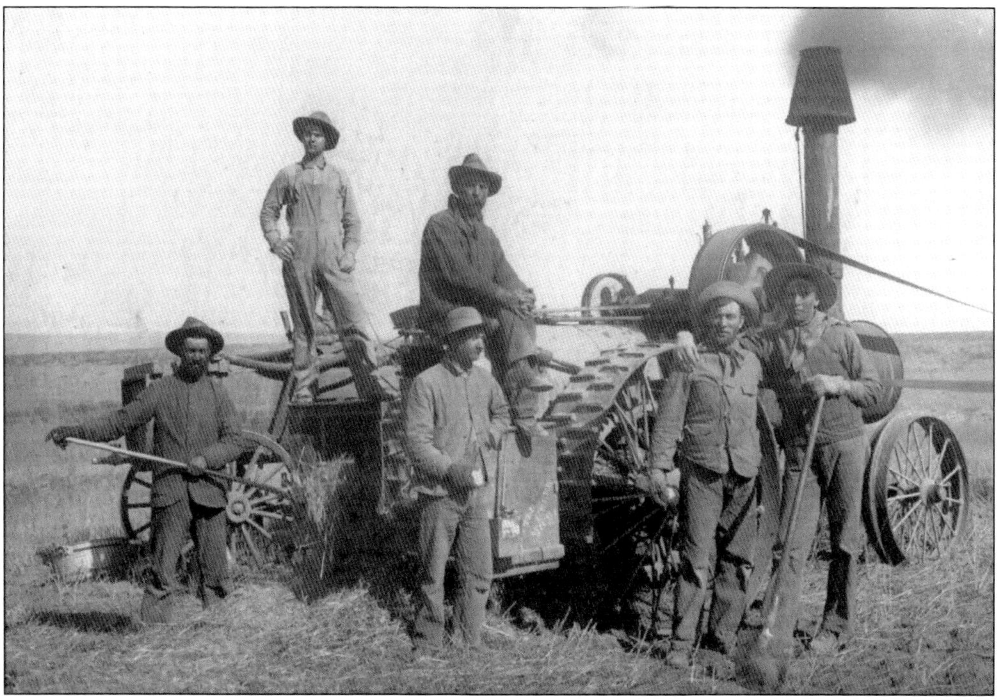

Homesteaders. Many homesteaders worked other jobs to support their families and the homestead. A number of homesteaders harvested wheat in the Palouse country south of Spokane. In the early years, it took long days, from sunrise to sunset, as well as many men, horses, and heavy equipment to harvest crops. Note the heavy steam tractor being used.

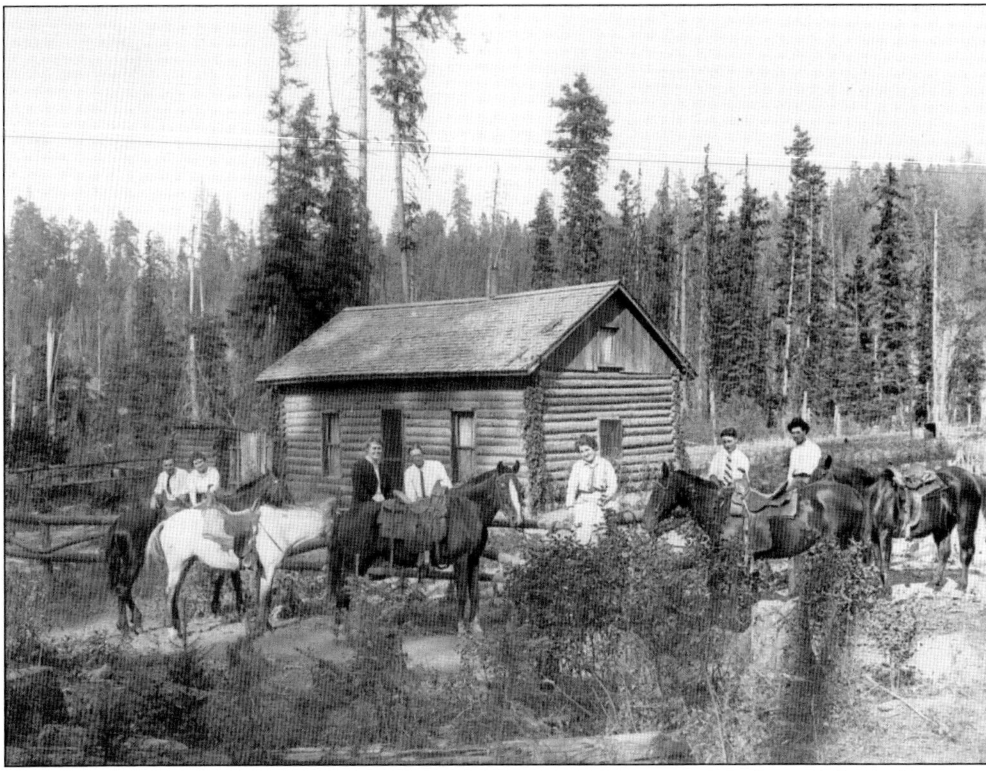

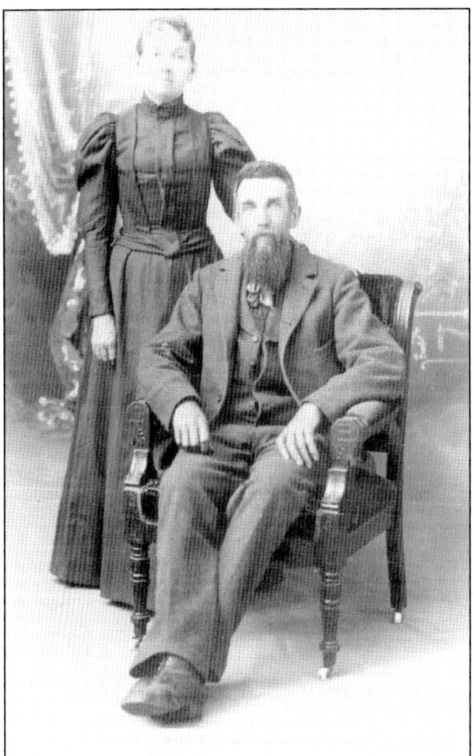

Phil and Winifred LaSota. The LaSotas were early settlers in the north end of the county. Phil's homestead was in Aladdin (Cronin). He married Winifred in 1917 and worked at the Ohio Match Company for several years. They did a little prospecting from time to time. Later, he became postmaster at Metaline Falls from 1935 to 1955.

Robert Payne and Sarah Jared. Robert Payne, Sarah Jared, and their four children came to Washington in 1880 and settled at Calispel Lake. Later, they moved close to Usk. The family lost its first house in the 1894 flood.

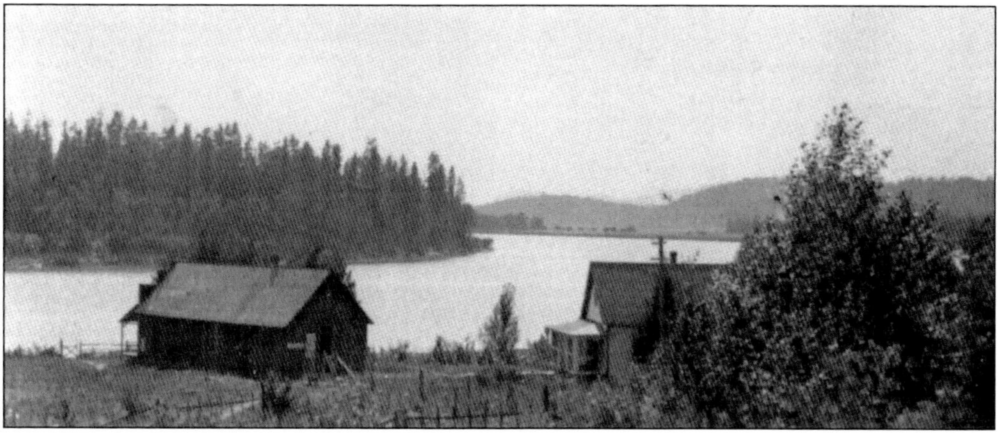

Gardiner Landing. Robert and Sarah Jared moved to Gardiner Landing in 1904. With the help of other family members, they built a trading post, which included a store and post office. Robert became the first postmaster. Later, the little community became known as Jared, Washington. Today, it is home to the large Riverview Bible Camp.

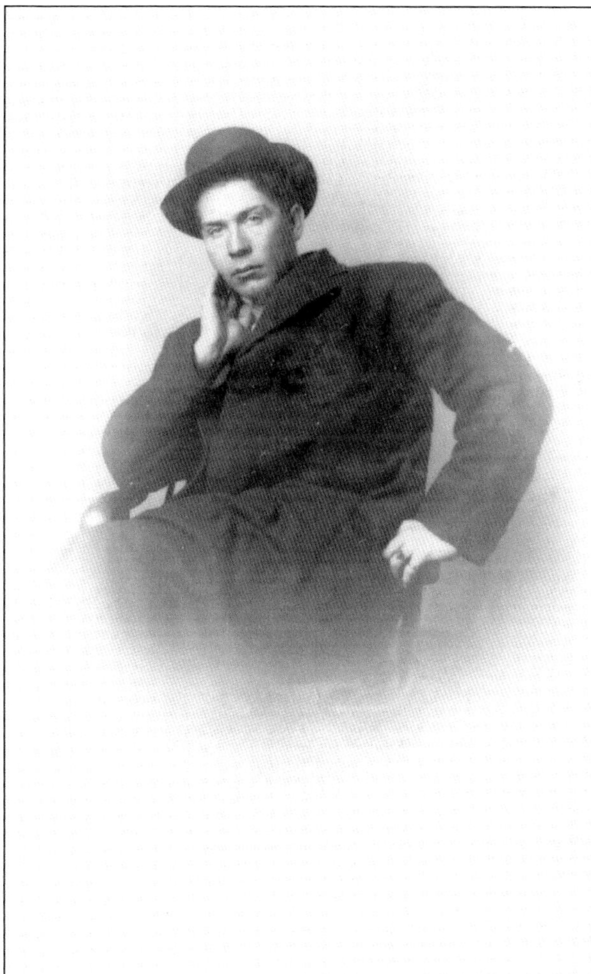

Oscar Wolf. Wolf was the publisher of the Metaline Falls newspaper, *Metaline News*. He was the brother of Fred Wolf, publisher of the *Newport Miner* newspaper. Oscar Wolf and his wife made important contributions to their community. It was an exciting day when the first slim newspaper appeared on the dirt streets of the pioneer community in 1911.

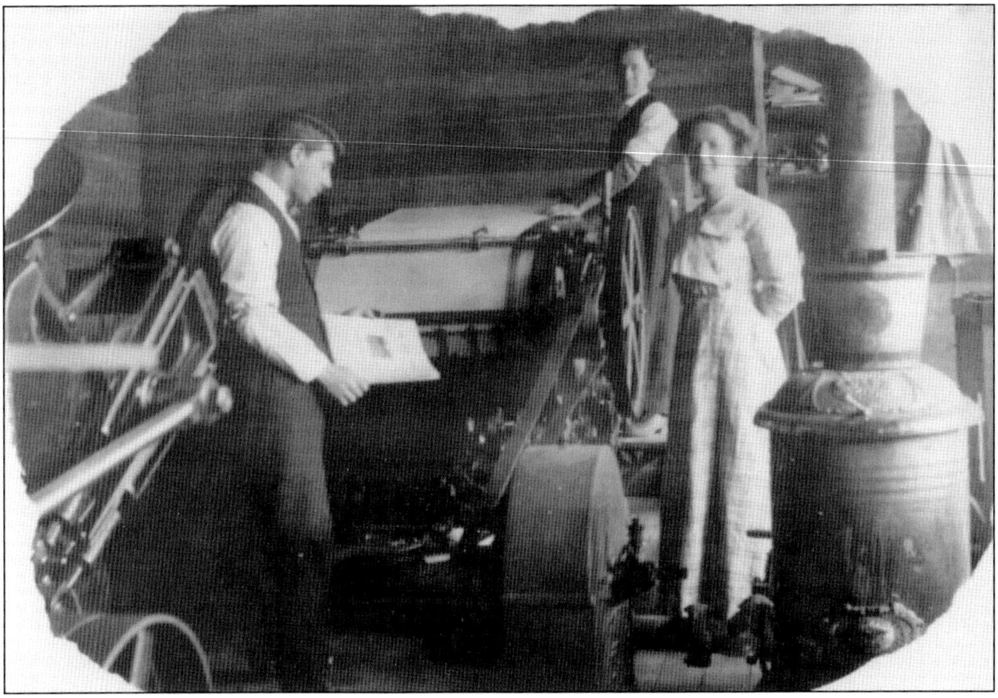

METALINE NEWS. The Metaline Falls newspaper office staff is getting ready to print the local news. Note the early printing equipment. Many local newspapers at that time were the only source of community and world news. The staff would usually pick up the news by visiting with members of the community.

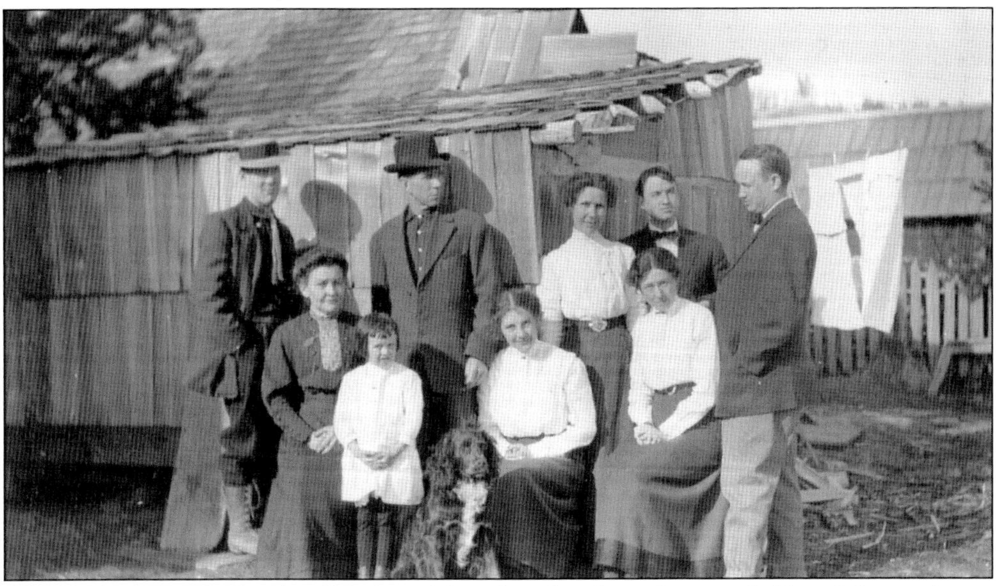

READING FAMILY. The Reading family and friends gather for a photograph. From left to right are (first row) Carlie Trumbull, Donna Jean, and two unidentified women; (second row) unidentified, Fred Williams, Bess Reading, Harry Reading, and Fred Trumbull. Harry Readings, a lawyer, had a homestead, and he assisted Oscar Wolf with the *Metaline News* paper. The Readings and Trumbulls were friends and came from Evert, Michigan.

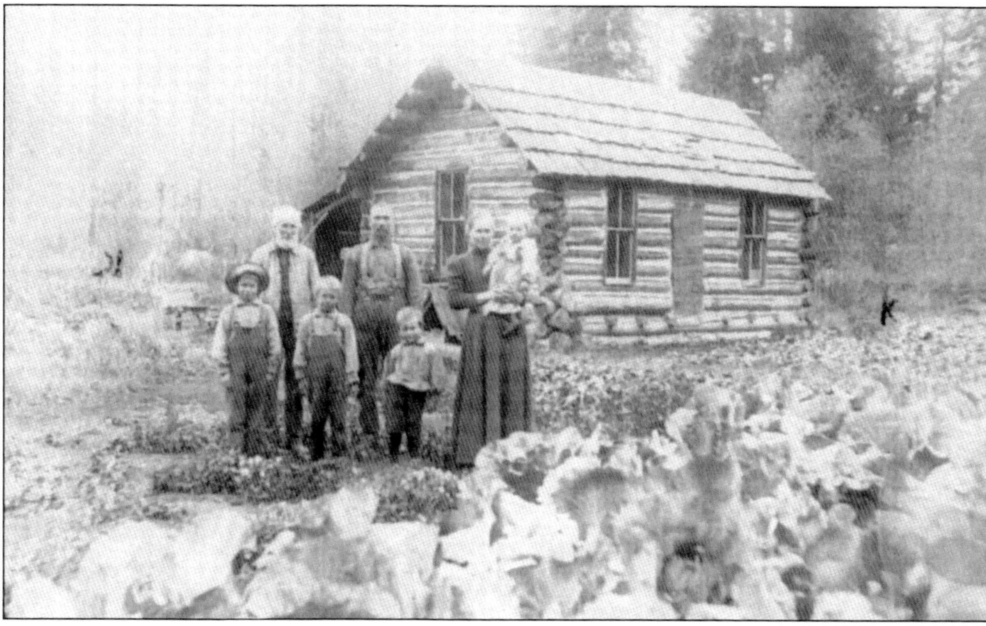

Wooding Family. Wes (right rear) and Jennie Wooding (front, holding baby) and their boys were homesteaders near the Tiger community, named after George Tiger. Wes had to go work in the mines, and Jennie worked the homestead. She wrote articles for the *Spokesman Review* about her experiences of gardening, building, and adding rooms to their cabin while caring for a new baby and young boys.

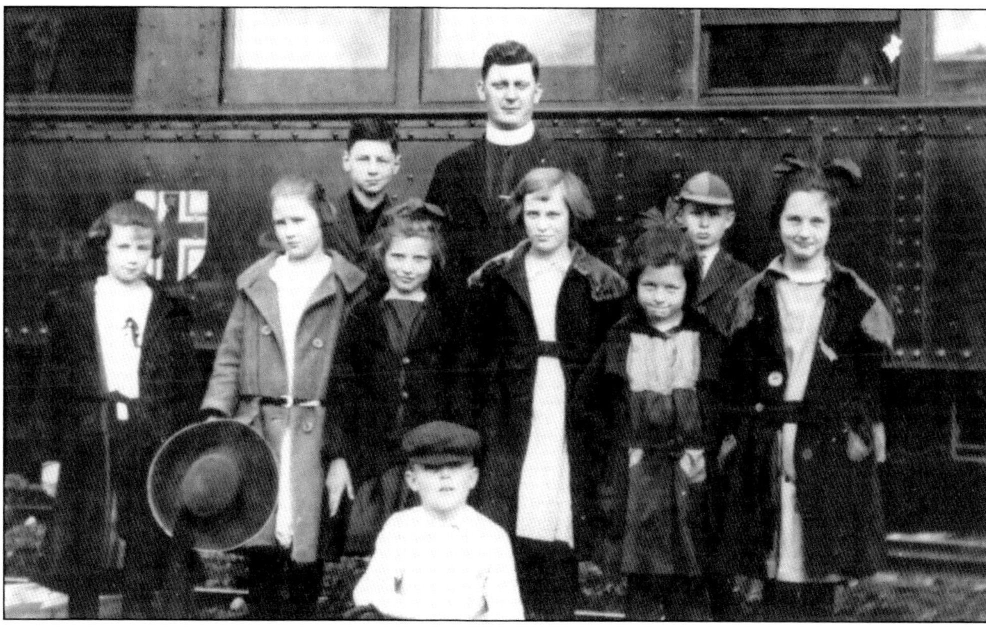

Catholic Church on Wheels. Father John J. Callanan is with a group of young people who were attending classes at the Church on Wheels in May 1923. The specially designed railroad car traveled the length of Pend Oreille County in the summer. The car had a chapel with an organ and could seat 75 people. There were also living quarters for the chaplain, superintendent, and porter.

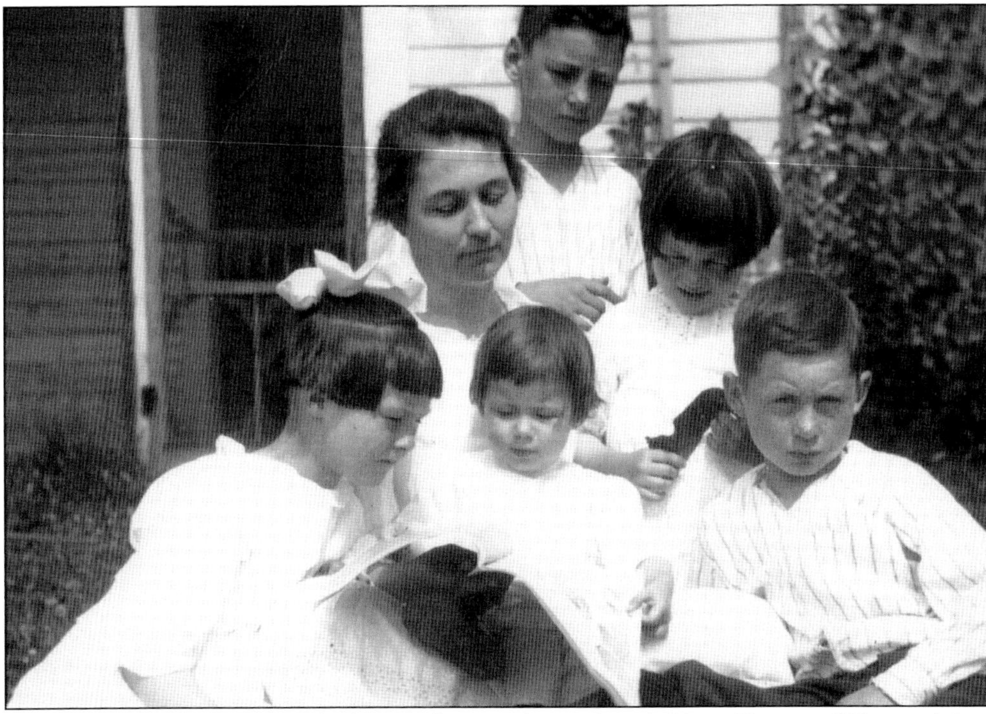

CRAWFORD FAMILY. Eliza Crawford is seen here reading to her children. Harry and Eliza and their five children were all very musically talented and contributed to countless programs, dances, marching bands, and church programs in the Ione area. Everyone in the family played several different instruments. They were the mainstay of St. Bernard's Catholic Church in Ione.

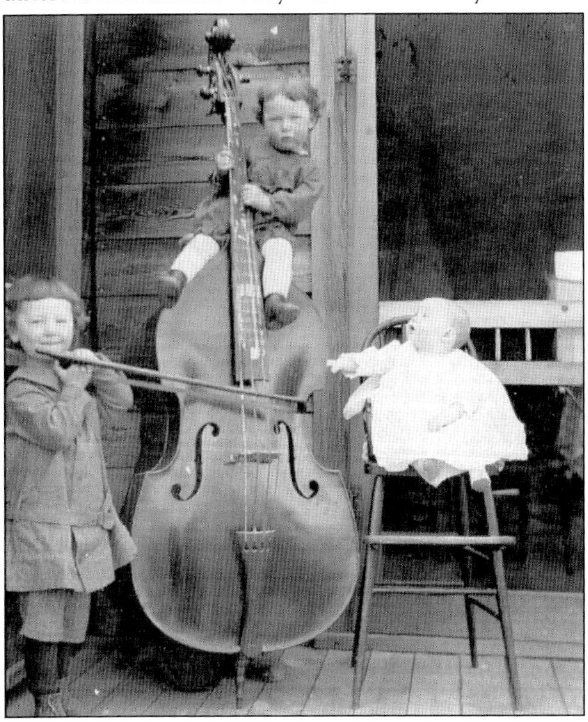

CRAWFORD CHILDREN. This staged photograph shows three musical Crawford children. Hugh holds the bow, little Harry sits on the neck of the bass viol, and baby Eleanor is in the high chair. In later years, Hugh wrote several articles for *Big Smoke*, the annual publication of the Pend Oreille Historical Society, about the family's musical history in Ione.

Sylvester Cusick. Sylvester and Mary Cusick and their family were old-time pioneers who settled in the Calispel Valley. Sylvester (1833–1903) married Mary C. Weir in 1859. They eventually settled at Locke, Washington, and raised herds of cattle. Sylvester and Mary were parents of Joe Cusick, founder of Cusick.

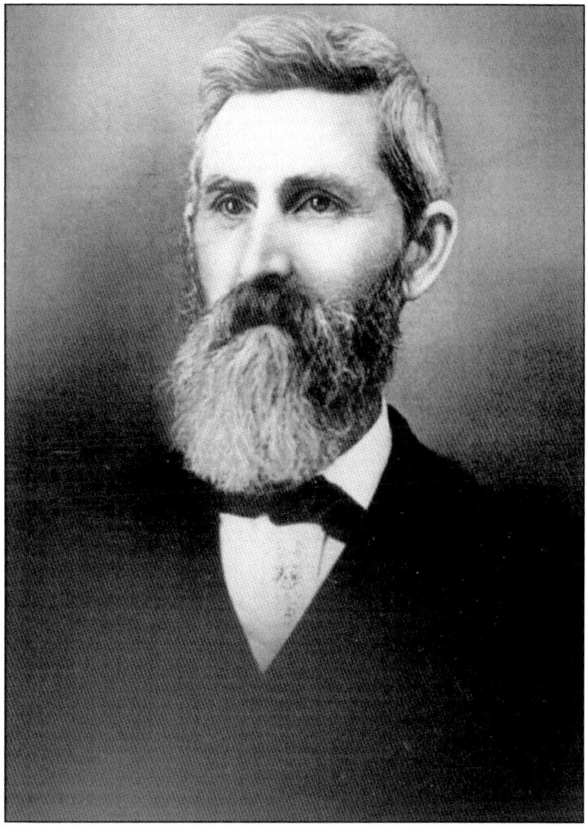

Winifred Cusick. On a doctor's recommendation, Winifred "Fred" C. Cusick (far right) moved to the Calispel area in 1886. The son of Sylvester and Mary Cusick, he married Lydia Bauer (second from right) in 1892. Fred, a farmer, was instrumental in establishing the Ponderay Creamery Association in Usk. He and his brother Joe built and operated the *New Volunteer* and *Elk* steamboats.

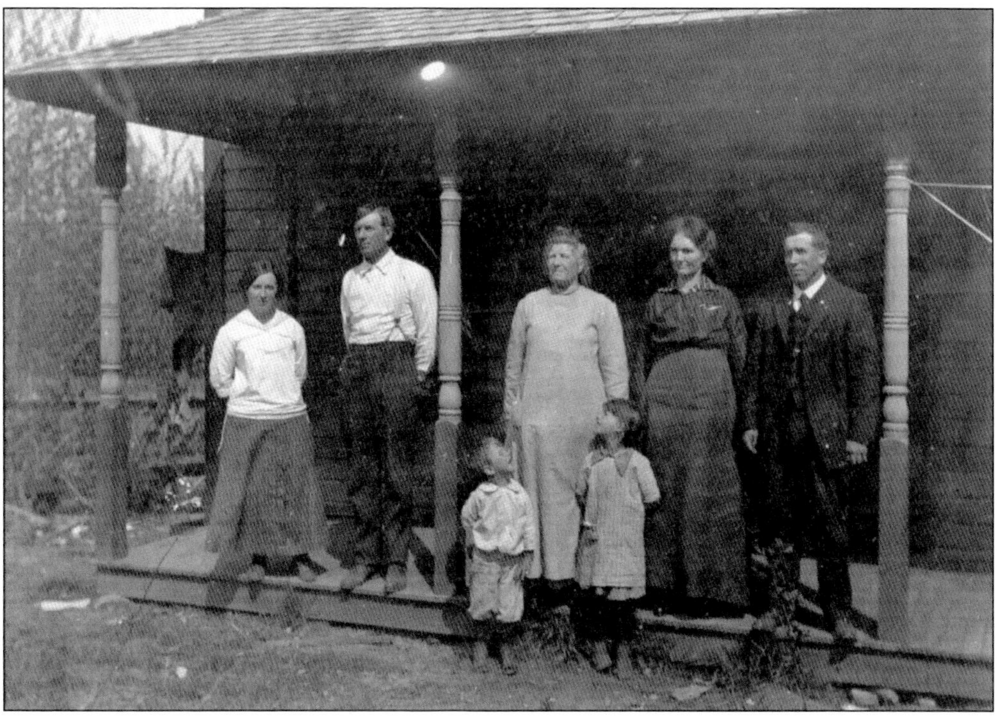

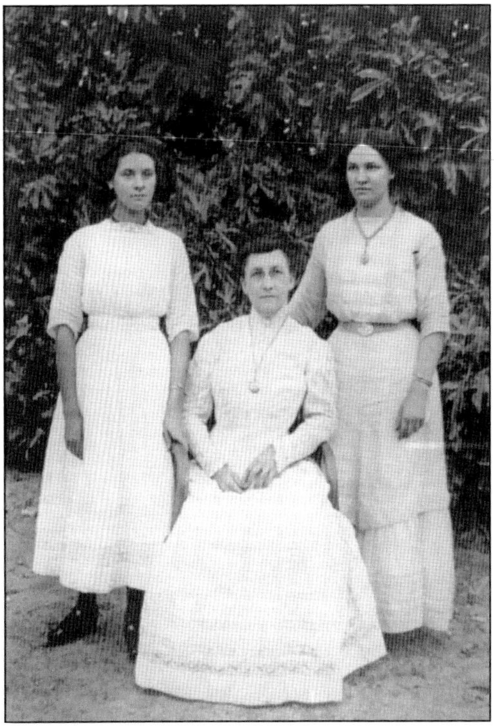

Cusick Sisters. Joe Cusick's three sisters are, from left to right, Coral Jean, Mary Ellen, and Jenny Cusick. Two of the sisters became teachers in the one-room schools that were common in the area at that time.

Mr. and Mrs. Joseph Cusick. Early homesteader Joe Cusick founded the town of Cusick. A colorful character, he owned and operated the steamboats *Red Cloud*, *Volunteer*, and *New Volunteer*, and, with brother Fred, the *Elk* steamer. The boats were sold in 1906 to the Pend Oreille Navigation Company. Joe Cusick was sent to the state penitentiary for four years for killing Harry Kilburn. Cusick died in California.

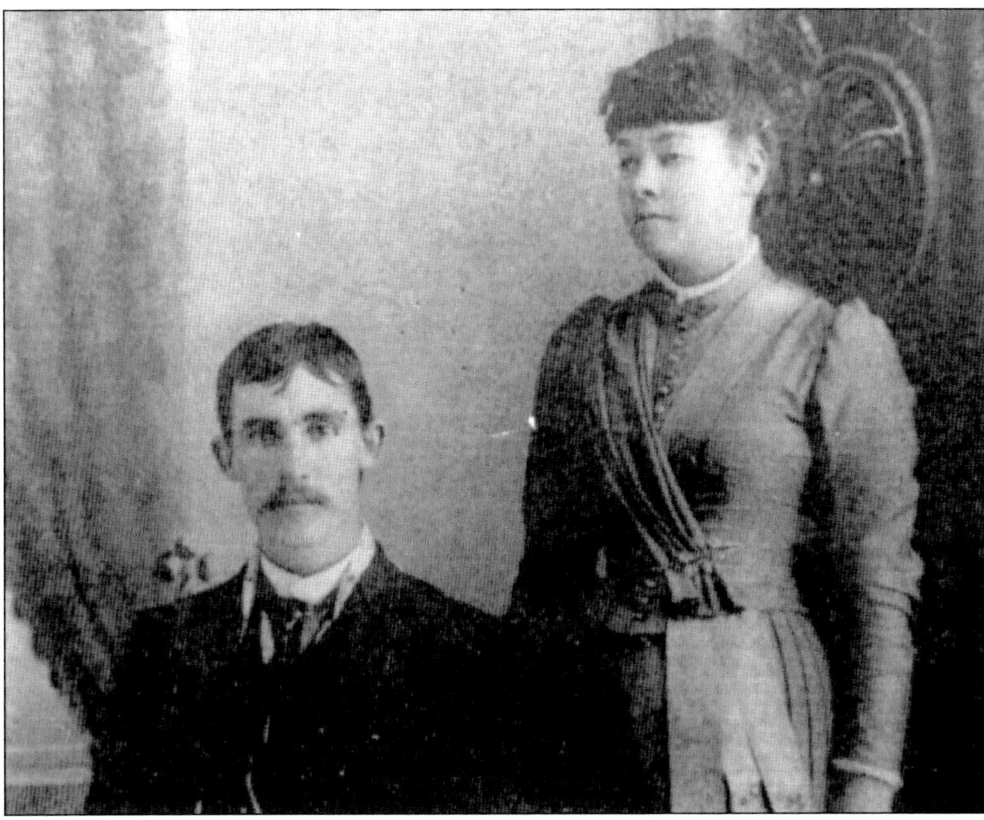

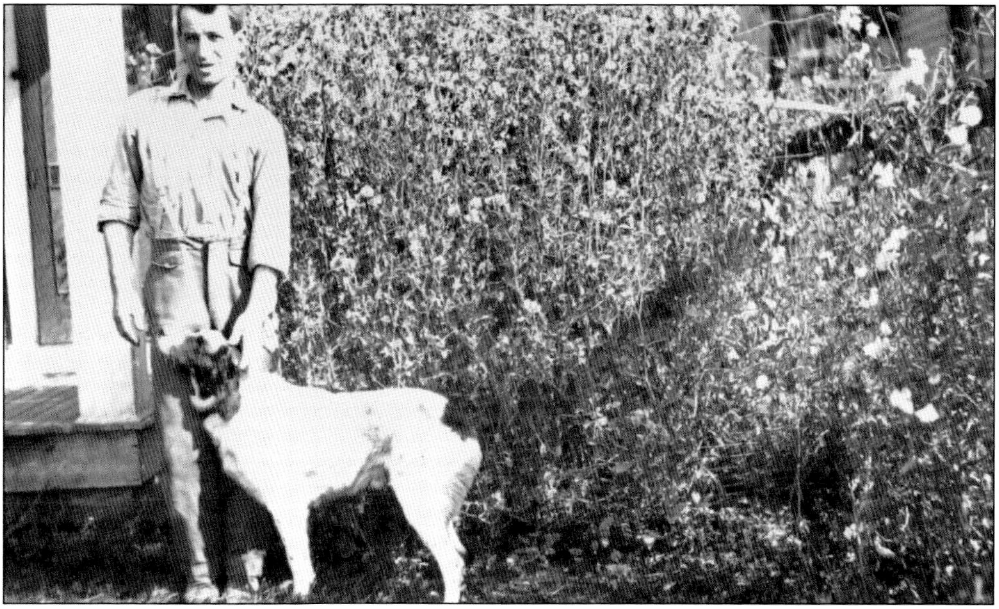

Adam Wike. An early settler in Cusick, Adam Wike came to the area in 1904. He taught school for a session and then became a partner with his brother in a general store. He was a leader in the community, served on the school board, and coached baseball teams. In addition, he was a rodeo booster and was influential in organizing the county fair.

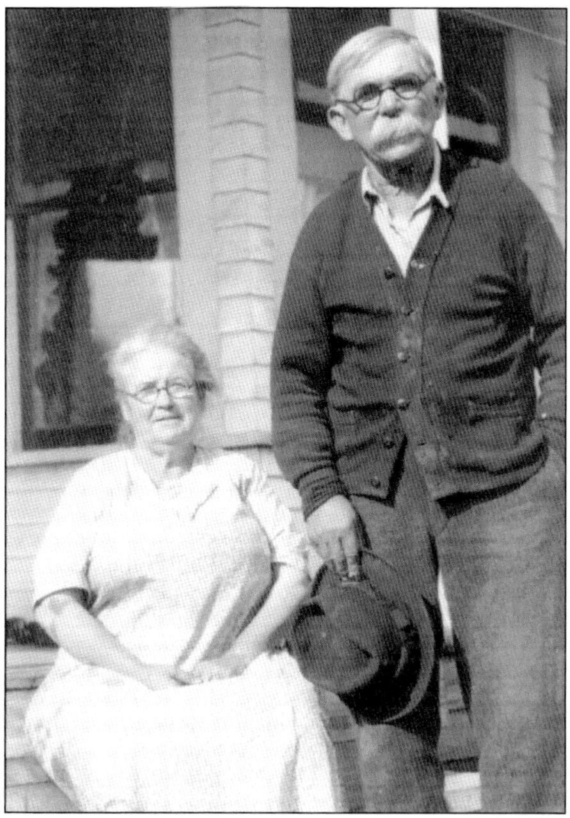

William J. and Ida Fountain. William Fountain was born in 1860 in Kentucky and came into the Washington Territory in 1884. He taught in the first public school in 1889 and 1890. William married Ida in 1896, and they settled and farmed in the Locke, Washington, area. He was a commissioner for both Stevens and Pend Oreille Counties. He and his extended family built up one of the largest ranches in the county.

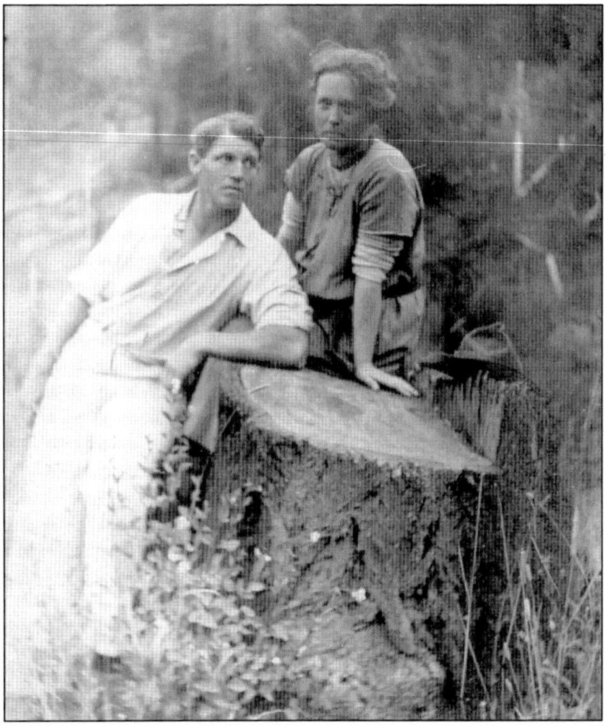

Alex and Laura Bradley. These college-trained homesteaders lived near Tacoma Creek, Washington, in the early 1900s. Alex, a mining engineer, had done gold mining in Alaska. Laura was a botany teacher. They carved out a home for their children in the wilderness in the middle of the Pend Oreille region.

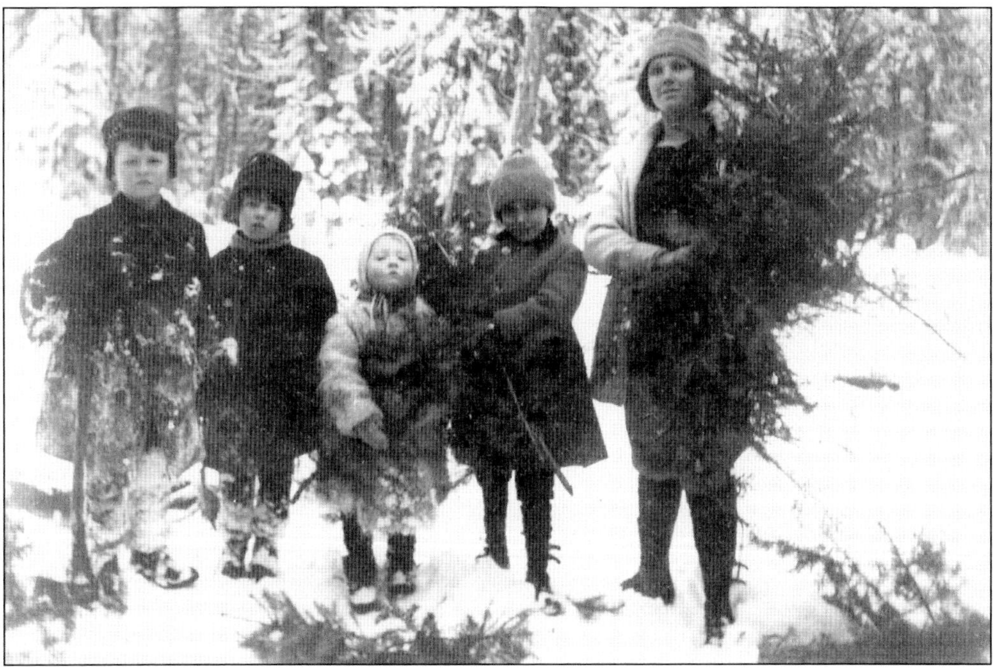

Stuart and Robin Bradley. Here, Stuart (far left) and Robin and friends gather small Christmas trees, which they then sent to relatives. Stuart Bradley was born in 1907 in Chicago and moved with his parents, Alex and Laura Bradley, to the Tacoma Creek area. He became an outstanding marine lawyer and historian. He and his family have supported the Pend Oreille County Historical Society and Museum for years.

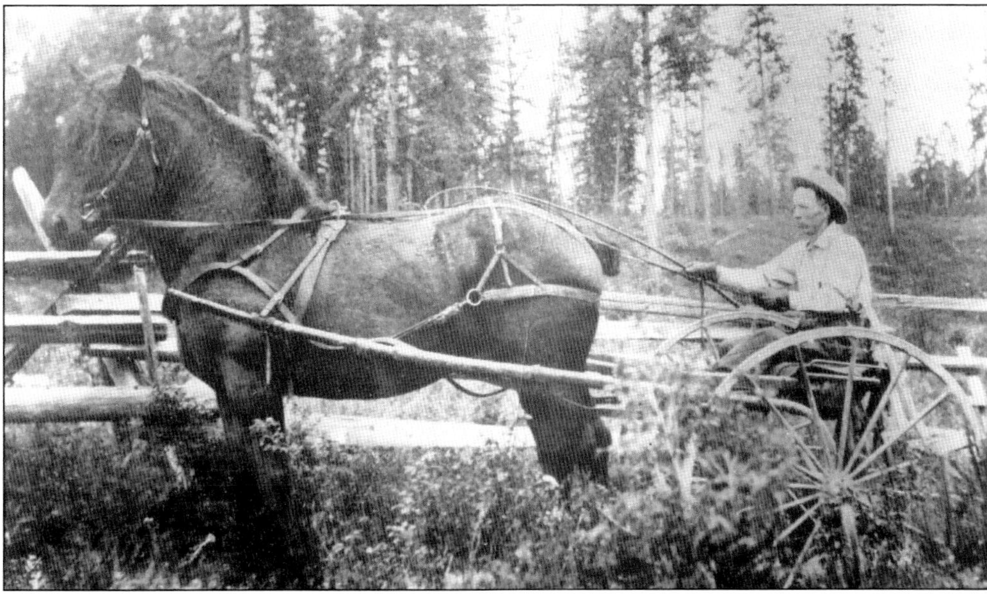

Bob Proctor. Born in New Hampshire in 1869, Proctor came to Newport in 1892. He homesteaded in the Marshall Lake, Washington, area, ran restaurants, and raised horses and cattle. Here, he drives his purebred Belgium stallion. Thousands of horses were used in logging camps and on farms for hauling freight.

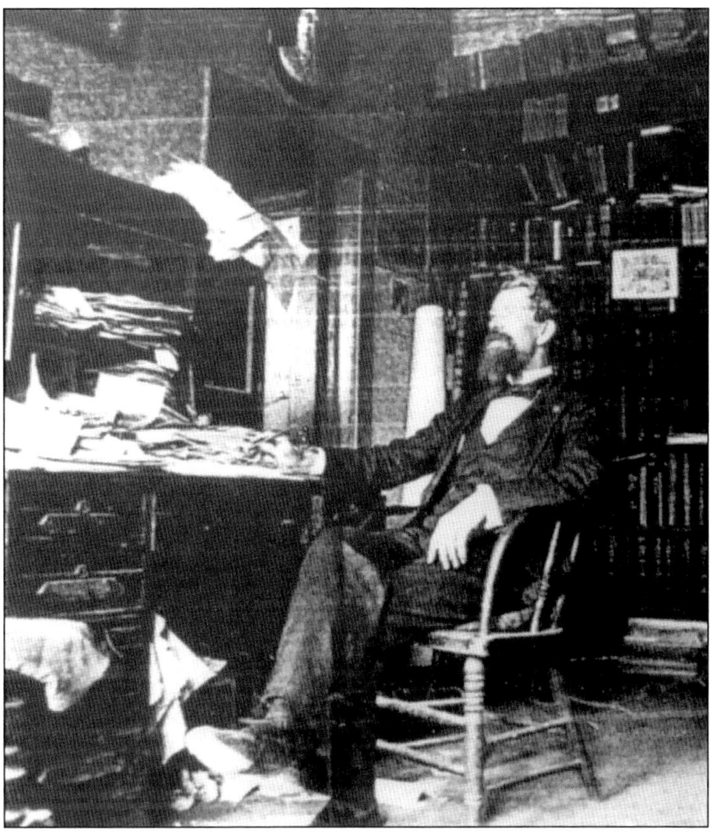

Charles Talmadge. A leader in the formation of Newport, Talmadge owned and operated the Silver Birch farm. He was president of the Newport Washington Land Company and was involved with the *Newport Miner* newspaper in the early years.

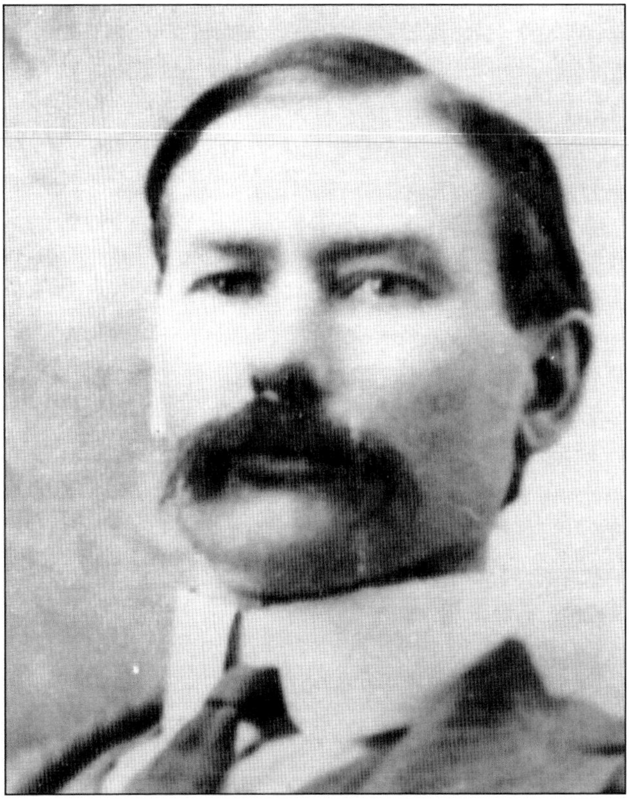

Tom. J. Kelly. One of the early businessmen in Newport was Tom Kelly. In 1896, he owned and ran one of the first general stores in the infant community of Newport. Kelly, the first mayor of Newport (1903–1906), was a strong supporter of the schools and the community.

Jessie Cass Scott. An early-day boardinghouse, the Cottage House, was run by Jessie Cass Scott in the late 1800s. It was located on Fourth and Warren Streets in Newport. The story is told that, when the local train was running close to Newport, the engineer would blow the whistle a number of times and let Scott know how many passengers would be eating at her boardinghouse.

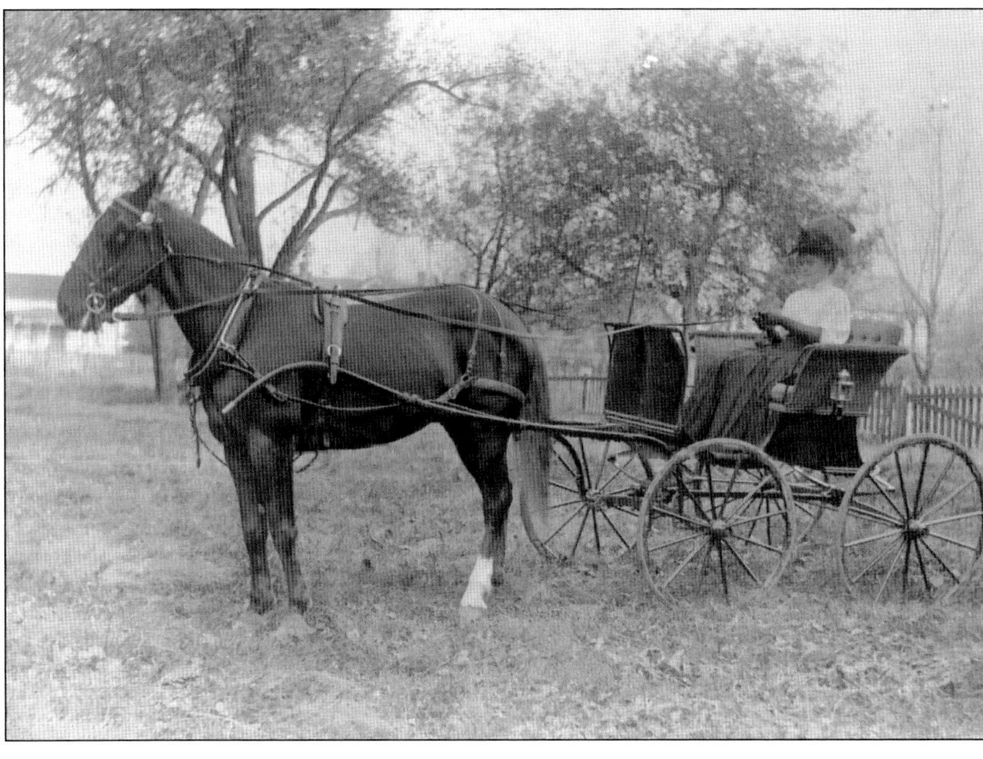

Dr. and Mrs. George Sutherland. The Sutherlands came to Newport in 1902. George, a chiropractor, was instrumental in starting the first water system in town. He ran a general mercantile store in the first brick building in town in 1903. He was a commissioner for both Stevens and Pend Oreille Counties. Dr. Sutherland, mayor of Newport in the 1930s, passed away at 94.

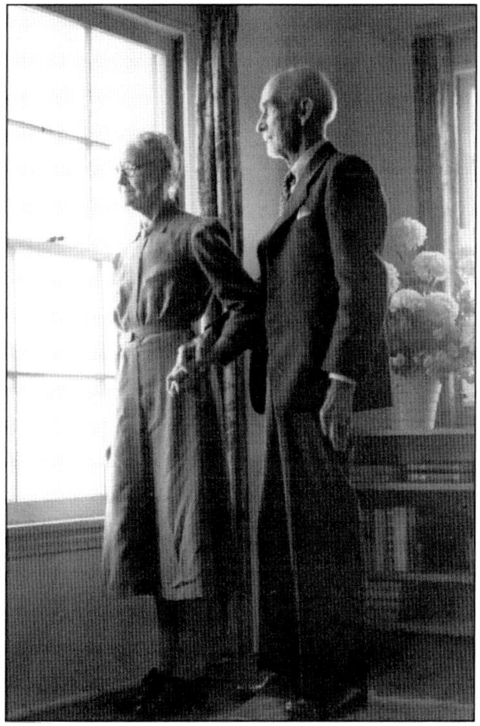

Sutherland Building. The first brick building in Newport, a mercantile store, used bricks from the local plant. It was built in 1903 and was owned by Dr. George Sutherland. The brick plants were located between Newport and Priest River, Idaho, and employed a number of people from both communities. Following several disastrous fires, most new buildings in Newport were constructed with bricks.

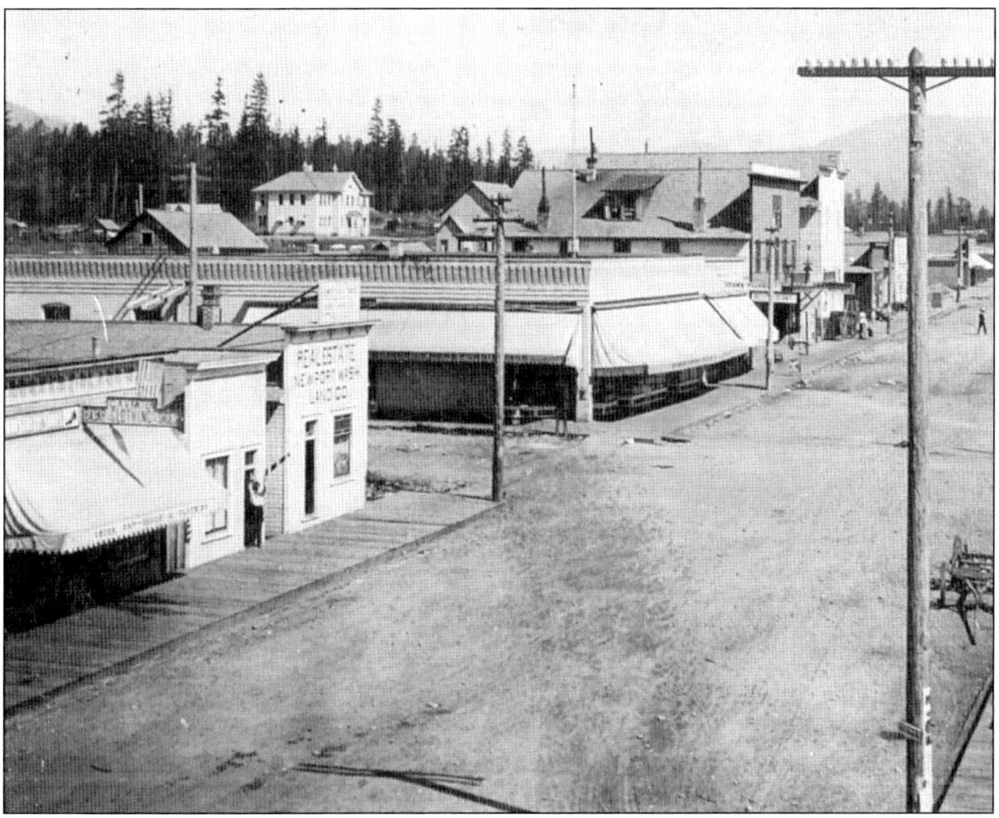

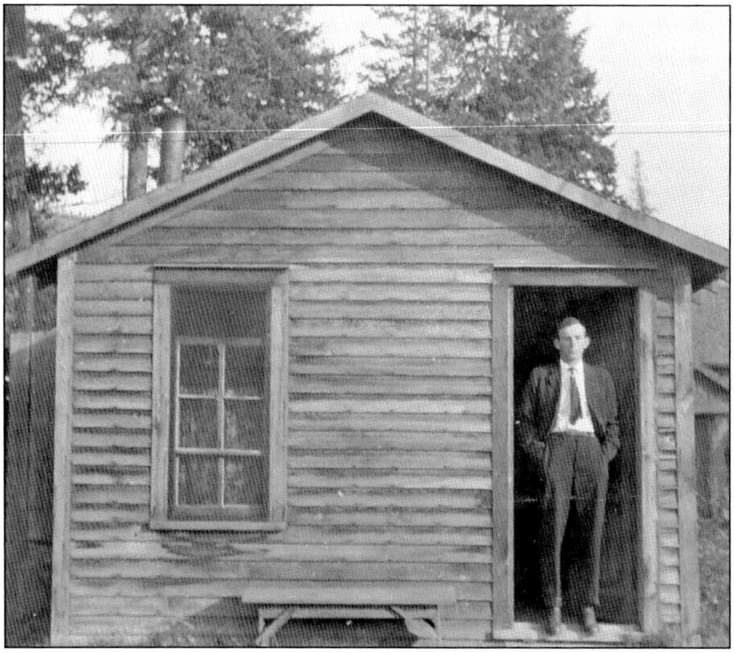

Charles Barker. A strong supporter of and contributor to the history of Newport and Pend Oreille County, Barker was a riverboat purser, prospector, miner, and amateur historian. He held all the offices in the county courthouse in Newport.

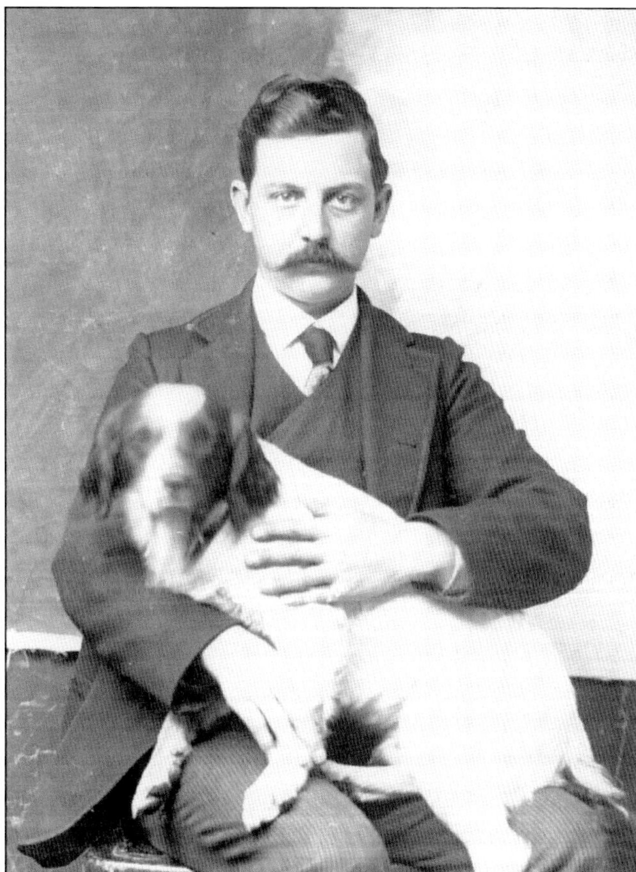

Charles Fiedler. The three-story Antler Hotel, two opera houses, and other buildings were owned and operated by Newport businessman Charles Fiedler. He was a strong supporter of Newport and Pend Oreille County. Fiedler is pictured here with one of his favorite dogs.

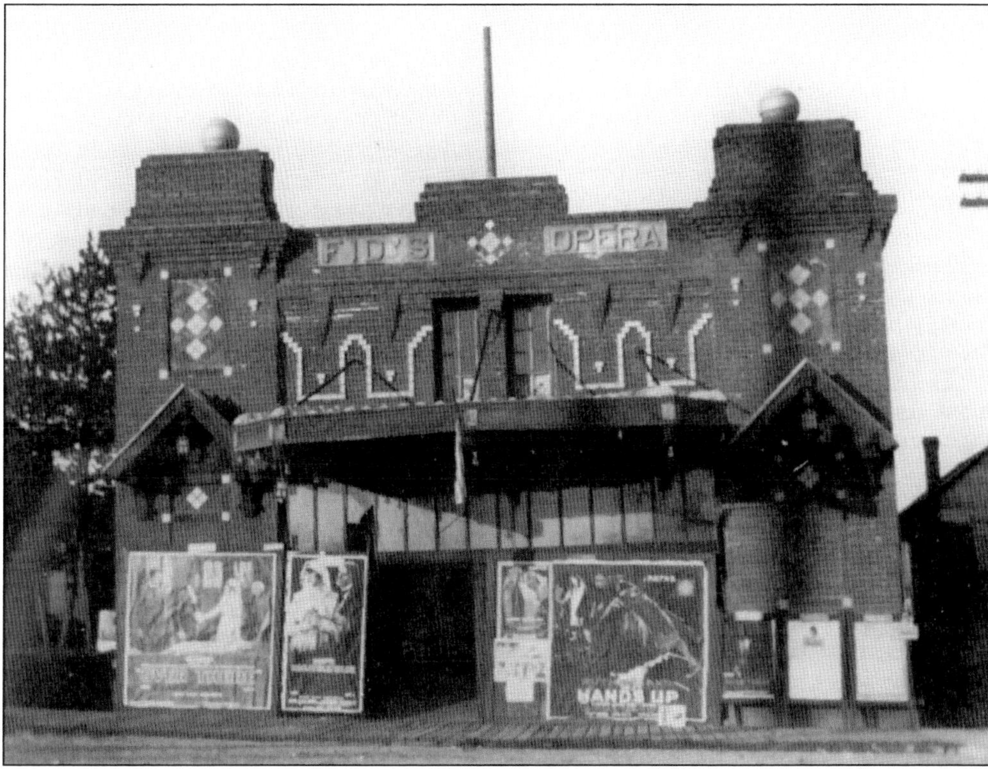

Newport Opera House. Charles Fiedler built the solid steel theater and playhouse in 1911. The first performance was *The American Girl* by the Jeanne Russell Company, a repertoire organization. Many school and community programs were put on at the opera house. Over the years, the sturdy building has housed various businesses.

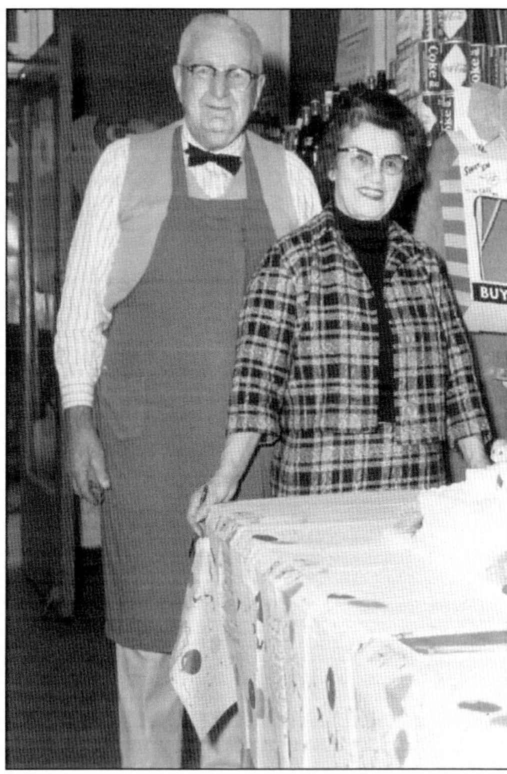

Mr. and Mrs. Robert Owen. Members of the Owen family have operated the popular grocery and deli store in the Sutherland Building since the late 1930s. Bob Owen played Santa Claus for the Newport children for many years. He was mayor of the town from 1952 to 1963. The Owen family have been strong contributors to and supporters of the community. (Courtesy of Alice Owen.)

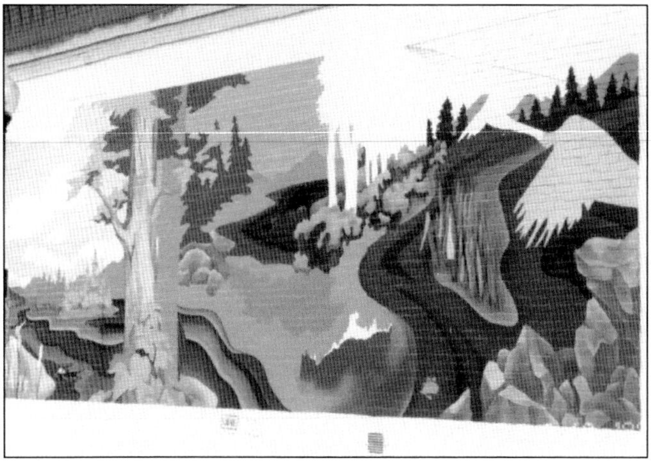

Newport Mural. The mural painted on the wall of the Sutherland Building depicts Newport as the gateway into the Pend Oreille Valley. In the early days, the community was a port for steamboats and had depots for the Great Northern and Idaho & Washington Northern Railroads. It was the business and shopping center for the area. Thousands of pioneers passed through Newport in the early days.

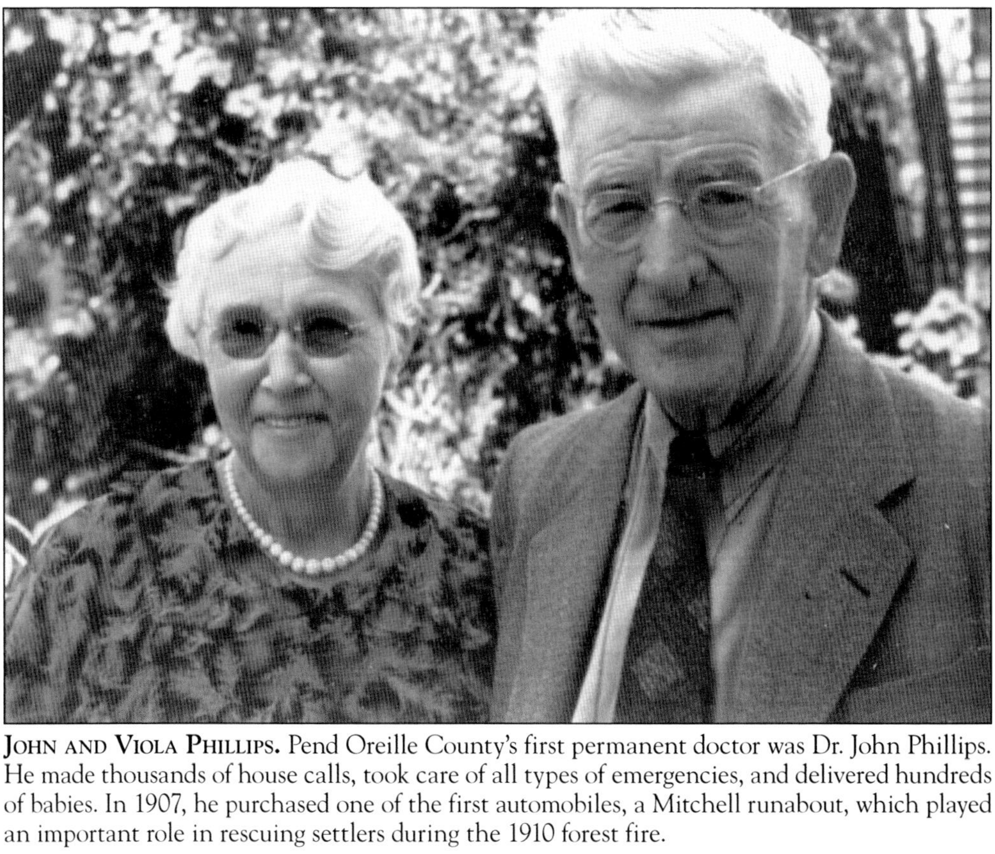

John and Viola Phillips. Pend Oreille County's first permanent doctor was Dr. John Phillips. He made thousands of house calls, took care of all types of emergencies, and delivered hundreds of babies. In 1907, he purchased one of the first automobiles, a Mitchell runabout, which played an important role in rescuing settlers during the 1910 forest fire.

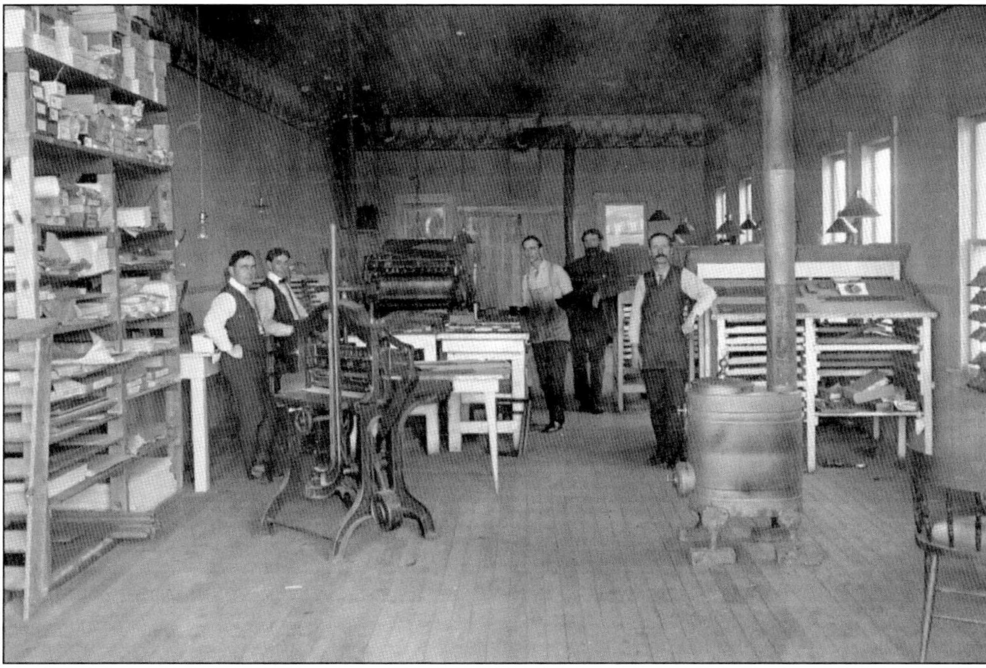

Newport Miner Office. This is the *Newport Miner* newspaper office and print shop in Newport. In the early years, newspapers were the only source of local and world news. Ralph Braddock and Fred Wolf, along with other members of the staff, are pictured here. Wolf, as editor of the newspaper, played an important role in the history of the county.

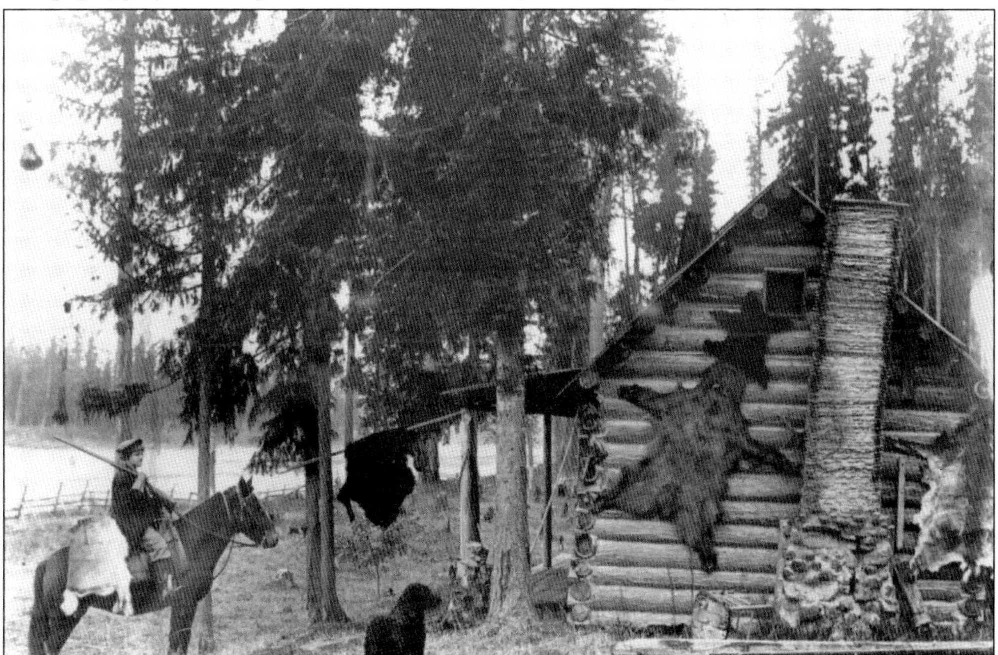

U.S. Anderson. Anderson sits on her pony in front of her small log cabin. This is an interesting example of a well-built log cabin, with a "wattle and daub" chimney, made of clay-mud and twigs and sticks. Such chimneys were common in early days, as pioneers had to use the resources at hand.

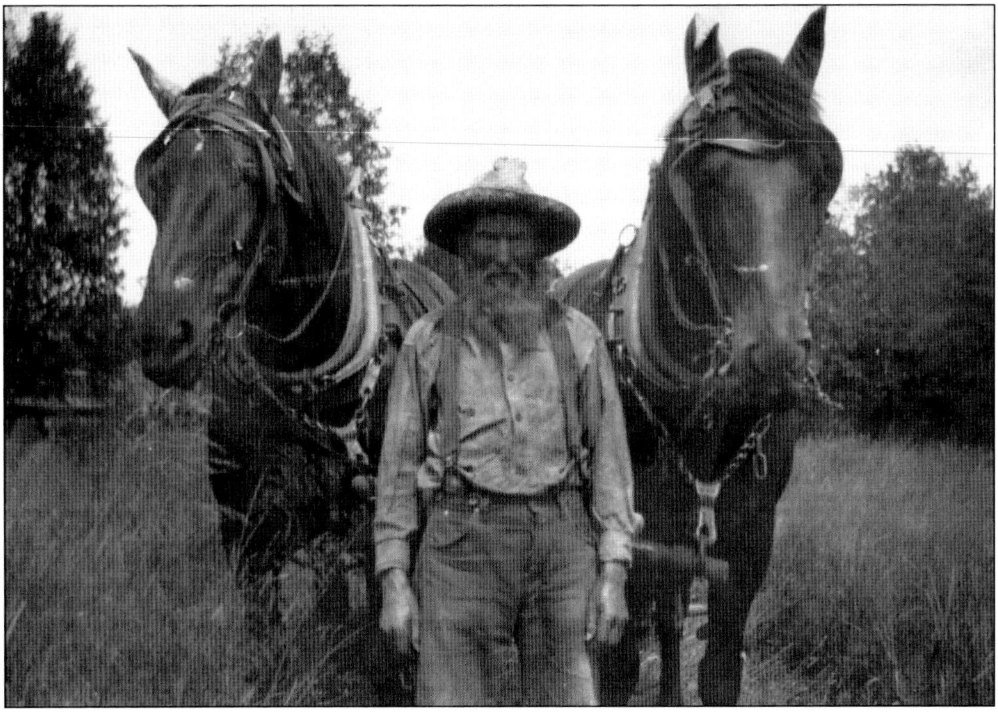

George Byxbe. One of the early settlers in Spring Valley, Washington, was George Byxbe. He never married or had children, but was very supportive of education and graciously donated land for a one-room schoolhouse and a teacher's cabin. He lived to be over 100 years old. Pioneers often donated land and erected and supported schools for their children.

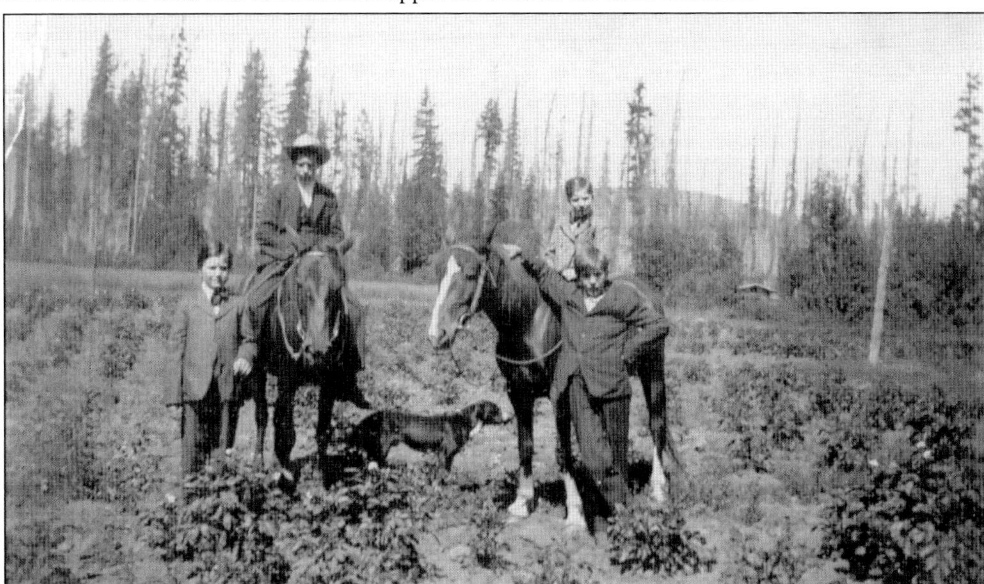

Wooding Family. The Woodings were homesteaders in Tiger, Washington. While Wes worked in the mines, Jennie managed her family, cared for the homestead, ran a store, was a beloved midwife, and supported the school and community. Today, the tiny community of Tiger is home to the Tiger Museum.

Four

Steamboats and Railroads

The transportation of people and goods is a contributing factor to the history of a region. For centuries, the Indians used a network of well-worn trails, streams, and rivers to travel from one place to another. When the first white people came into the region, they also used the river and rode horses or hiked the Indian trails. Initially, most of the pioneers settled along the Pend Oreille River and depended on canoes, makeshift rafts, and rowboats. When the population increased enough to make it profitable, large steamboats—the *Ione*, *Spokane*, *Newport*, *New Volunteer*, and others—began to make regular stops along the river.

J.C. Langile and Kremkran and others had a boatbuilding business near Newport, constructing the wooden hulls for steamboats, tugboats, and ferries. Machinery for the large steamboats was built in Portland, Oregon, and other places and shipped to Newport. There were a number of boat landings along the river, and pioneers could flag down smaller steamers and launches. The glory days of the large steamboats lasted until 1910.

In the late 1800s, the Great Northern Railroad was being built from Minneapolis to Seattle. The railroad came through Newport in 1892. The attractive depot was completed in 1910. With the arrival of safe and dependable transportation, homesteaders and settlers started pouring into the region. In the summer, Spokane residents would often take the Great Northern train to Newport, board one of the large steamboats, and take excursion trips to Usk, Cusick, and other small communities for baseball games, horse races, and picnics. The Idaho & Washington Northern Railroad (I&WN), owned and operated by Fredrick Blackwell, reached Metaline Falls in 1910. At the time, it was considered the best railroad in the State of Washington. Soon, there were several trains running the length of the region, carrying passengers as well as freight from the mines and sawmills.

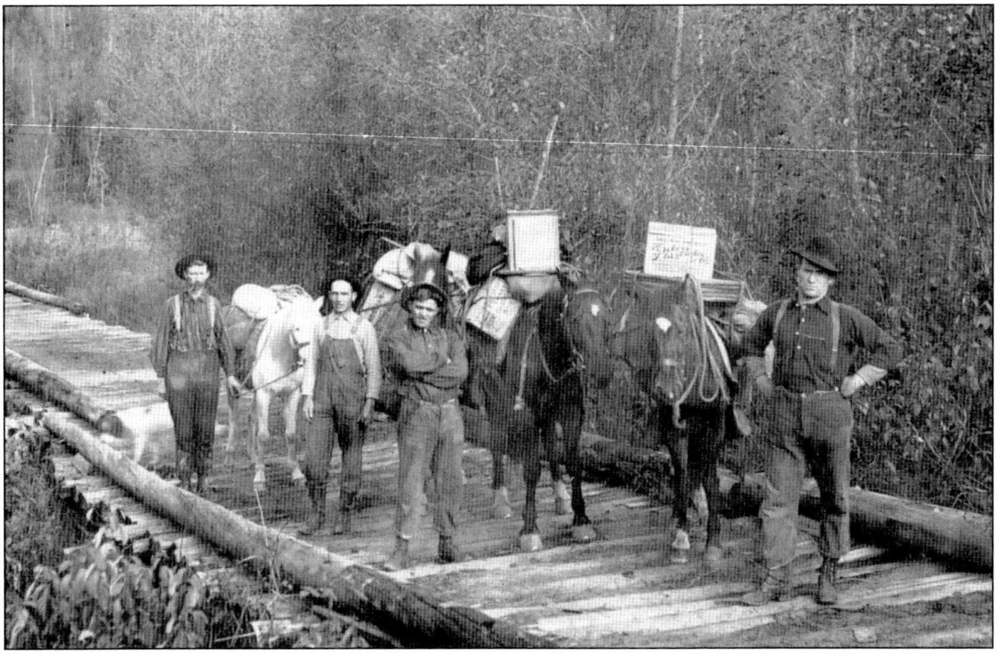

Pack Trains. Pack trains of horses or mules carried supplies for surveyors, prospectors, miners, and isolated pioneers. In the early days, horses or mules carried out ore from the primitive mines to railheads. In more recent years, pack trains carried supplies to surveyors, workers, and men living in forest-fire lookout towers on high peaks.

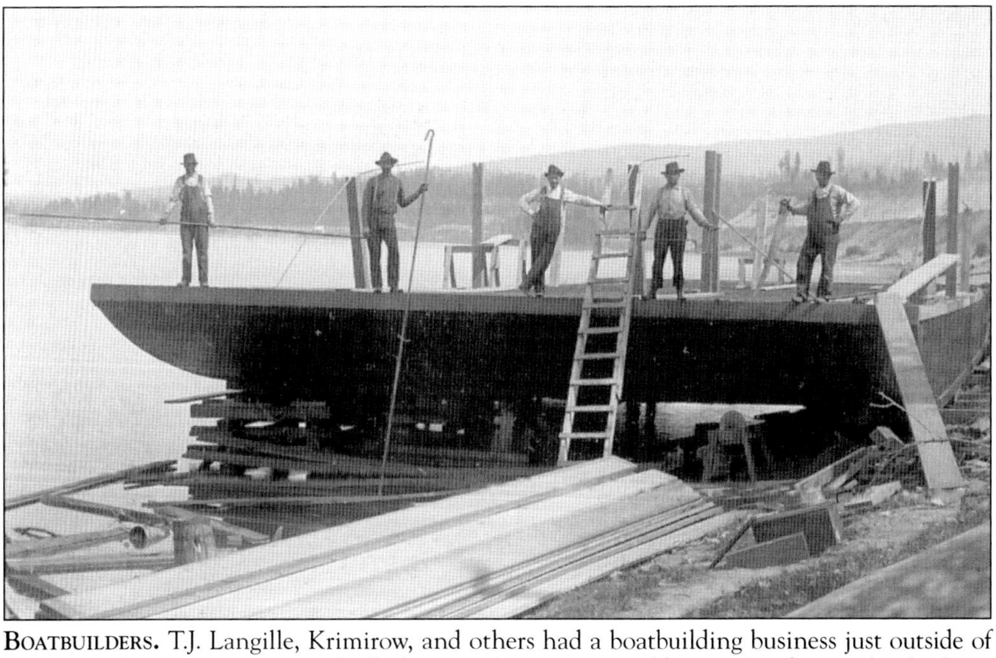

Boatbuilders. T.J. Langille, Krimirow, and others had a boatbuilding business just outside of Newport. They constructed the hulls for steamboats, tugs, and barges. Machinery for the large steamboats was manufactured in Portland, Oregon, and other places and shipped to Newport. The lumber was sawed at the Standard Sawmill in Newport. Seen here are Tom Strayer (far left) and Boyd Strayer (far right).

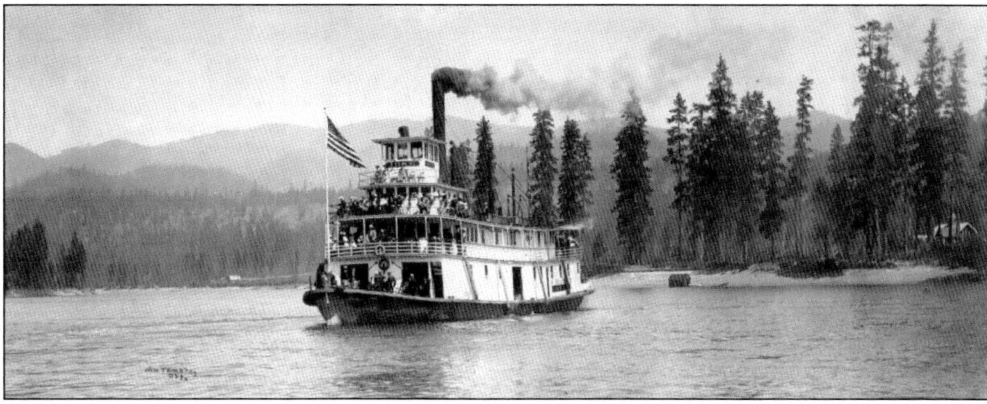

IONE. "Floating Palace" and "River Queen" were nicknames of the steamboat *Ione*. Built in 1908, it had furnished staterooms, a carpeted ladies' parlor, and a luxurious dining room. Often during the summer season, 500 people from Spokane would enjoy Sunday excursions and float along the Pend Oreille River to events at Cusick, Usk, and Ione.

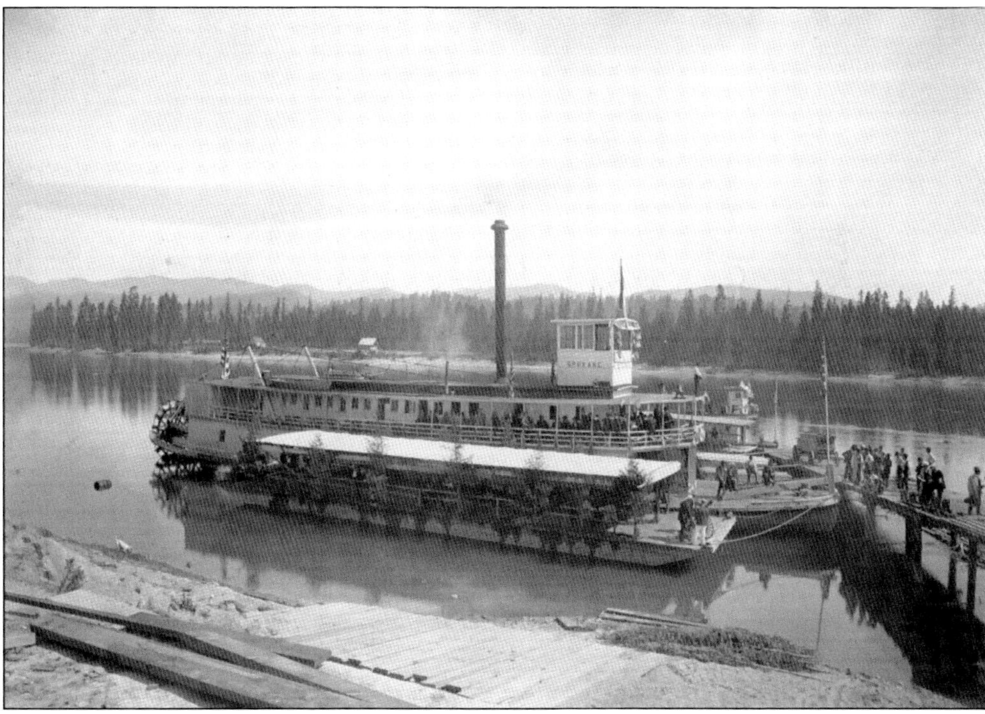

GOETZ PICNIC. Here, the steamboat *Spokane* and a barge are docked at Newport. Dutch Jake Goetz, well-known businessman and gambler in Spokane, rented the vessels for his employees' annual picnic along the Pend Oreille River. They used the barge for dancing and other entertainment. Goetz would often bring his cannon along to start the fun.

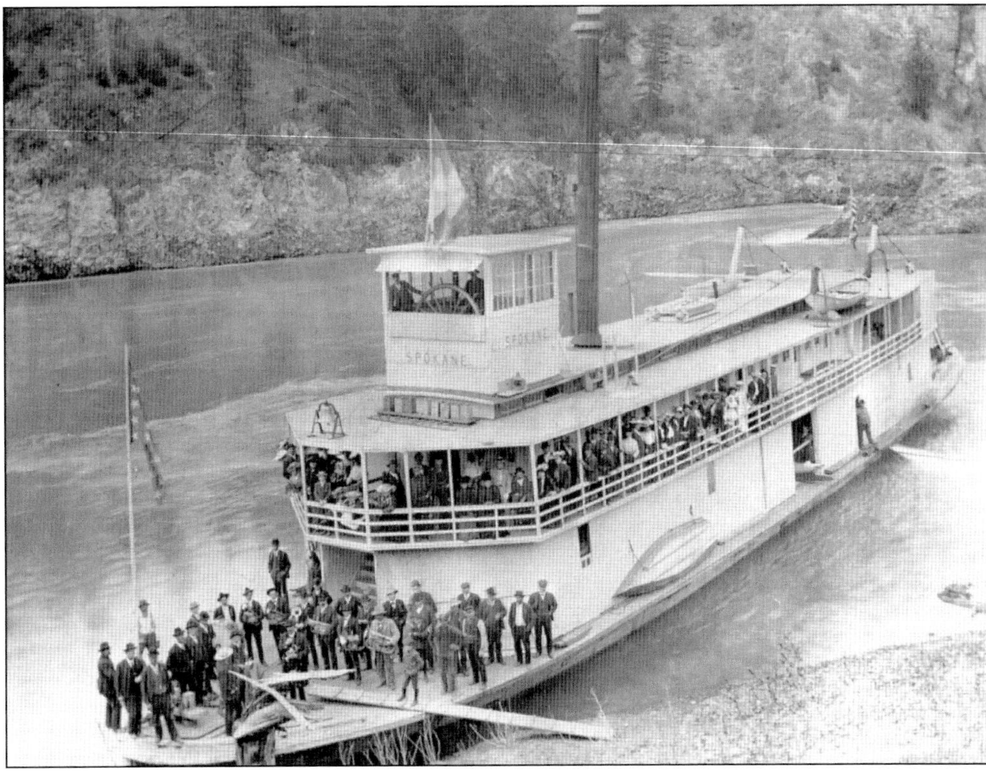

SPOKANE. This big steamboat was built in 1903 for the Pend d'Oreille River Navigation Company. The *Spokane* could carry 200 passengers on Sunday excursions. The Newport City Band is on the deck, ready to serenade the passengers A few years later, the beautiful, sturdy steamboat was converted into a tugboat for one of the large sawmills.

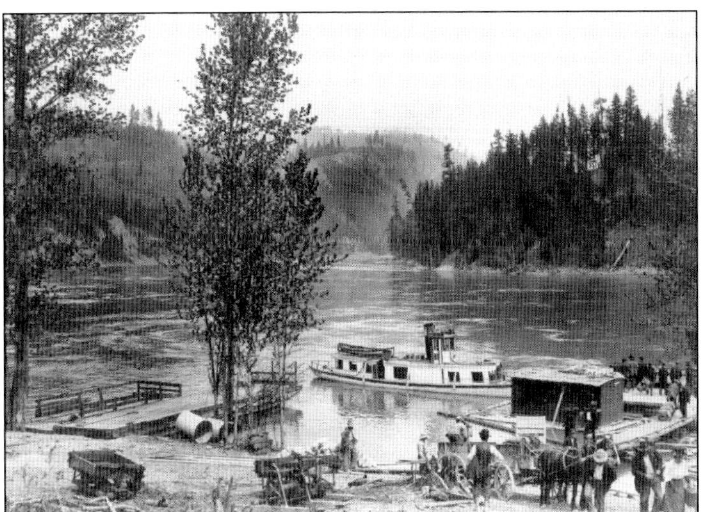

STEAMBOAT LANDING. This is one of the very primitive boat landings along the banks of the Pend Oreille River. Note the horses and wagons. Settlers who lived along the river could flag down a steamer if they needed transportation.

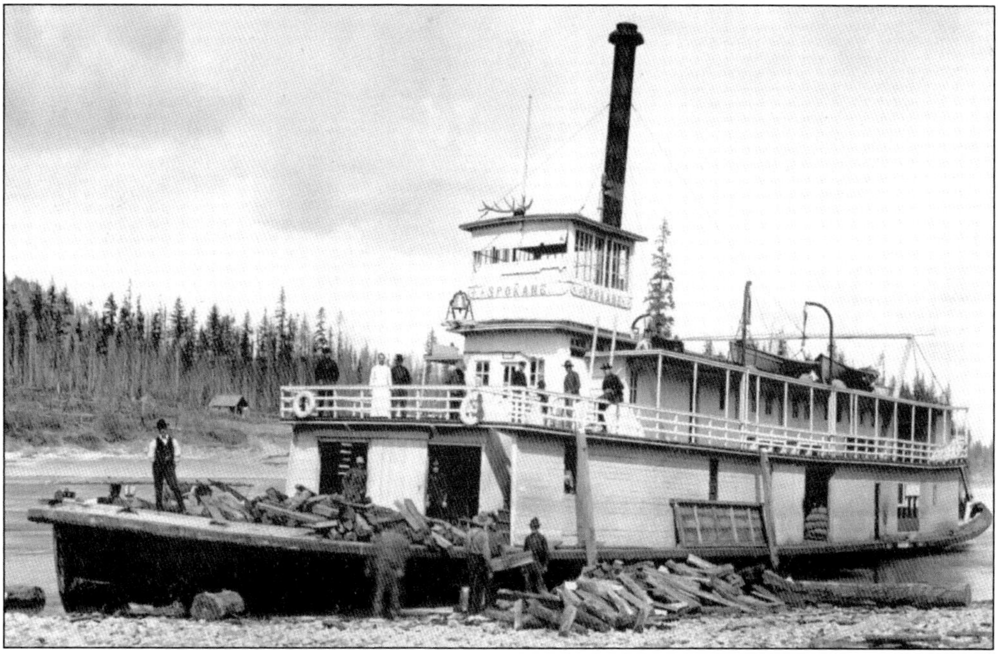

CORDWOOD FOR STEAMERS. The large steamboats burned cordwood for fuel. Dry tamarack wood was considered "lifesavers" by pioneers, since they could cut and stack the wood along the river and get a couple of dollars for each cord. Some of the smaller steamboats were converted to use oil boilers.

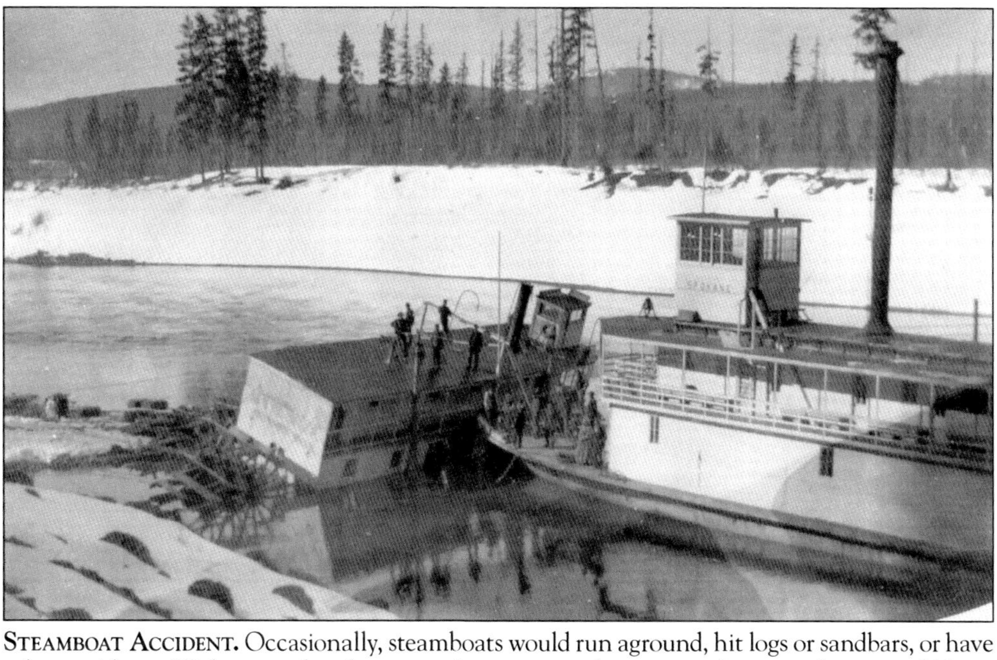

STEAMBOAT ACCIDENT. Occasionally, steamboats would run aground, hit logs or sandbars, or have other accidents. Without modern heavy equipment, men, horses, or other steamboats would have to be used to solve the problems. Here, the larger steamer is attempting to push the smaller boat back into the current of the river. Since the river would often freeze in the winter, steamboats and ferries were laid up until spring.

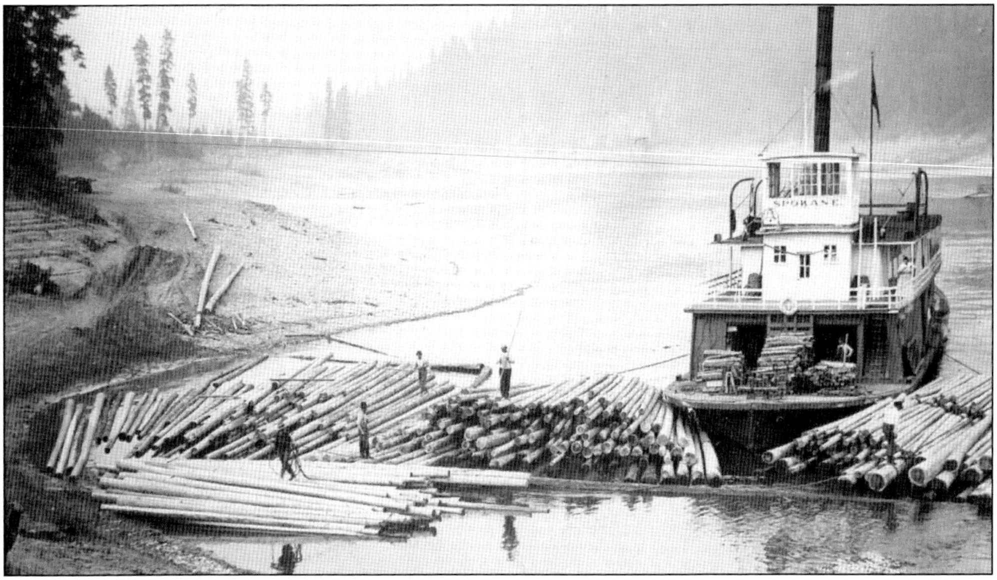

TUGBOAT. During slack times in the summer, steamboats were hired by the large sawmills and used as tugboats. The boats would either push or tow logs to their destination. After railroads were running in the county, some of the steamers became permanent tugboats, others were scrapped, and several were used on other rivers or lakes.

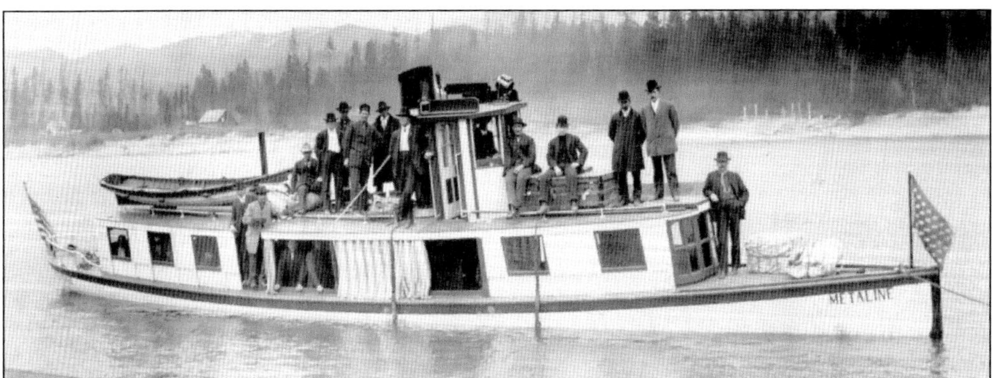

METALINE LAUNCH. In 1908, Napoleon LeClerc brought a 25-passenger launch from Coeur d'Alene, Idaho, to the Pend Oreille region. It often made round trips from Newport through Box Canyon to Metaline. It had a tubular boiler and triple-expansion engine placed near the middle of the boat. It was remodeled several times and was laid up late in 1909.

LeClerc Brothers. Napoleon LeClerc (pictured) was born in 1863 in Quebec, Canada. He and his brothers Arsen, Felix, and Joe came to the Pend Oreille region in 1887. Napoleon, Arsen, and Felix had a 900-acre ranch. Napoleon owned and piloted the small *Metaline* steamer. He was a prospector and helped to start the Calispel Creamery Company in Usk. The LeClerc Creek Road and LeClerc Creek are named after the brothers.

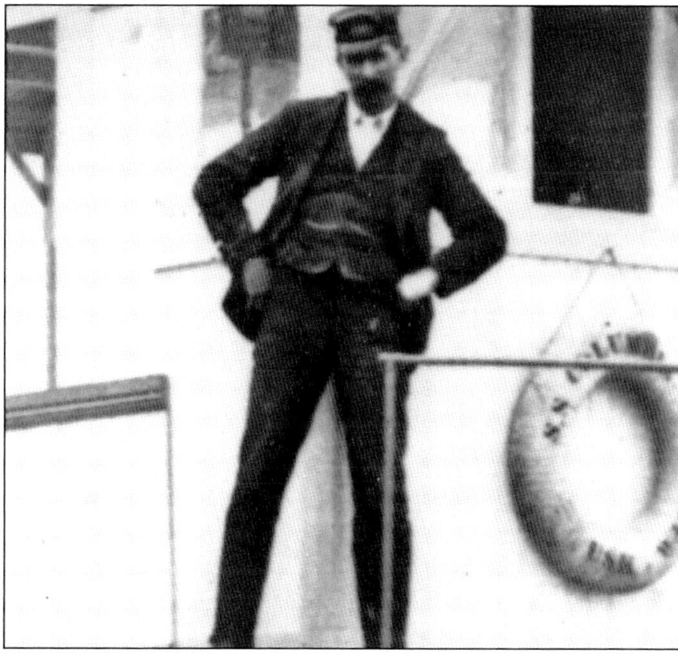

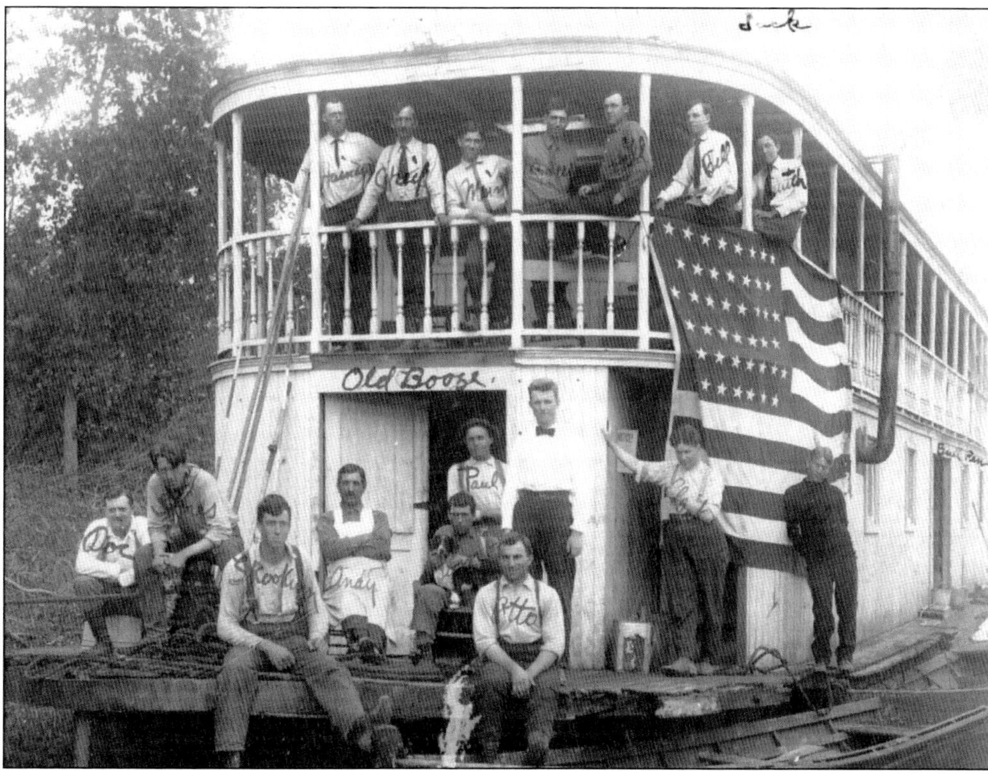

New Volunteer Steamboat. The *New Volunteer* ("Old Booze") was owned and operated by Joe Cusick, a boat pilot. It was built in 1901 for Cusick and was retired in 1905. The story was told that, on slow river trips, Joe would report an engine problem. Soon, a hot poker game would be started. Once Joe had "cleaned out" his passengers, the boat was repaired.

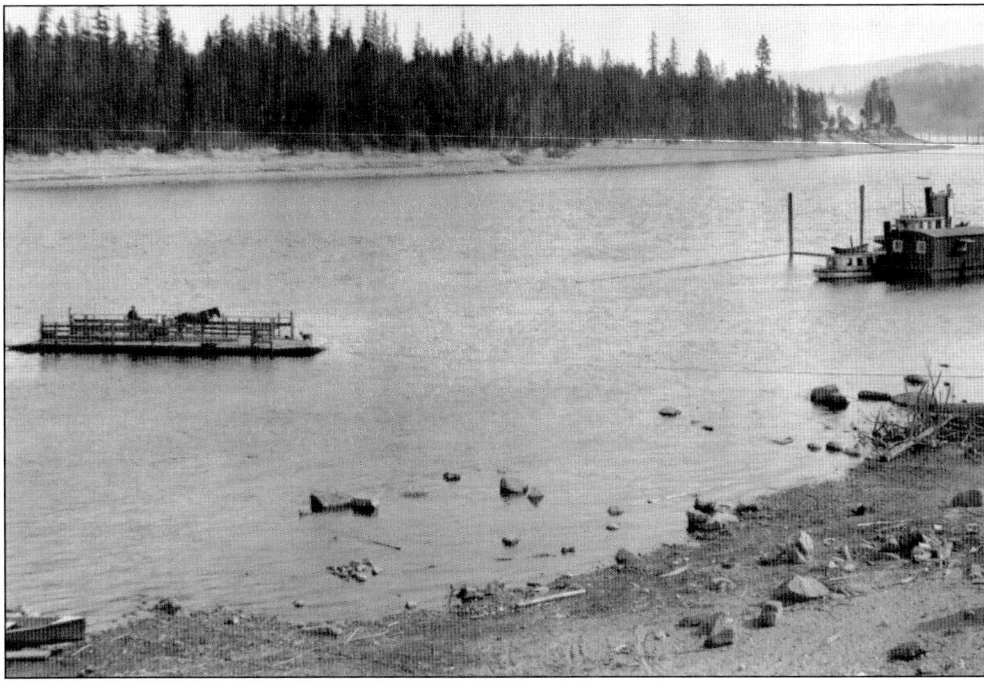

NEWPORT FERRY. The Newport Ferry operated from 1891 until 1927, when the Interstate Bridge was constructed. The fare was 10¢ for walk-on passengers and 25¢ for cars and wagons. After 9:00 p.m., the fare went up to 50¢. The ferryman was on duty every day, 24 hours a day.

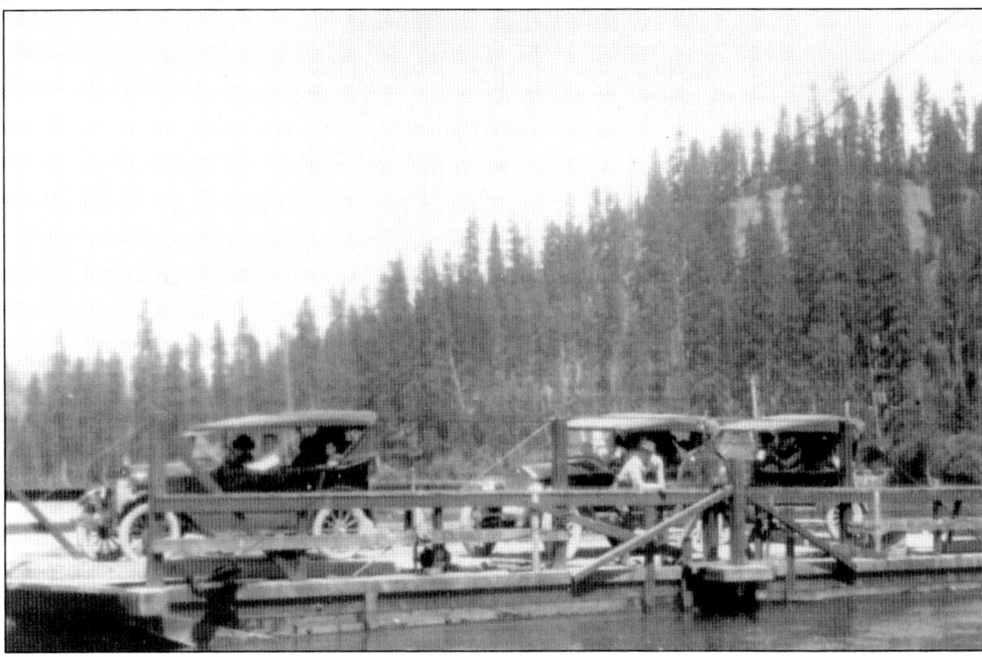

RUBY FERRY. Ruby Ferry was built in 1913 and operated until 1923, when the ferry tower collapsed, injuring a motorist. Prior to the building of bridges across the Pend Oreille River, ferries performed a vital service in connecting people on both sides of the river. Here, there are three cars on the ferry. A passenger leans over the railing.

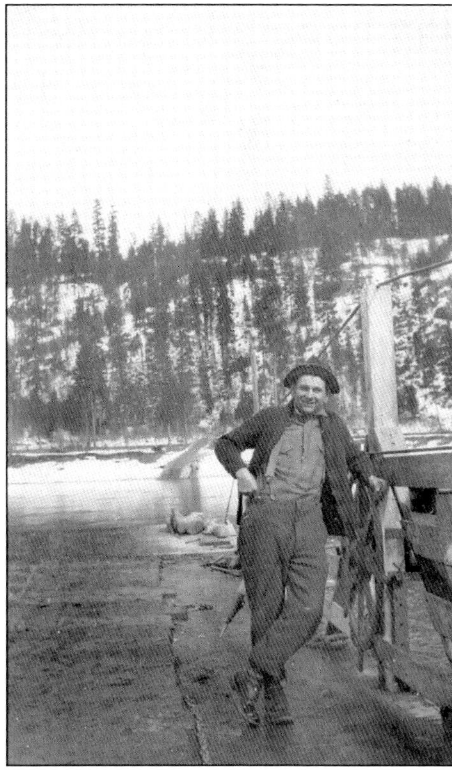

Otto Wilmer. Otto "Dutch" Wilmer, a ferryman, was a popular, friendly man who loved sharing all the local news, gossip, and stories of his adventures, especially the incident of being struck by lightning. For his favorite passengers, he shared his "ginger ale" out of his toolbox.

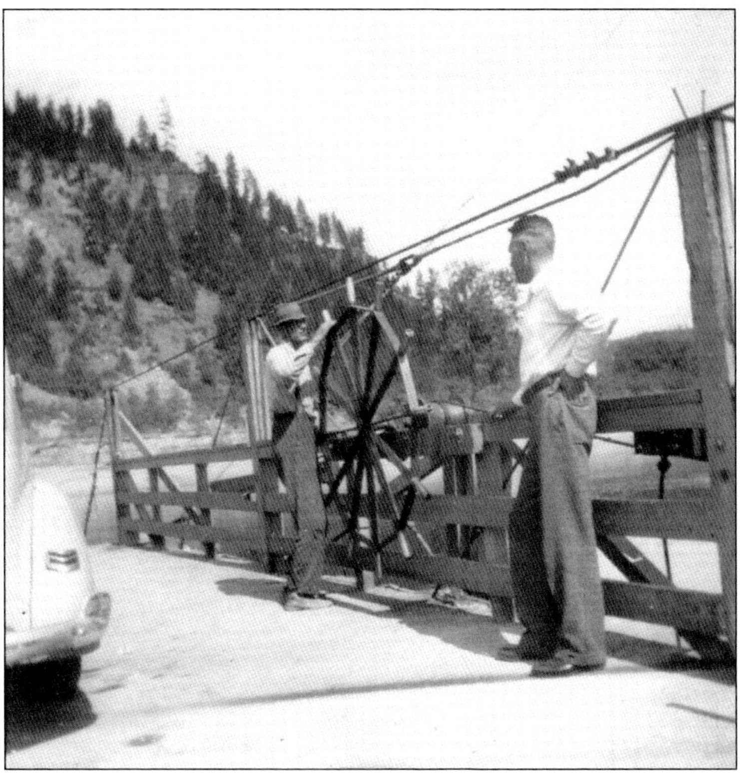

Earl Middleton. As a young man, Middleton came to the county and settled in Ruby, Washington. He operated the Ruby Hotel, was a deputy sheriff, and was a ferryman on the Ruby Ferry. He remembered the year when sheep were ferried across the Pend Oreille River to graze in the Selkirk Mountains.

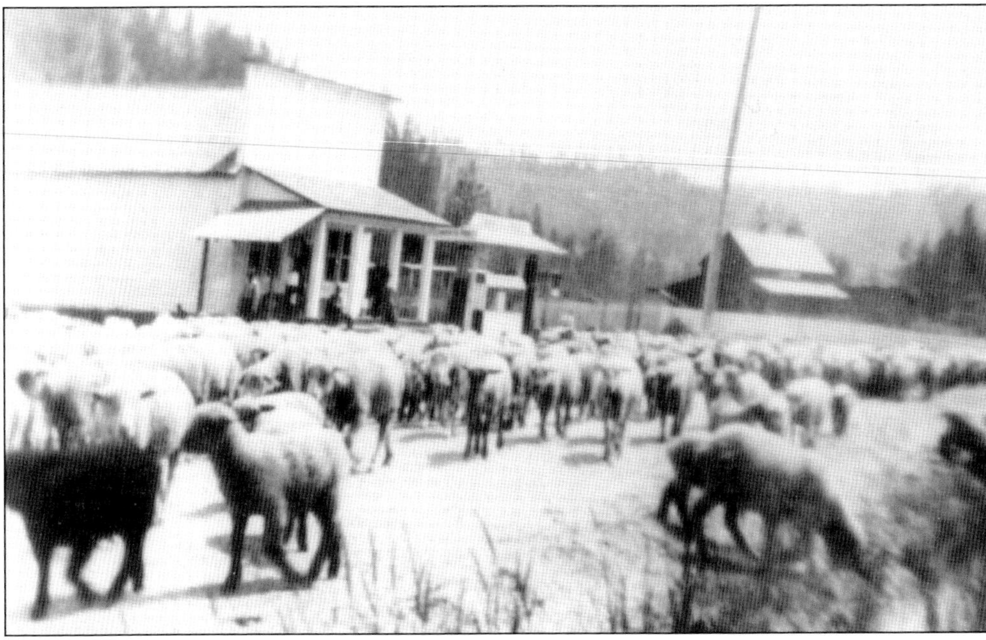

Flock of Sheep. Here, sheep have just come off the Ruby Ferry at Ruby. Their herders were taking them into the mountains for the summer. Thousands of sheep and their herders were shipped by carloads from central Washington to Pend Oreille County. Once in a while, there were disagreements between cattle farmers and sheep herders about sharing pastureland.

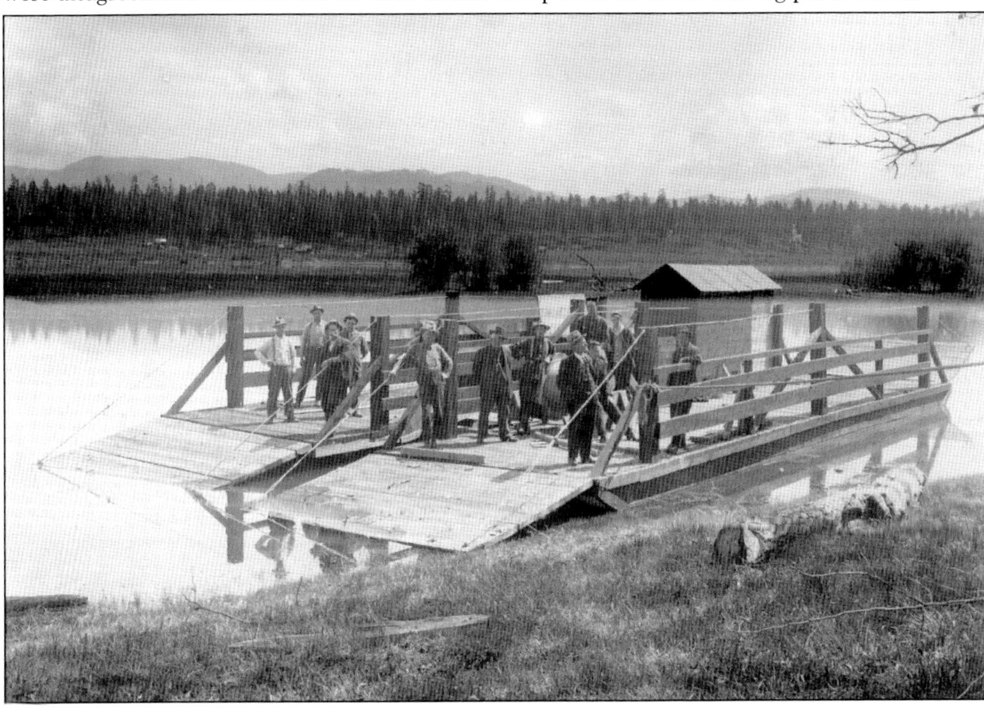

Usk Ferry. This ferry was unique, as it had two landing aprons and decks. It could carry twice as much freight. In the fall, the ferry carried hay and herds of cattle across the Pend Oreille River. None of the ferries could run when the river had slush or was frozen over.

Ferry Towers. High wooden towers anchored heavy wire cables that helped guide the ferries across the Pend Oreille River. Bill Piper, an amateur historian in Newport, often told stories of climbing the towers to fill the large grease cups at the top. It was a scary job, but it was necessary to keep the ferries running smoothly.

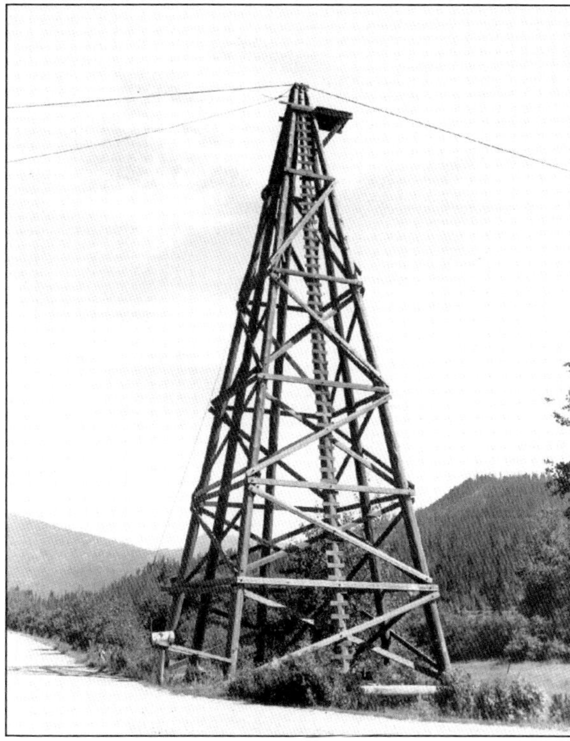

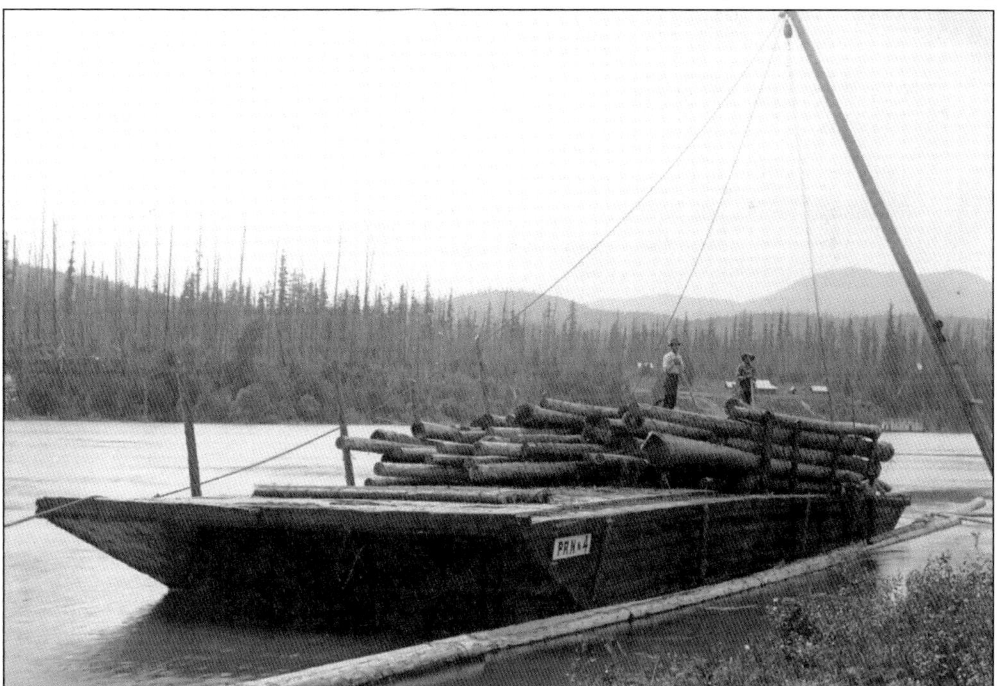

Poles on a Barge. Barges carried electric, telephone, or telegraph poles, logs, logging camp buildings, hay, and animals. The poles were barged from Metaline Falls to Newport and then sent on to Spokane and other destinations.

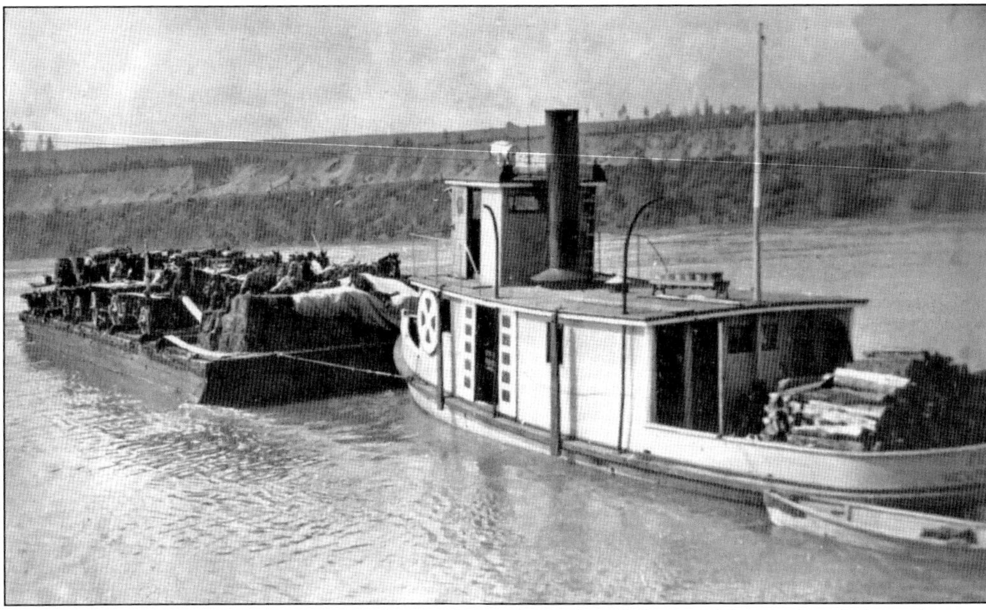

FIDELITY TUGBOAT. The *Fidelity* is pushing a barge loaded with hay and horses headed to a logging camp. Note the cordwood on the deck of the tugboat. Large sawmills, such as the Panhandle and Diamond Match Lumber Companies, had several tugboats.

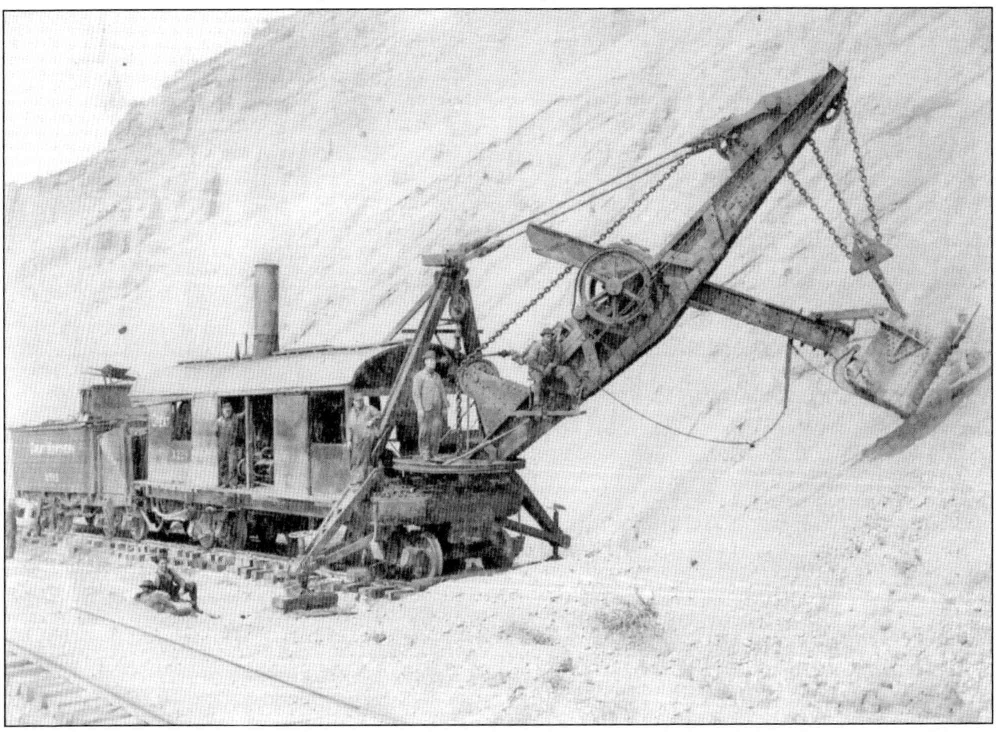

GREAT NORTHERN RAILROAD. Jim Hill's goal for his Great Northern Railroad was to reach into areas that had industrial potential. In the early 1900s, Pend Oreille County was rich in timber and ore resources. The Great Northern Railroad started surveying, clearing land, and laying track into the Pend Oreille region in the late 1800s. The railroad reached Newport in 1892.

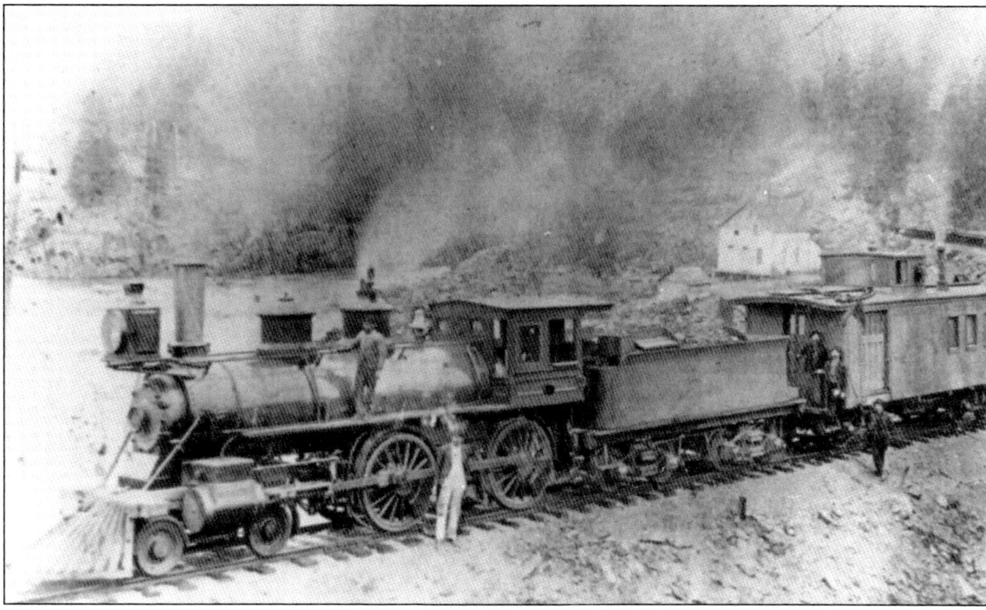

GREAT NORTHERN TOUR TRAIN. This short Great Northern tour train was taking passengers on a short trip over the railroad bridge to catch a glimpse of the river roaring between the rocks at Albeni Falls. Hundreds of people rode the Great Northern trains to Newport for Sunday steamboat excursion trips.

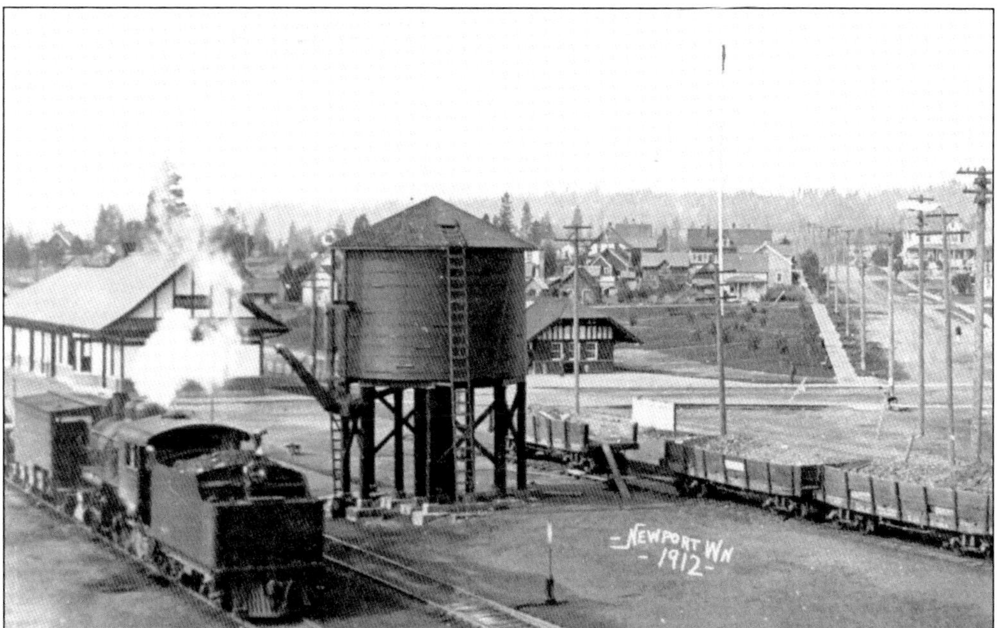

GREAT NORTHERN RAILROAD DEPOT. Seen here are the train, the new Great Northern depot (left), the Idaho & Washington Northern depot (center), and part of Newport in 1912. The depot was built by J. Skinner Contracting of Spokane in 1910. The exterior was constructed of Minnesota red brick. Inside, there were ladies' and gentlemen's waiting rooms and ticket and telegraphy offices. The waiting-room ceiling was 14 feet high and had massive chandeliers.

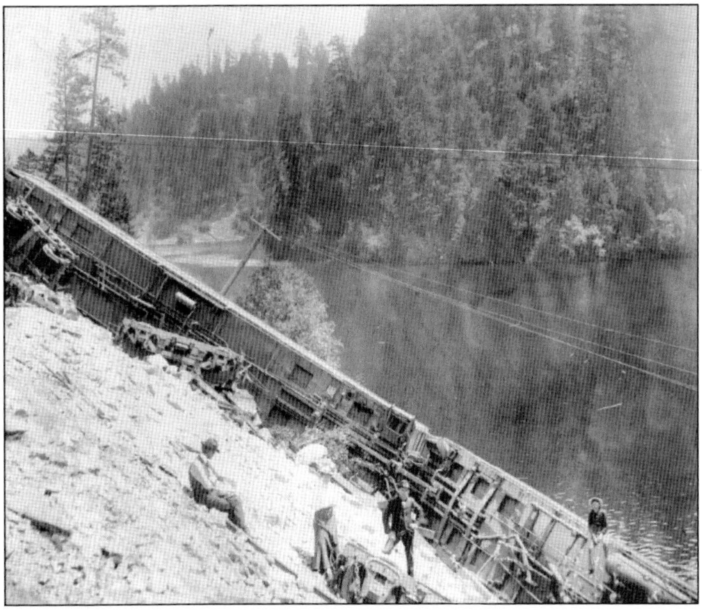

Great Northern Wreck. In 1906, a Great Northern train wrecked at Chain Lakes, between Newport and Spokane, Washington. The westbound Great Northern Railroad No. 3 jumped the tracks just as it emerged from a tunnel. The passenger cars were thrown on the side of the hill and into the water. Ed Munson, Mr. Bell, George R. Strickland, George Curtis, T.J. Dolbow, and an unidentified man were killed. Many people were injured.

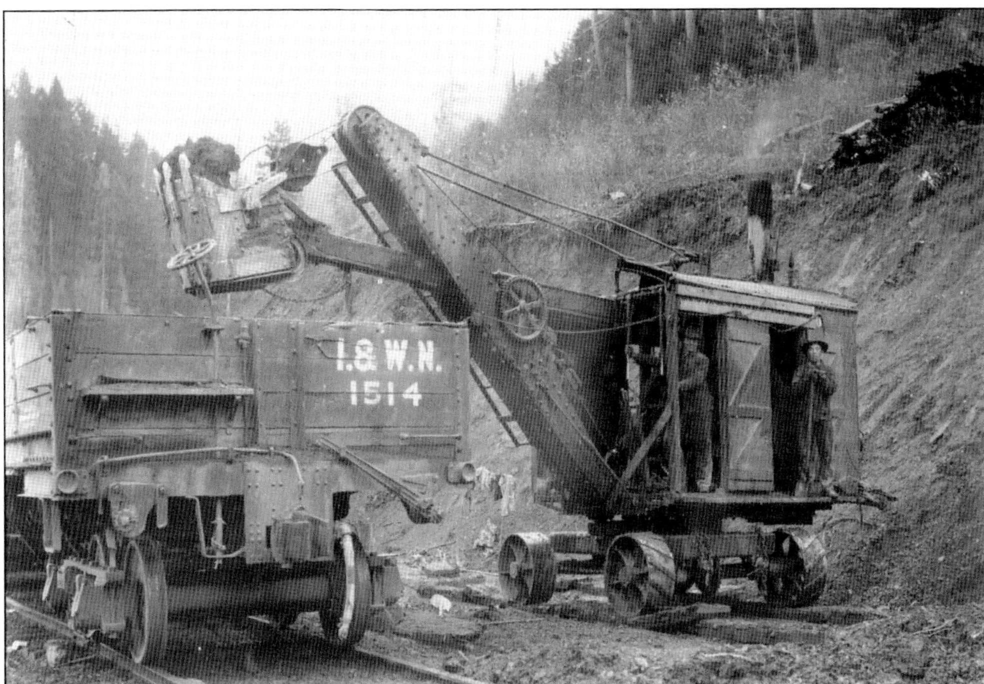

Idaho & Washington Northern Railroad. Fredrick Blackwell owned and operated the Idaho & Washington Northern Railroad (I&WN). It reached Newport in 1908. Workers started laying track through Pend Oreille County to Metaline Falls. Blackwell's Spirit Lake Lumber Company sawmill crews and other laborers worked on constructing the line up to Metaline Falls.

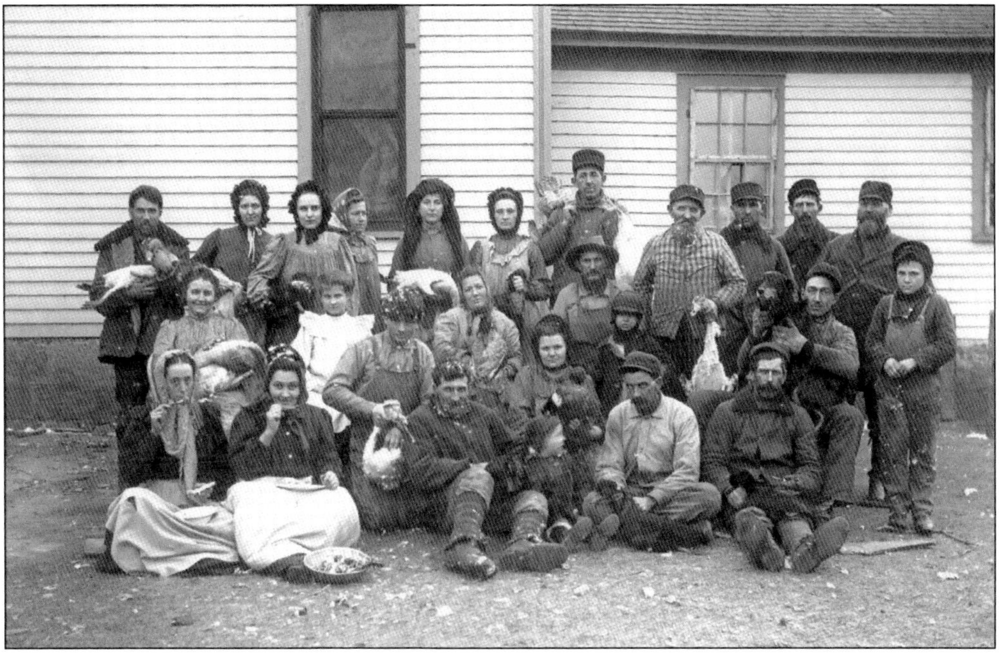

Railroad Workers. Here, Serb railroad laborers and their families take a lunch break. At times, Fredrick Blackwell had over 2,000 people working on his railroad. Large crews had to survey, clear the land, and lay the railroad track. Blackwell often had crews from the Spirit Lake sawmill and laborers from other parts of the world working on the railroad. It was hard, backbreaking work.

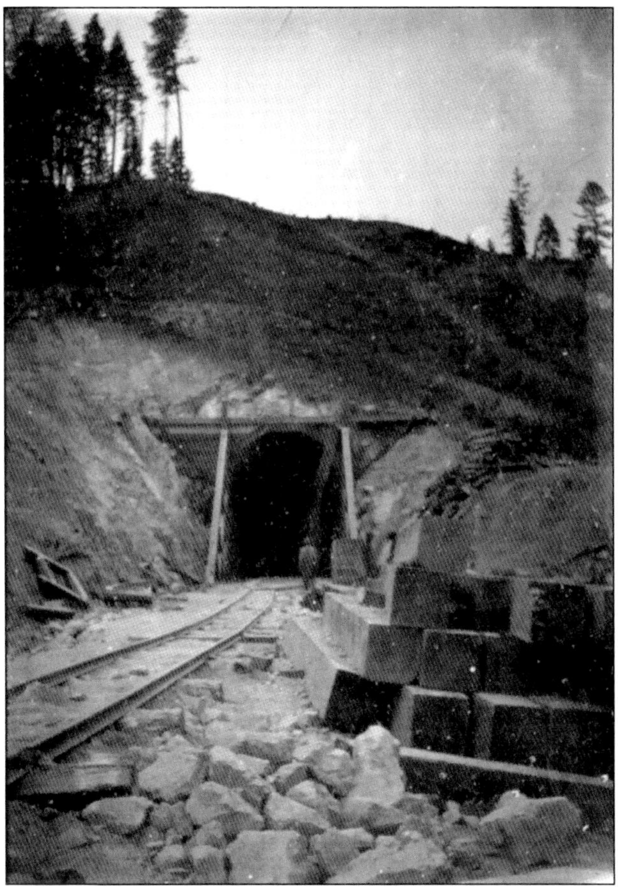

Blueslide Tunnel. The 1,100-foot Blueslide railroad tunnel was constructed through the mountain just north of Blueslide, Washington, in 1909. Construction of the tunnel took six months to complete, with 300 men working two shifts, drilling and dynamiting. During construction, two men were killed. The night foreman was killed when some rocks collapsed, and Eli Anderson was shot during the celebration at the end of the project.

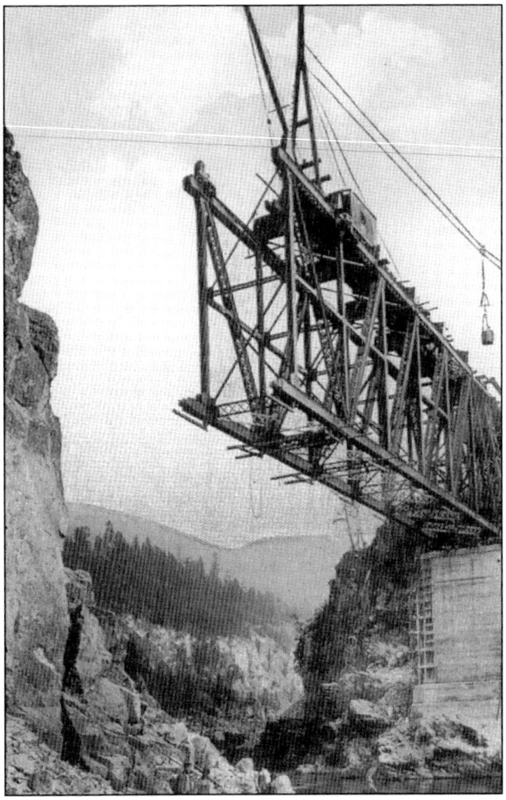

Box Canyon Cantilever Bridge. Box Canyon Bridge is a piece of historic American engineering. Plans called for using the cantilever construction method to build the bridge only from one end. The land end was loaded with 600 tons of steel rails as a counterweight for the 700-ton channel span. The bridge material was manufactured by the Pennsylvania Steel Company of Steelton, Pennsylvania. The bridge was constructed by McCreary and Willard of Spokane.

Railroad Construction. Here, railroad crews lay track through a cut in the mountains in the northern part of the county. The rugged terrain meant that the construction was more time consuming and much more expensive than what was anticipated by Fredrick Blackwell. The railroad reached Metaline Falls in 1910.

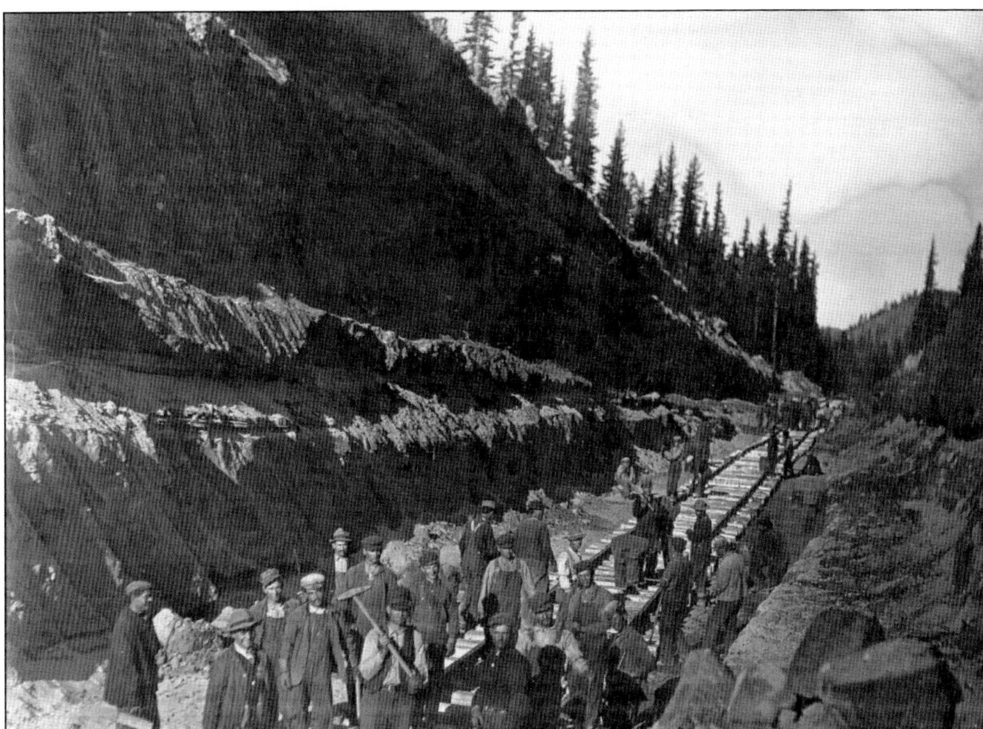

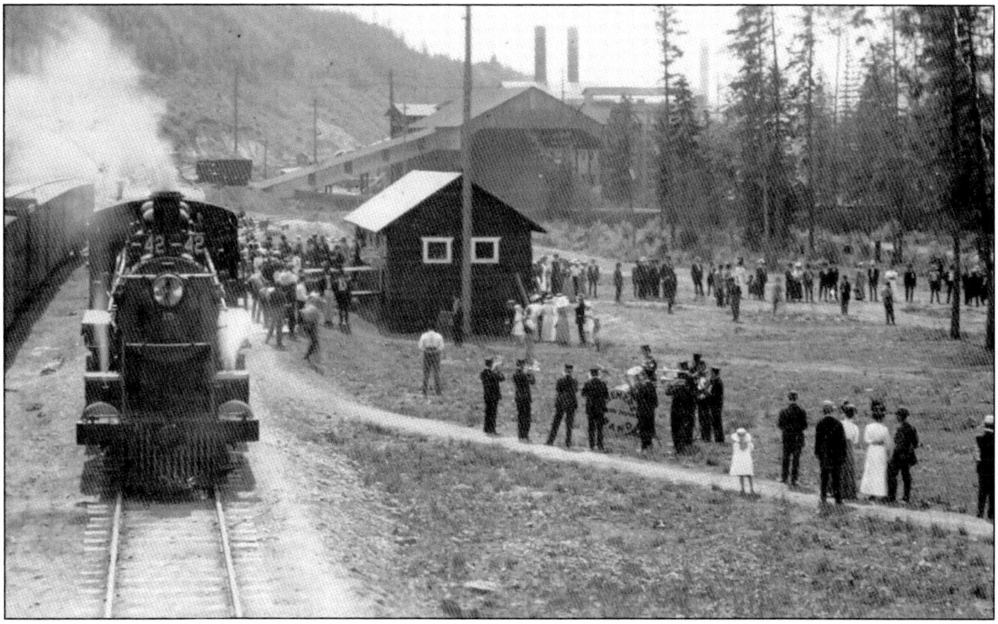

TRAIN AT METALINE FALLS. The Idaho & Washington Northern Railroad arrived at Metaline Falls in 1910. The I&WN provided fast, safe, dependable, and frequent service between Spokane and northern Pend Oreille County. The future of the county looked bright, with the completion of the cement plant in Metaline Falls and the Panhandle Lumber Company in Ione.

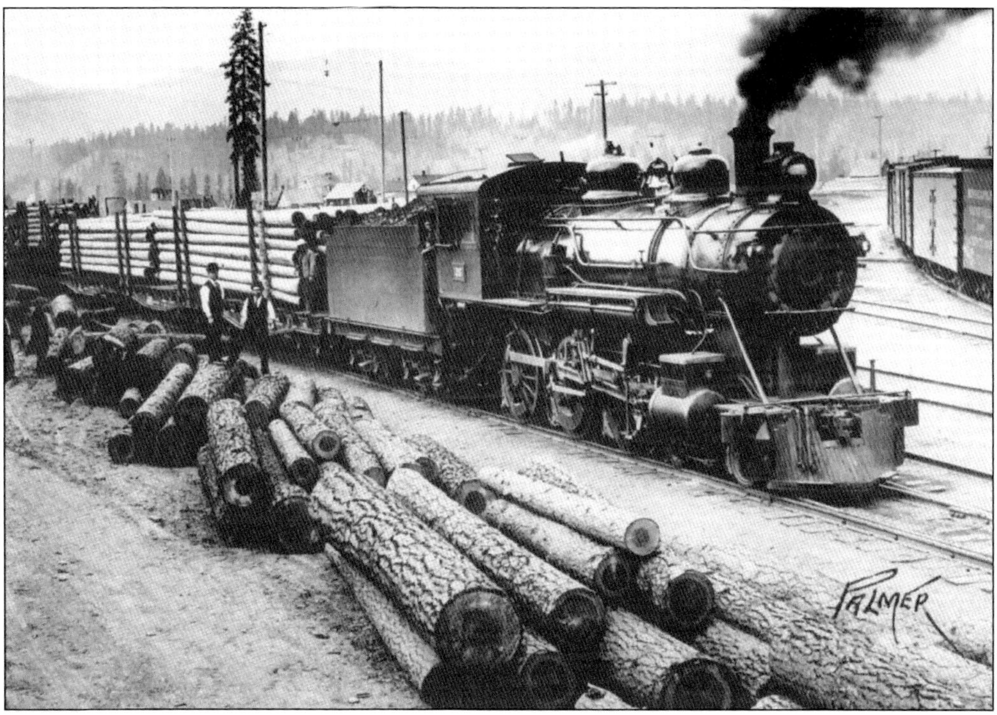

HAULING POLES. The Idaho & Washington Northern Railroad was the only rail system to run throughout Pend Oreille Company. At that time, it was not unusual for four trains to run daily in the county.

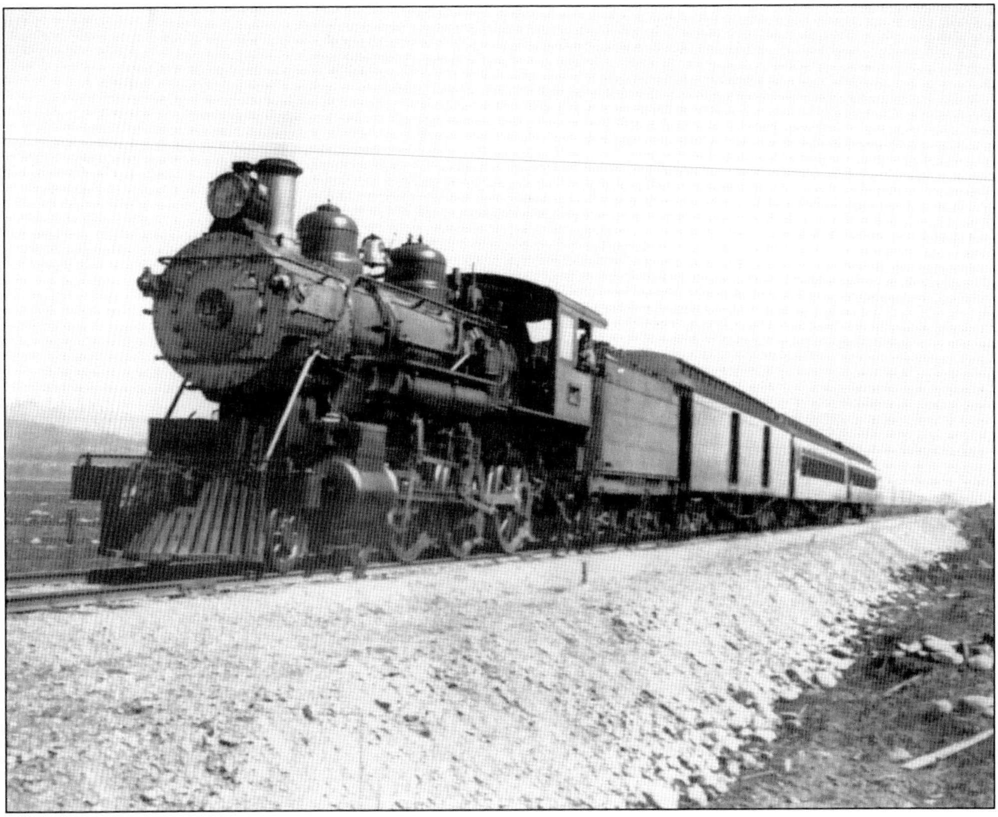

Blackwell Road. Early pioneers called the Idaho & Washington Northern Railroad the "Blackwell Road." This c. 1910 photograph shows the shiny, well-run train traveling somewhere in Pend Oreille County. The "Blackwell Road" was sold in 1916 to the Milwaukee Railroad. Today, the Pend Oreille Valley Railroad runs over the old I&WN tracks from Newport to Metaline Falls.

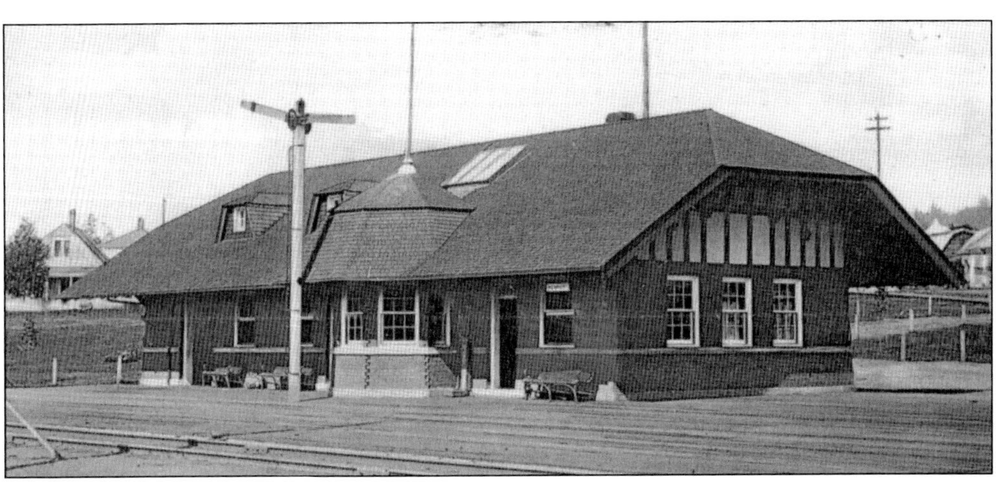

I&WN Depot. The Idaho & Washington Northern Railroad Depot in Newport was designed by Kirkland Cutter in 1907–1908. The Milwaukee Railroad bought the I&WN in 1916 and ran it until the 1970s. The Pend Oreille County Historical Society purchased the building, which was dedicated as a museum in 1978.

I&WN Brochure. This brochure tells the story of Fredrick Blackwell's Idaho & Washington Northern Railroad, which ran from McGuires, Idaho, to Metaline Falls from 1910 to 1916. It was considered one of the best and most well-run railroads in the State of Washington.

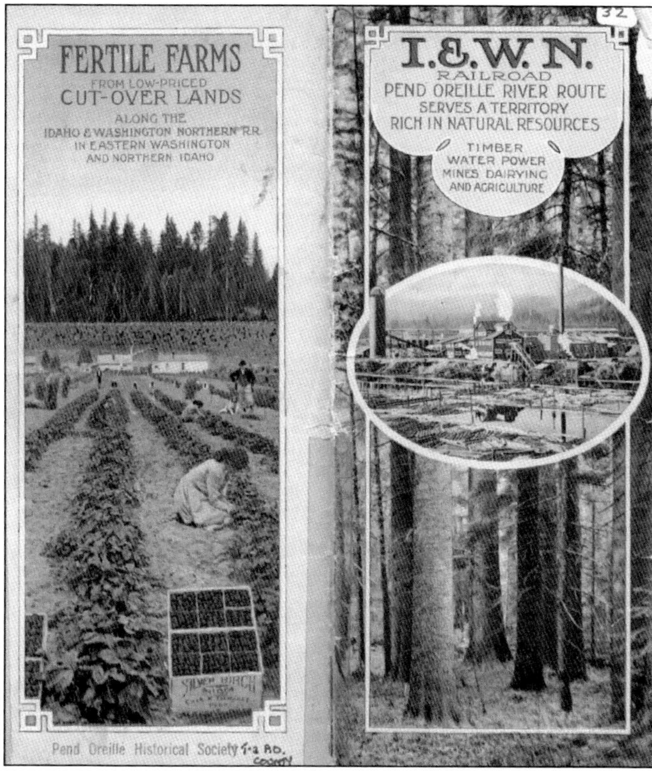

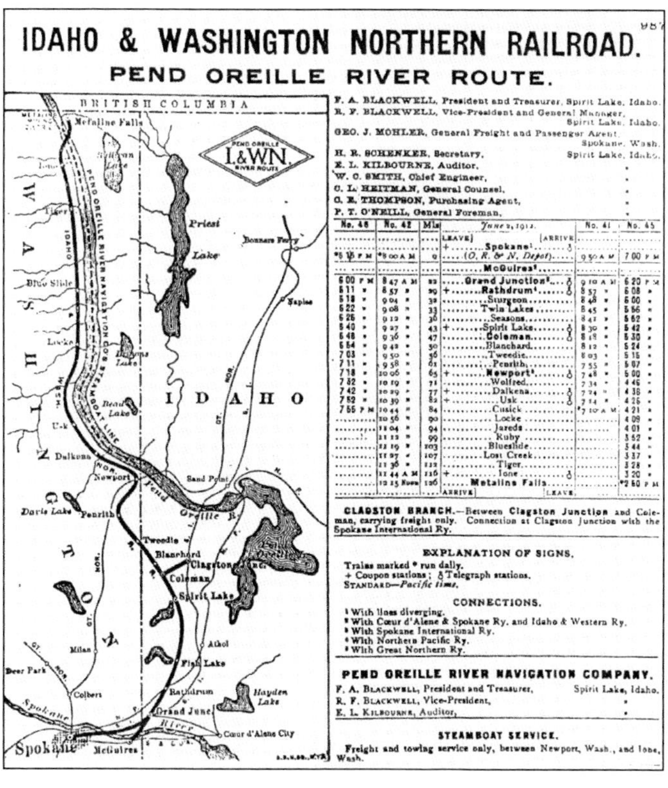

IDAHO & WASHINGTON NORTHERN RAILROAD.

PEND OREILLE RIVER ROUTE.

F. A. BLACKWELL, President and Treasurer, Spirit Lake, Idaho.
R. F. BLACKWELL, Vice-President and General Manager, Spirit Lake, Idaho.
GEO. J. MOHLER, General Freight and Passenger Agent, Spokane, Wash.
H. R. SCHENKER, Secretary, Spirit Lake, Idaho.
E. L. KILBOURNE, Auditor, "
W. C. SMITH, Chief Engineer, "
C. L. HEITMAN, General Counsel, "
C. E. THOMPSON, Purchasing Agent, "
P. T. O'NEILL, General Foreman, "

No. 48	No. 42	Mls	June 2, 1912.	No. 41	No. 45
			LEAVE] [ARRIVE		
			+ Spokane[1] ♁		
*5 15 P M	*8 00 A M	0	(O. R. & N. Depot)	9 50 A M	7 00 P M
			McGuires[1]		
6 00 P M	8 47 A M	22	Grand Junction[2] ♁	9 10 A M	6 20 P M
6 11 "	8 57 "	29	+ Rathdrum[4] ♁	8 57 "	6 08 "
6 18 "	9 04 "	32	Sturgeon	8 48 "	6 00 "
6 22 "	9 08 "	33	Twin Lakes	8 45 "	5 56 "
6 26 "	9 12 "	36	Seasons	8 41 "	5 52 "
6 40 "	9 27 "	43	+ Spirit Lake ♁	8 30 "	5 42 "
6 48 "	9 36 "	47	Coleman ♁	8 18 "	5 30 "
6 54 "	9 42 "	50	Blanchard	8 12 "	5 24 "
7 03 "	9 50 "	56	Tweedie	8 03 "	5 15 "
7 11 "	9 58 "	61	Penrith	7 55 "	5 07 "
7 18 "	10 06 "	65	+ Newport[5] ♁	7 48 "	5 00 "
7 32 "	10 19 "	71	Wolfred	7 34 "	4 46 "
7 42 "	10 29 "	77	+ Dalkena ♁	7 24 "	4 36 "
7 52 "	10 39 "	82	+ Usk ♁	7 14 "	4 26 "
7 55 P M	10 44 "	84	Cusick	*7 10 A M	4 21 "
	10 56 "	90	Locke		4 09 "
	11 04 "	94	Jareds		4 01 "
	11 12 "	99	Ruby		3 52 "
	11 19 "	103	Blueslide		3 44 "
	11 27 "	107	Lost Creek		3 37 "
	11 36 "	112	Tiger		3 28 "
	11 44 A M	116	+ Ione ♁		3 20 "
	12 15 Noon	126	Metaline Falls		*2 50 P M
			ARRIVE] [LEAVE		

CLAGSTON BRANCH.—Between Clagston Junction and Coleman, carrying freight only. Connection at Clagston Junction with the Spokane International Ry.

EXPLANATION OF SIGNS.

Trains marked * run daily.
+ Coupon stations; ♁ Telegraph stations.
STANDARD—*Pacific time.*

CONNECTIONS.

[1] With lines diverging.
[2] With Cœur d'Alene & Spokane Ry. and Idaho & Western Ry.
[3] With Spokane International Ry.
[4] With Northern Pacific Ry.
[5] With Great Northern Ry.

PEND OREILLE RIVER NAVIGATION COMPANY.

F. A. Blackwell, President and Treasurer, Spirit Lake, Idaho.
R. F. Blackwell, Vice-President, "
E. L. Kilbourne, Auditor, "

STEAMBOAT SERVICE.

Freight and towing service only, between Newport, Wash., and Ione, Wash.

I&WN Timetable. This is an Idaho & Washington Northern Railroad timetable and schedule. The map shows the route of the train from McGuires, Idaho, to Metaline Falls. There were connections with other trains at the Idaho stop.

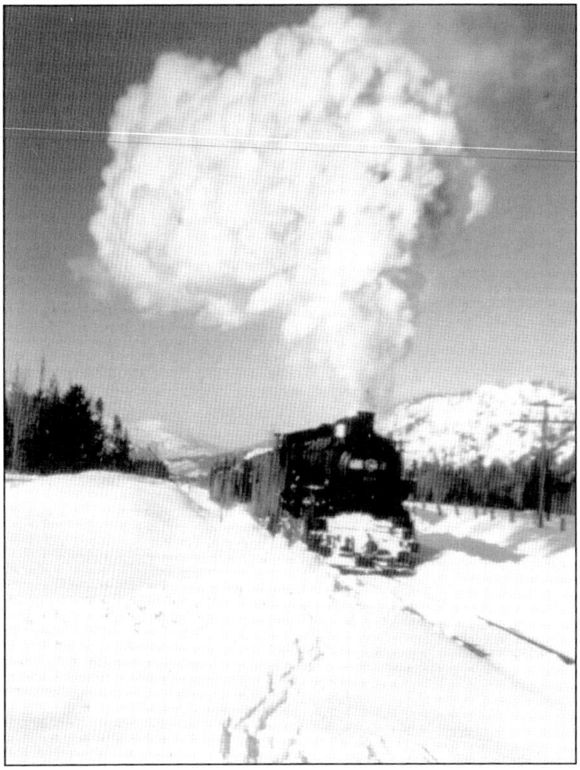

Milwaukee Railroad. The Milwaukee Railroad runs through a snow-covered valley in Pend Oreille County around 1920. Fredrick Blackwell suffered financial problems and had to sell his railroad to the Milwaukee line in 1916. Blackwell died seven years later.

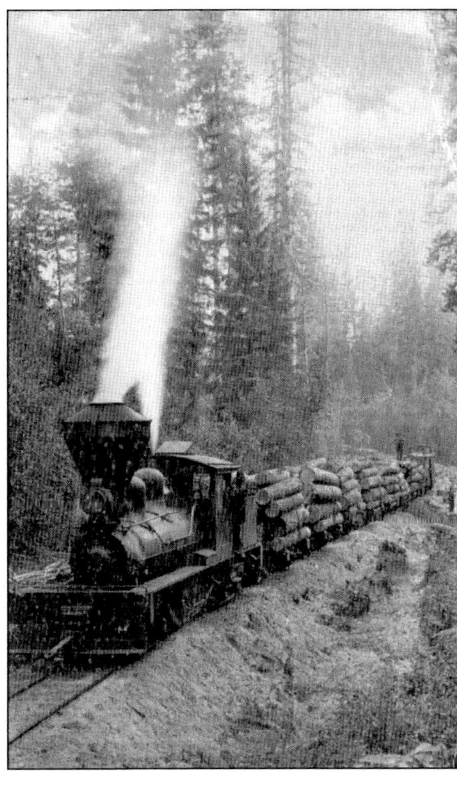

Logging Train. Narrow-gage, heavy-duty logging trains were used throughout Pend Oreille County. The Panhandle Lumber Company, the Diamond Match Lumber Company, and other companies used them to haul logs from the mountainous areas to unloading docks along the Pend Oreille River. Shay engines were used by the Panhandle Lumber Company on the LeClerc railway. Note the smoke resister on the engine.

Five

Mining and Lumber Industries

Mining and lumber played major roles in the history and development of Pend Oreille County. The region was rich in natural resources, and there was an insatiable demand for those resources throughout the country.

Following the creation of the new county, two very ambitious men made their mark. Lewis Larsen shaped the cement and mining industries, and Frederick Blackwell succeeded in the lumber industry. In 1911, Larsen started the Inland Portland Cement Company, which was purchased in 1914 by the Lehigh Portland Cement Company. The cement industry was the primary business in Metaline Falls for over 60 years. Cement from the plant was used in the construction of Grand Coulee Dam in central Washington and the Monroe Bridge in Spokane.

Lead and zinc mining in Pend Oreille County started to take off in the late 1920s with Larsen's formation of the Pend Oreille Mines & Metal Company. At the time, the US Geological Survey and US Bureau of Mines considered the mines the most promising in the country.

For years, Frederick Blackwell's Panhandle Lumber Company in Spirit Lake and Ione dominated the lumber industry. The mill at Ione was the first all-electric sawmill in the inland Northwest. Meanwhile, the large Diamond Match Lumber Company was quietly acquiring large tracts of prime timber acreage, and, by the 1920s, became a dominating company. At that time, 80 percent of its holdings were being used in the production of wooden matches. The large company had several sawmills in the county. The Diamond City mill had an aerial tram, which took match stock across the Pend Oreille River to Lost Creek. During the busy years of the lumber industry, there were hundreds of small sawmills producing lumber. Also produced, in addition to lumber, were poles, posts, and railroad ties. The poles were needed for the burgeoning electric, telephone, and telegraph systems throughout the country. When most of the timber was cut down or burned by forest fires, the lumber industry disappeared.

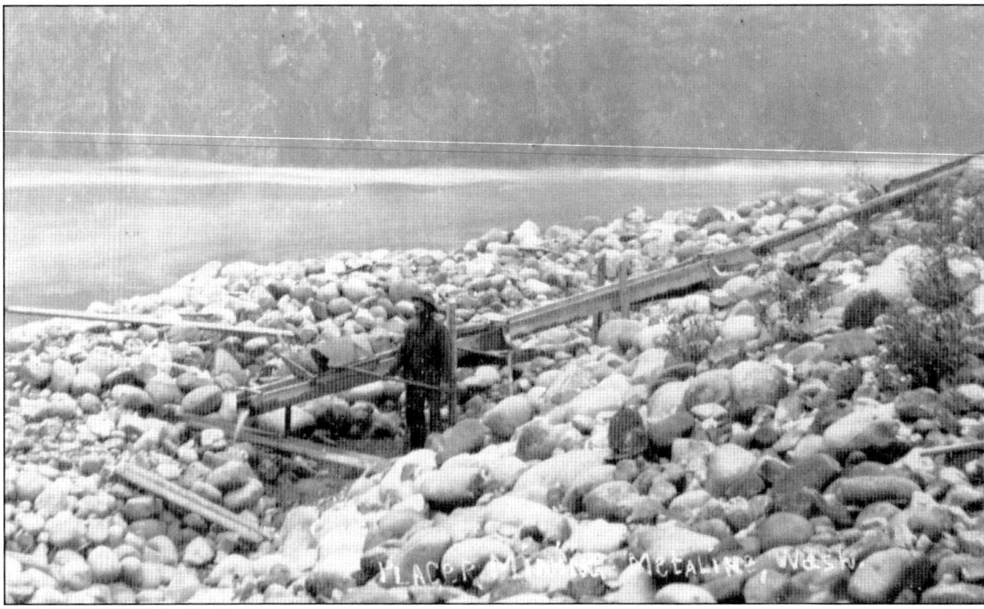

Gold Placer Mining Equipment. This is a placer mining setup along the Pend Oreille River. Prospectors in the 1800s entered the Pend Oreille region dreaming of another California gold rush. They panned for tiny flakes of gold that had broken off of rocks and been washed downstream.

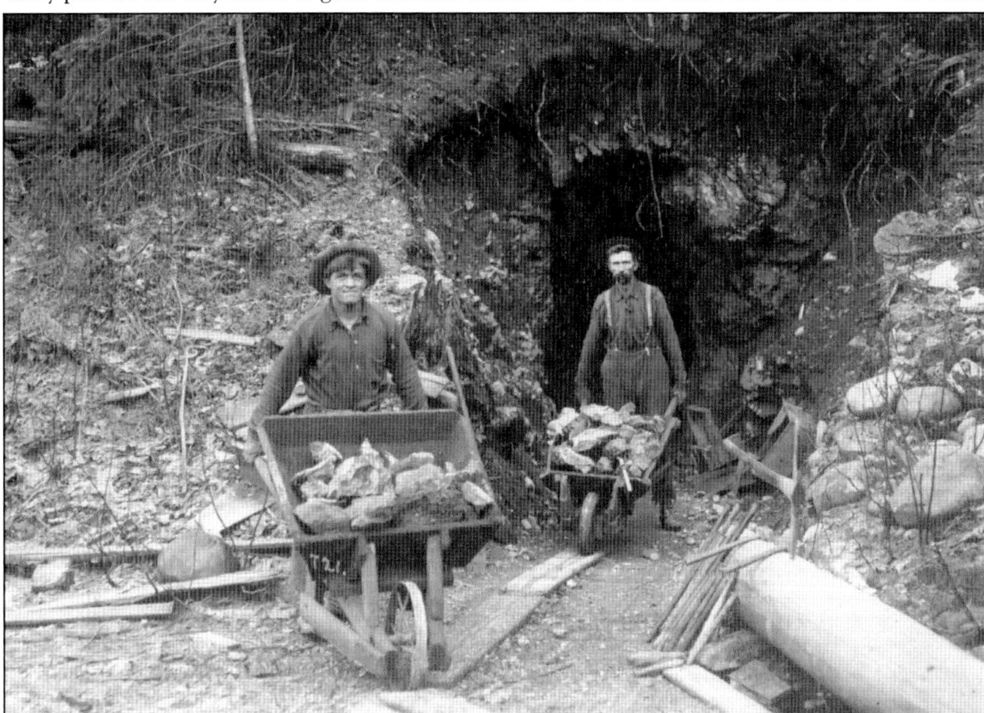

Pioneer Miners. The Morning Mine/Oriole Mine was located in the Metaline Falls area. Harry Bagnall (left) and Dick Stevens are working with wheelbarrows and shovels. Harry came into the area about 1910, and he and Dick worked in the mines and did a little prospecting. Harry Bagnall has a creek named after him.

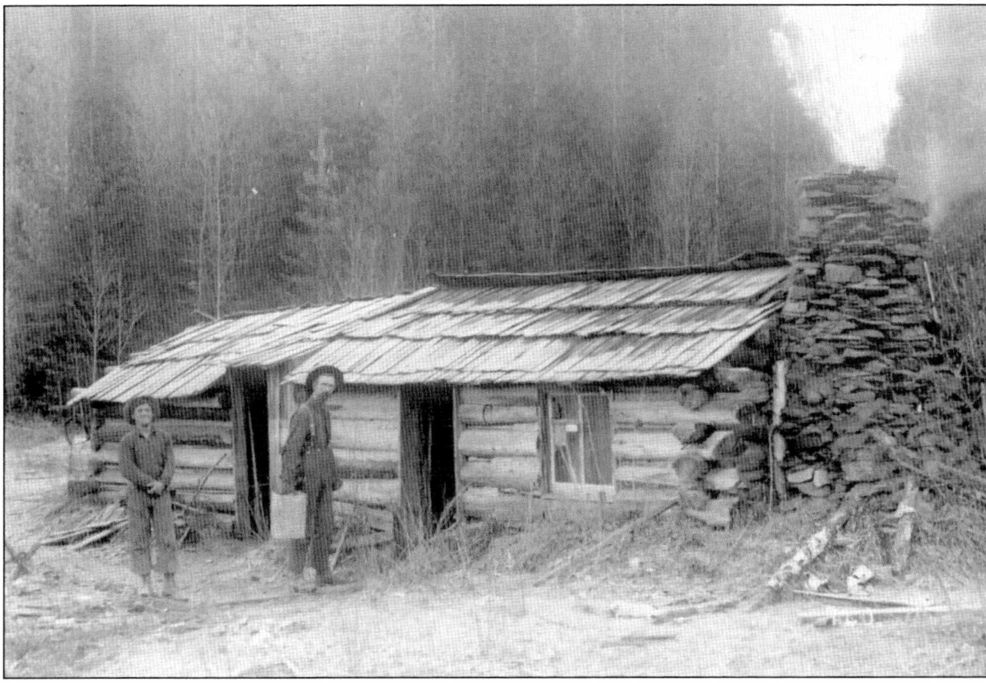

Miner's Log Cabin. Harry Bagnall (left) and Dick Stevens, the two miners seen here, picked up whatever mine work they could find and spent the rest of the time prospecting, hoping to hit it rich. Note the wattle and daub chimney.

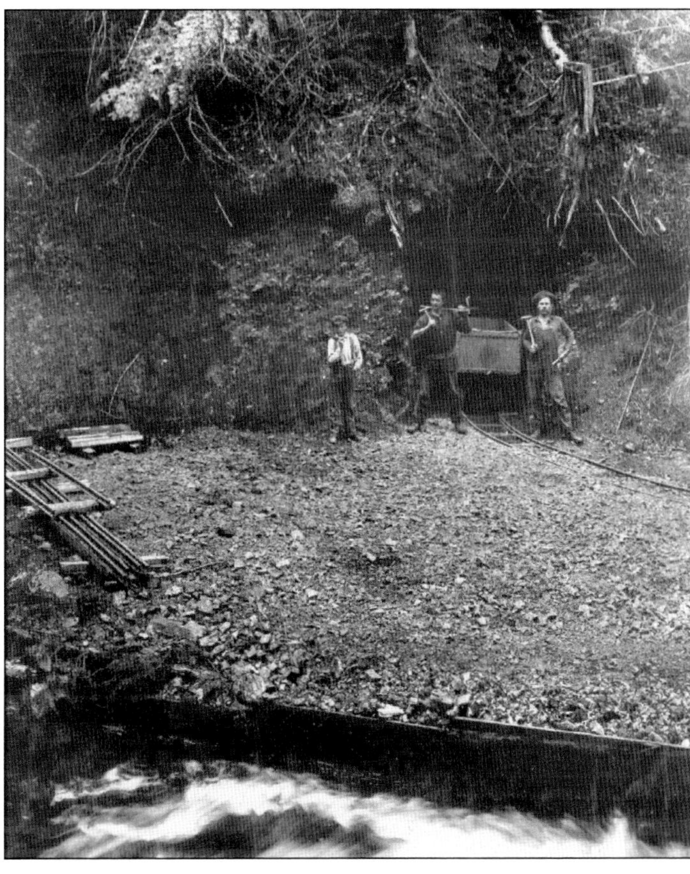

Josephine Mine. The zinc and lead Josephine Mine was located near Metaline Falls, Washington. It was discovered by C.W. Clark in the early 1900s and was sold to Lewis Larsen in 1909. It was worked until 1919 and then was closed for a period of time. Later, Larsen combined the Josephine Mine with others and formed the very profitable and successful Pend Oreille Mines & Metal Company.

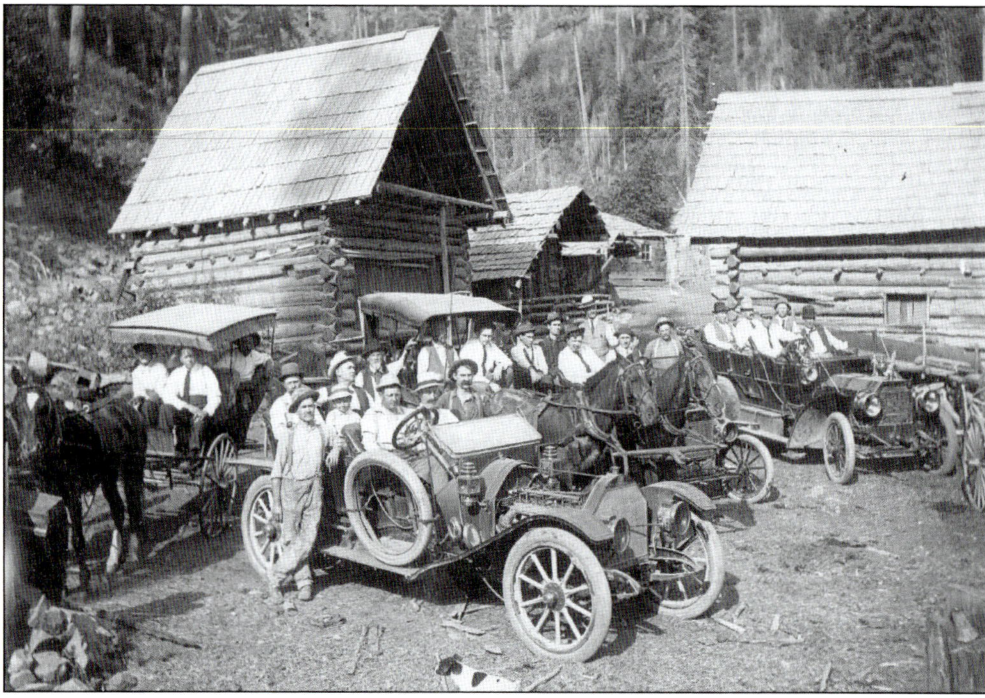

Bead Lake Mine. The Bead Lake Mine was located in the Newport Mining District. A concentrator mill was built in 1922. The volume of the mine was never substantial enough to become a paying proposition. A number of Newport people had claims on Bead Lake and other mines in the area.

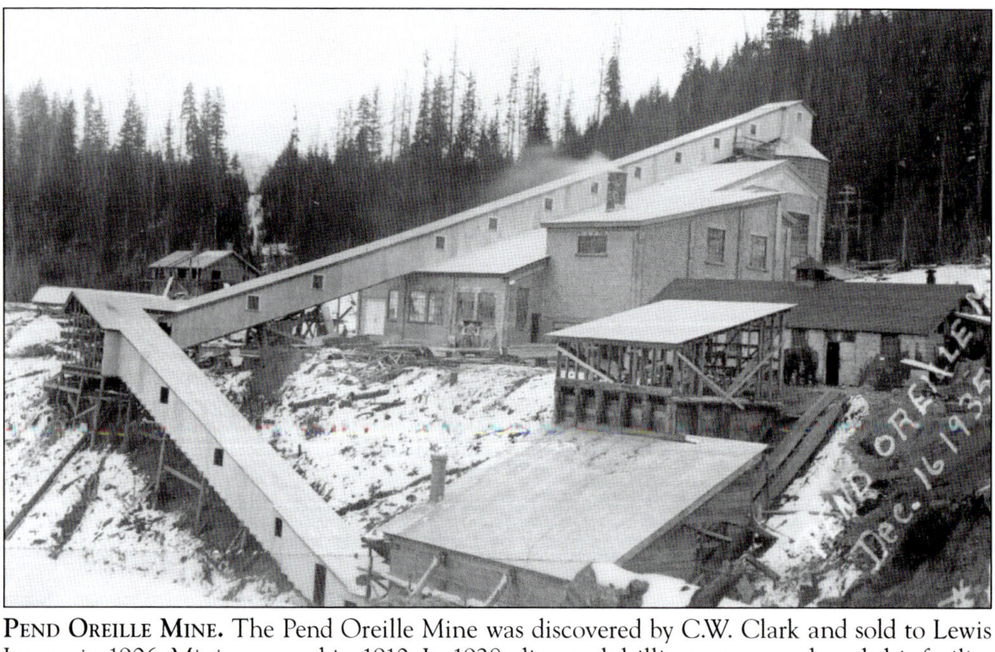

Pend Oreille Mine. The Pend Oreille Mine was discovered by C.W. Clark and sold to Lewis Larsen in 1906. Mining started in 1910. In 1928, diamond drilling was started, and this facility developed into the most productive zinc and lead mine in the district. Underground pumps were used to keep it dry.

Ore Concentrator. Seen here is an old ore concentrator building. Zinc and lead were the most common ores that were mined; however, sometimes slight concentrations of silver and gold were found. Zinc is used as a productive galvanizer for iron and steel, among other uses. Lead has many uses in batteries, pipe linings, X-ray equipment, and more.

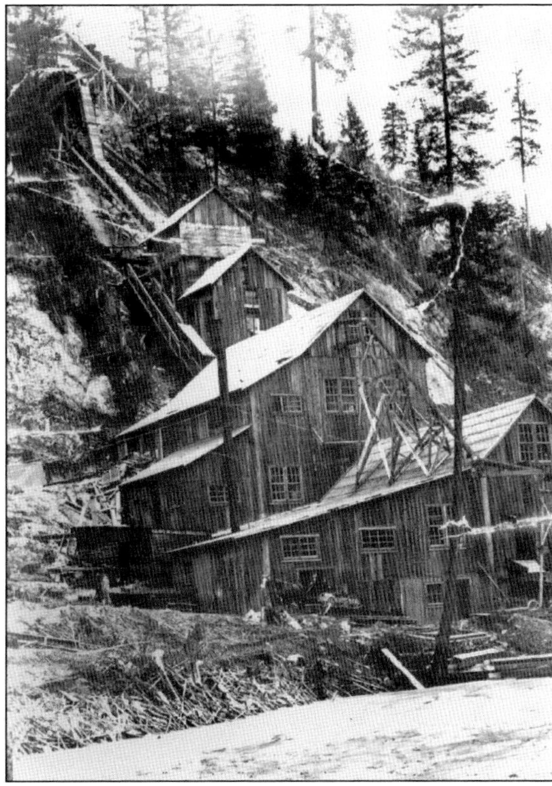

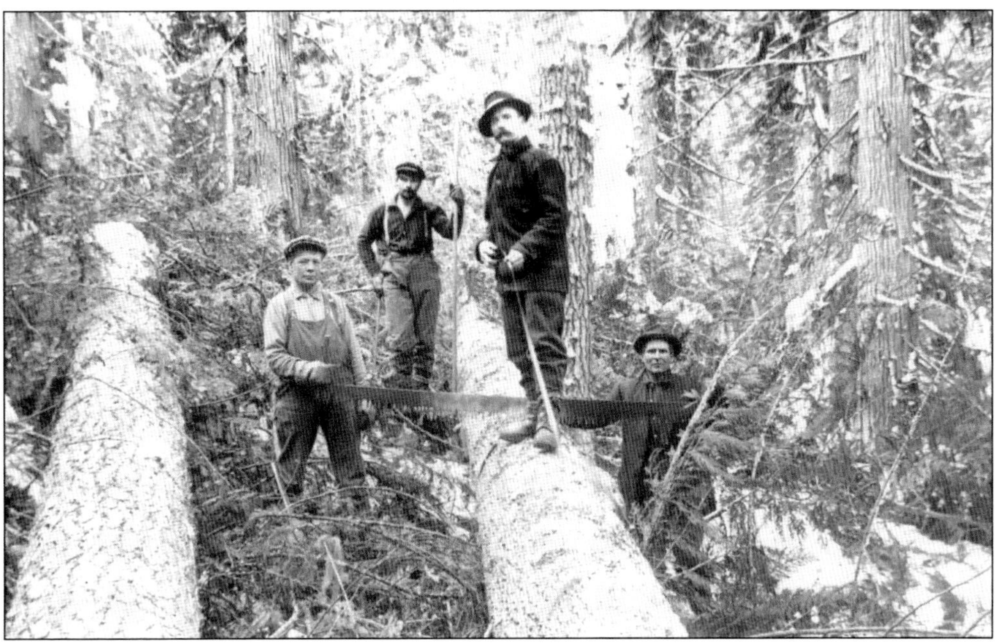

Logger's Tools. Old-time loggers pose with their tools. Crosscut saws were used to cut down trees and cut up logs. Axes, peaveys, wedges, and bottles of oil were the logger's basic tools. Skillful loggers would carefully keep their tools sharp and clean to make them work easier. Many laborers in logging camps worked from 10 to 12 hours a day, six days a week.

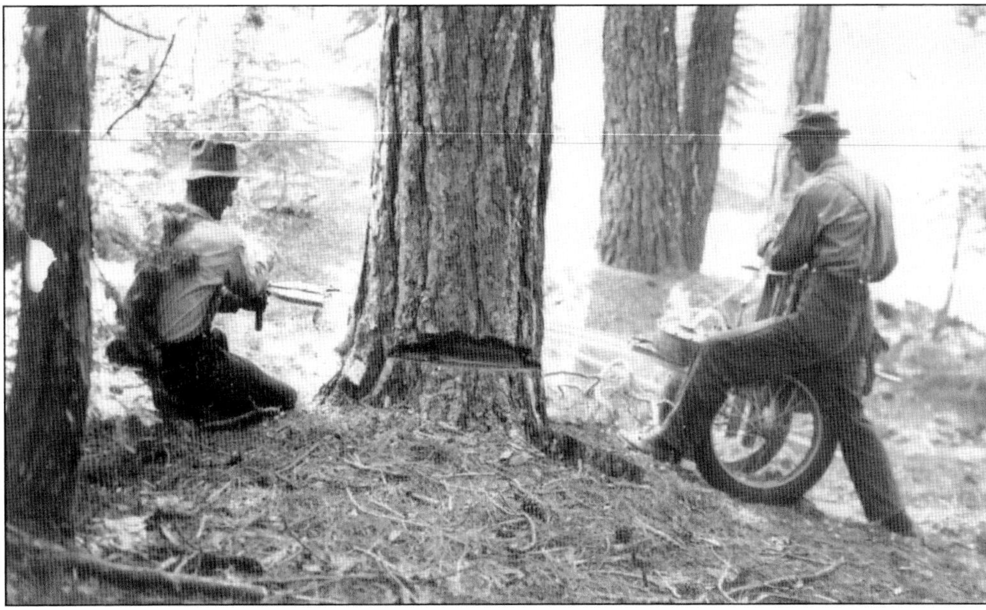

Early Chainsaw. When heavy, awkward chainsaws appeared, they made the work of cutting down trees and cutting logs somewhat easier. Logging was, and still is, dangerous work. Early newspapers reported stories almost every week of loggers being hit or killed by trees and cut by saws and axes.

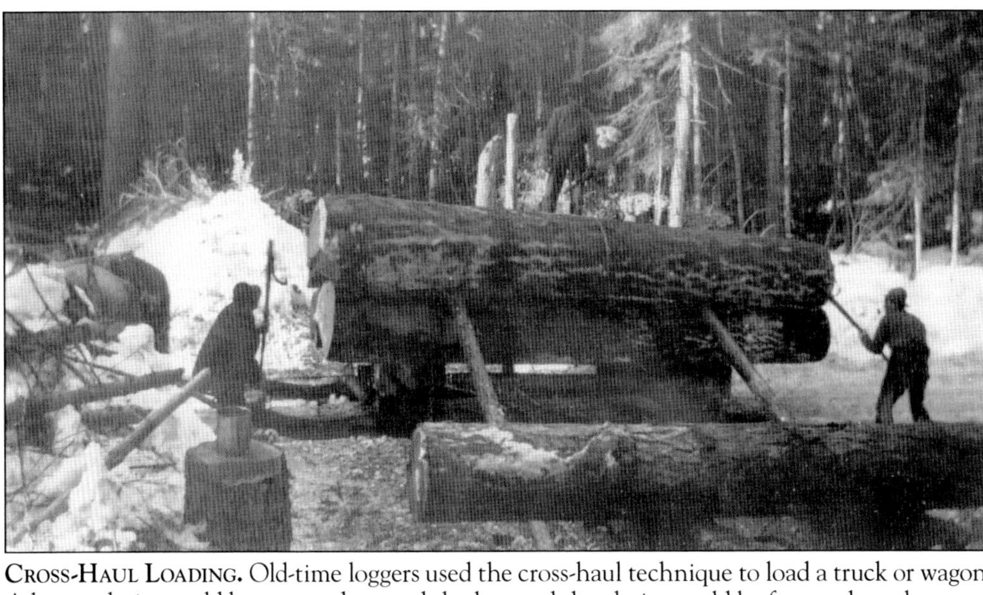

Cross-Haul Loading. Old-time loggers used the cross-haul technique to load a truck or wagon. A heavy chain would be wrapped around the log, and the chain would be fastened to a horse on the other side of the truck. Slowly, the two loggers would roll the log up on skids while the horse pulled on the chain.

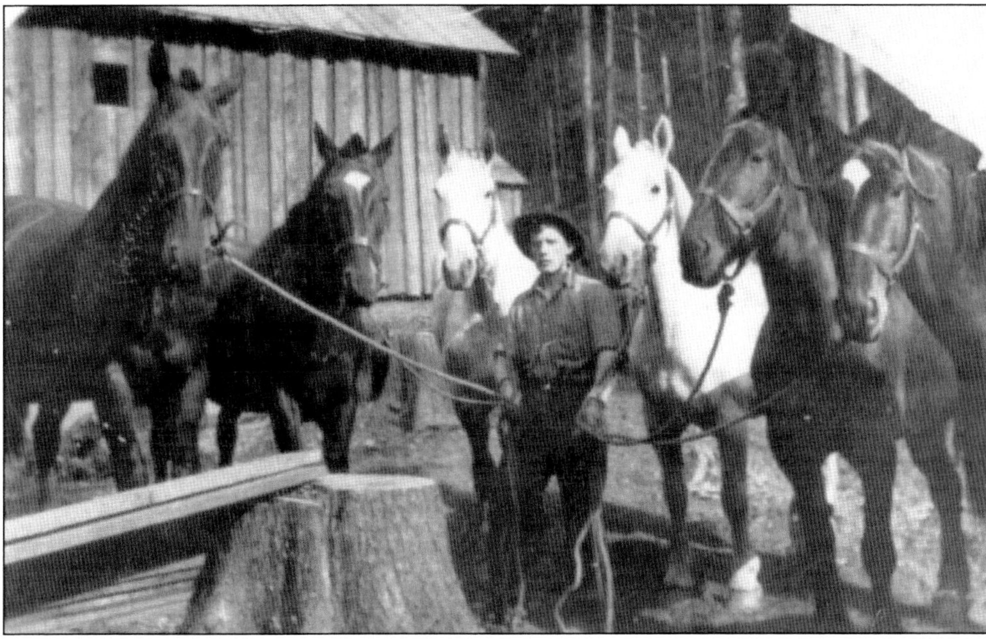

Logging Horses. Prior to modern equipment, logging required hundreds of horses, which had to be fed and cared for. Many logging camps had special workers to take care of the animals. Many farmers raised acres of grain, hay, and strong sturdy horses.

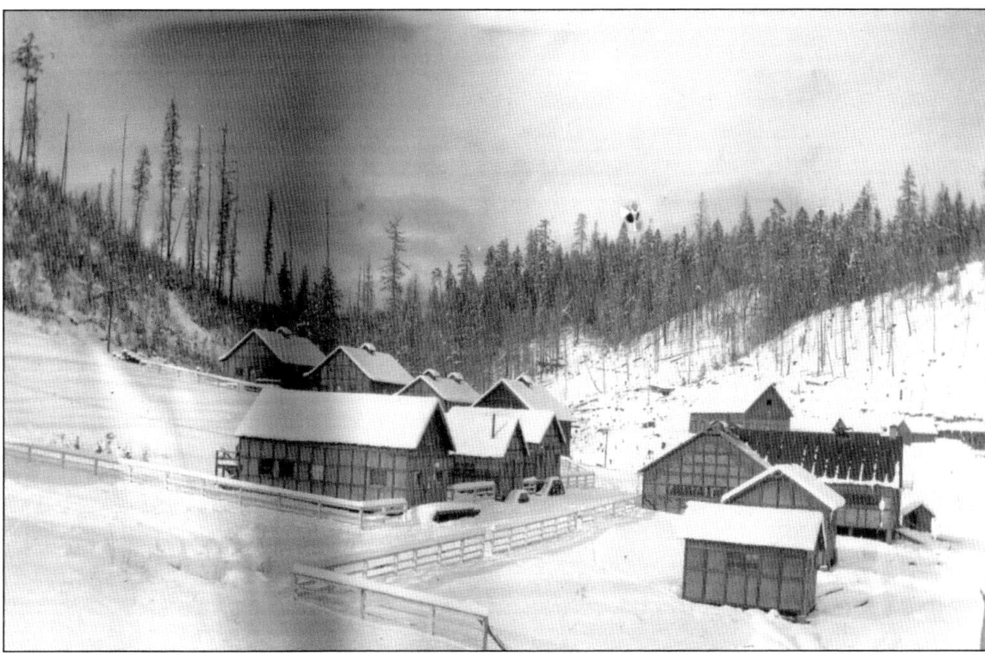

Logging Camp. The large Panhandle, Diamond Match, Ohio Match, and Dalkena Lumber Companies had logging camps. Single men, and married men whose homes were some distance away, would live in bunkhouses. Both the Panhandle and Diamond Match companies ran six to ten camps throughout Pend Oreille County. Men would live in the camp for weeks at a time.

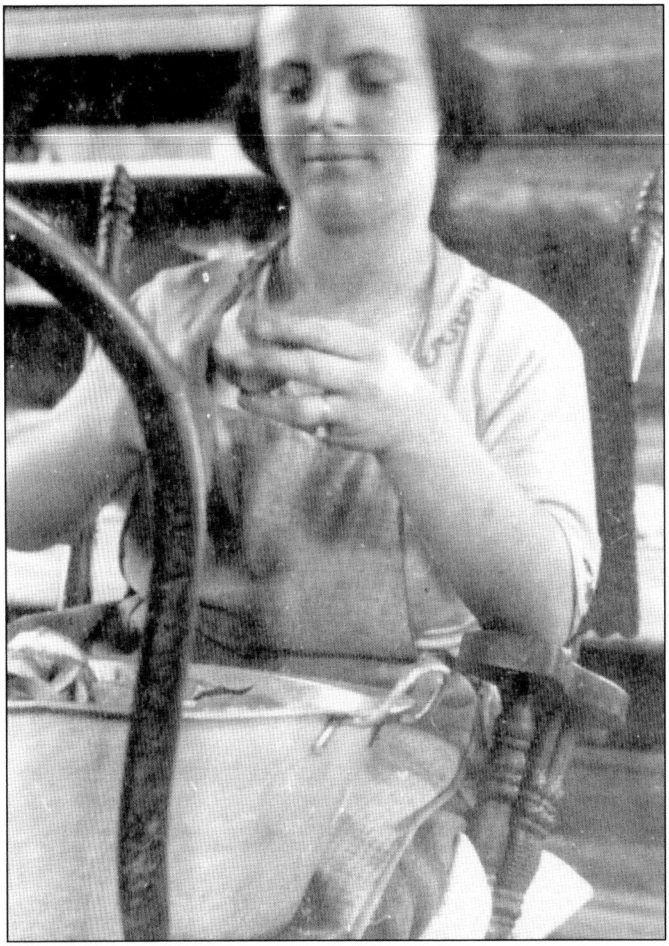

Logging Camp Cooks. Cooks and cook's helpers were vital to a well-run logging camp. The loggers worked long hours and expected good and generous amounts of food. The cooks were in charge of ordering, planning, and preparing tons of food each day. Often, the cook and his or her helpers lived at the camp during the week or longer. Much of the food was supplied by local farmers.

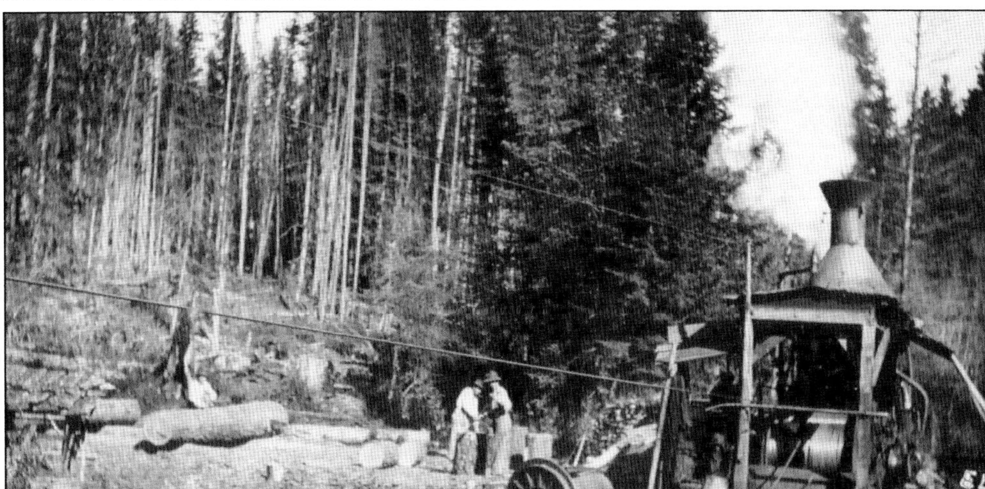

Steam Donkey. A steam or donkey engine is the nickname for a steam-powered winch that was used in logging. A cable would be carried out into the woods and attached to the log. After a signal was given, the machine would drag or skid the log to a landing, flume, or the river.

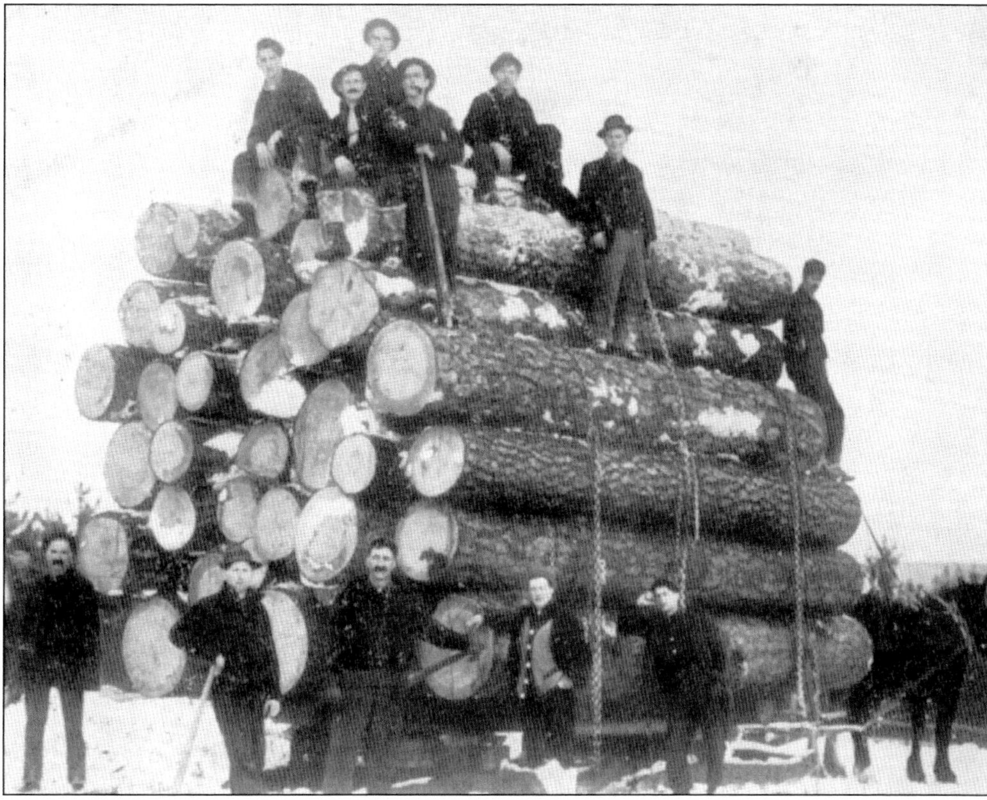

Logging Sleigh. Logging was usually done in the winter. Cross-haul loading was used to load the sleighs. Logging trails were sometimes sanded to keep the sleigh from going too fast. At other times, the trails would be iced, allowing the sleigh to be pulled easier. It was dangerous work for both the men and the horses.

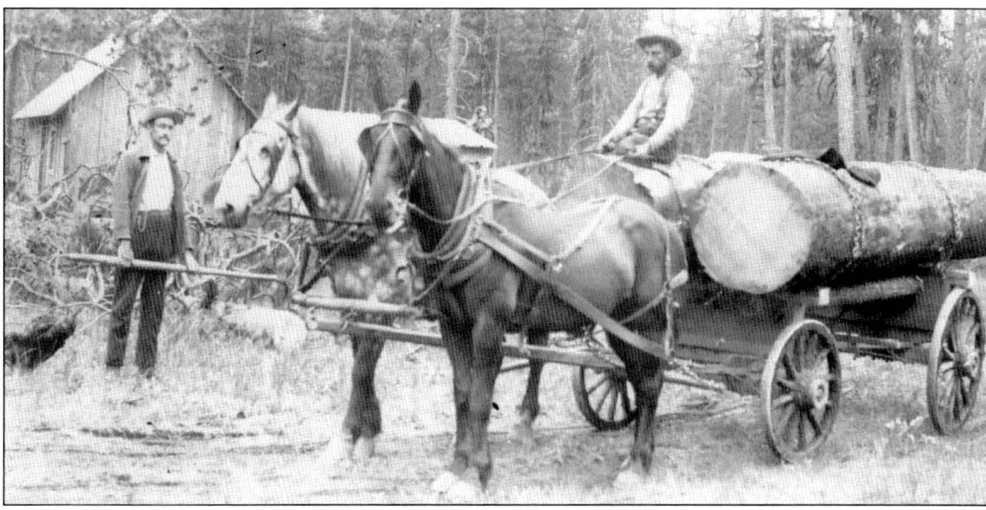

Logging Wagon. The virgin trees were so large that, sometimes, one or two logs would constitute a wagonload. Heavy-duty, sturdy wagons pulled by strong horses were used to haul the huge logs. It is estimated that, prior to the coming of the white man, 95 percent of the Pend Oreille region was covered with dozens of different species of trees.

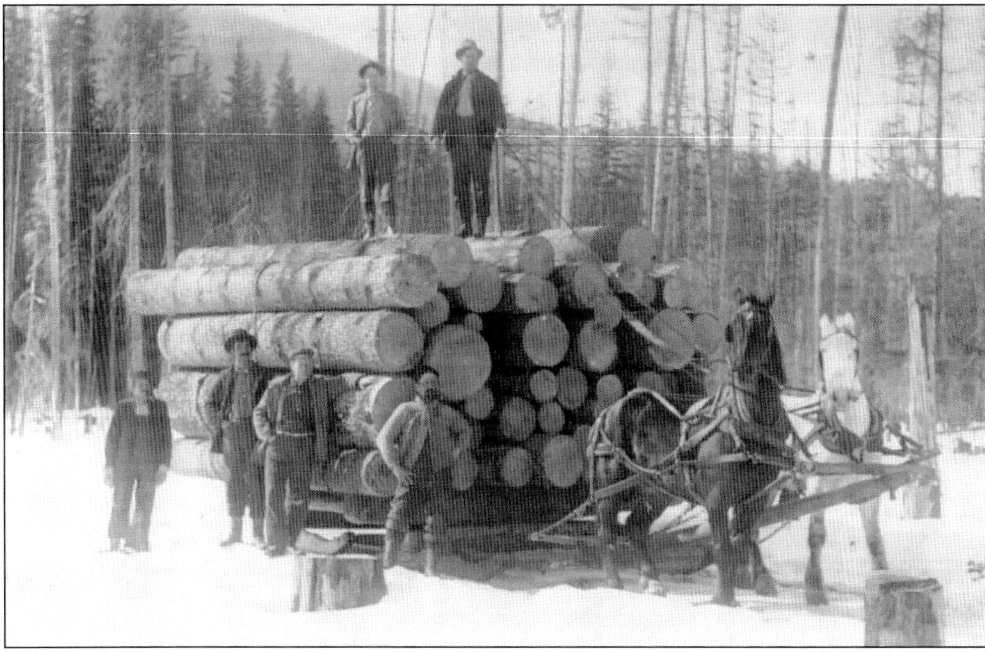

Load of Logs. Shown here are Roy Rauch (center, in front of logs), his logging crew, and a record load of 11,800 board feet of logs in the early 1900s. The sled load is pulled by a team of horses down an icy roadway. The logs would probably be milled in Newport and shipped by rail to Spokane. Note the cutover forest.

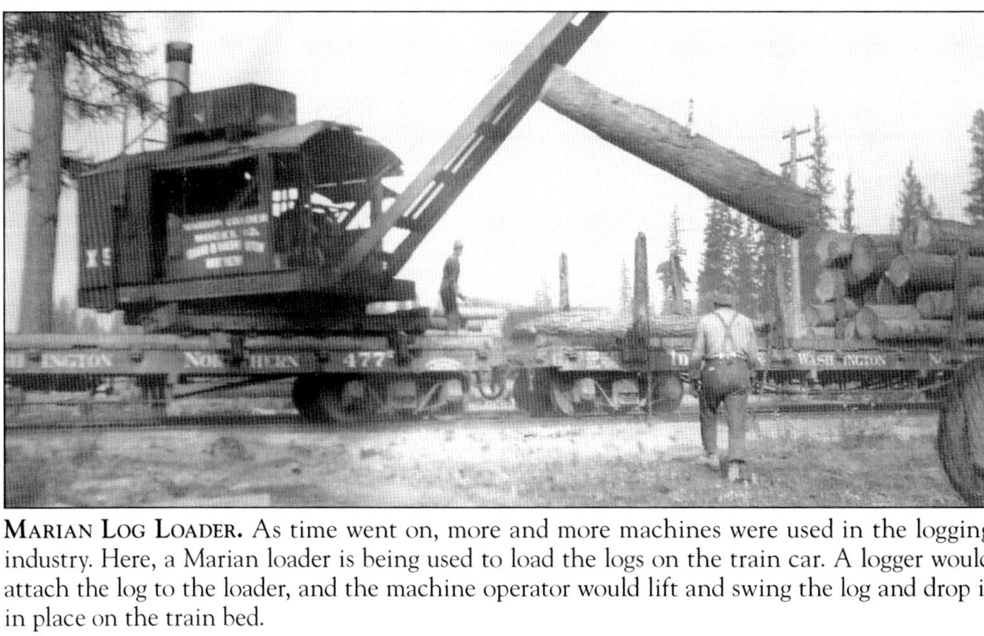

Marian Log Loader. As time went on, more and more machines were used in the logging industry. Here, a Marian loader is being used to load the logs on the train car. A logger would attach the log to the loader, and the machine operator would lift and swing the log and drop it in place on the train bed.

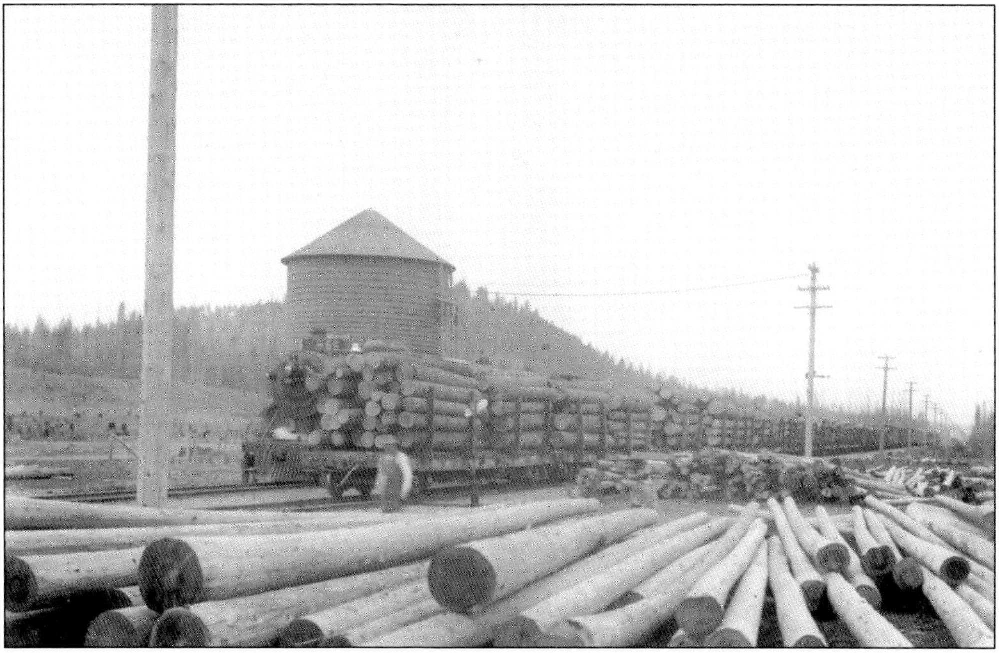

Pole and Log Landing. The clean, peeled poles are carefully piled beside the train tracks. Loggers in the woods, using axes, would peel yellow pine or fir poles. There was a big demand for telephone and telegraph poles all over the country. Carloads of logs were shipped to Spokane and other places.

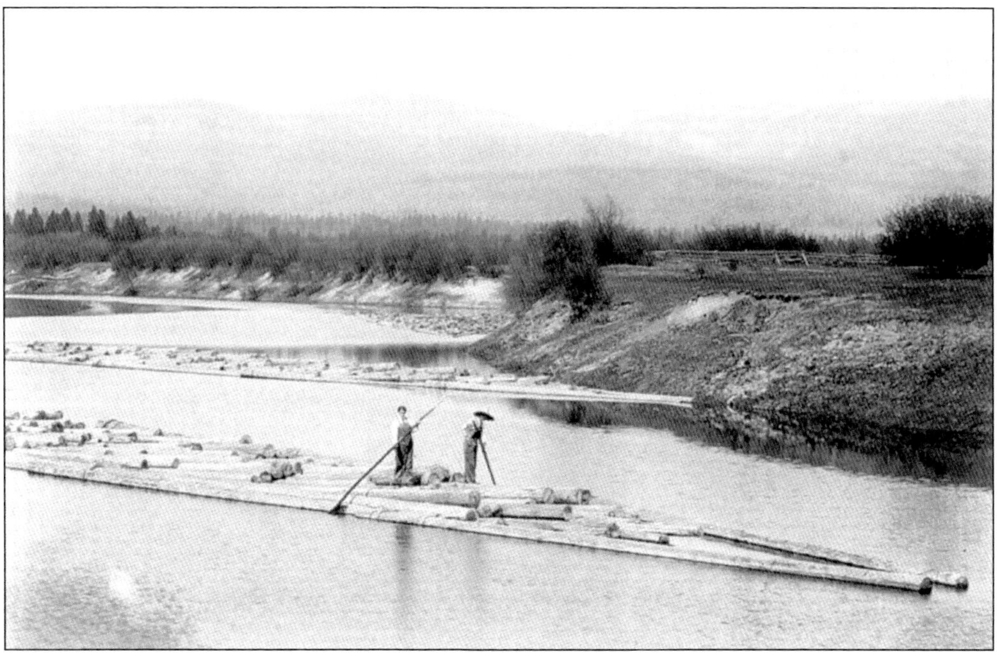

Boom of Logs. River loggers, often called "river pigs," placed heavy chains and hooks on connecting logs, which then enclosed hundreds of logs. The loggers then floated the booms downriver. Sometimes, the logs were collected at the mouth of a river. Here, men are guiding logs to a landing or a sawmill log pond.

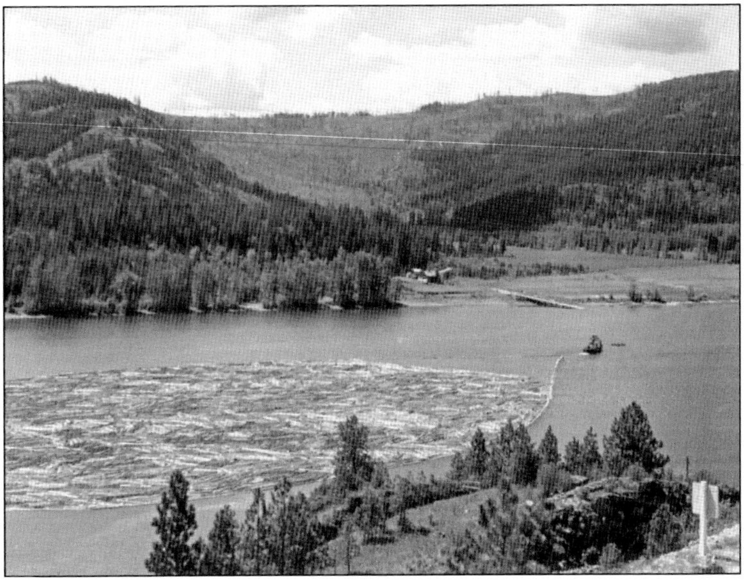

Tugboat and Log Boom. A tugboat pulls a boom of logs somewhere on the Pend Oreille River. The logs were corralled with chained logs and then towed by the tugboat to a sawmill.

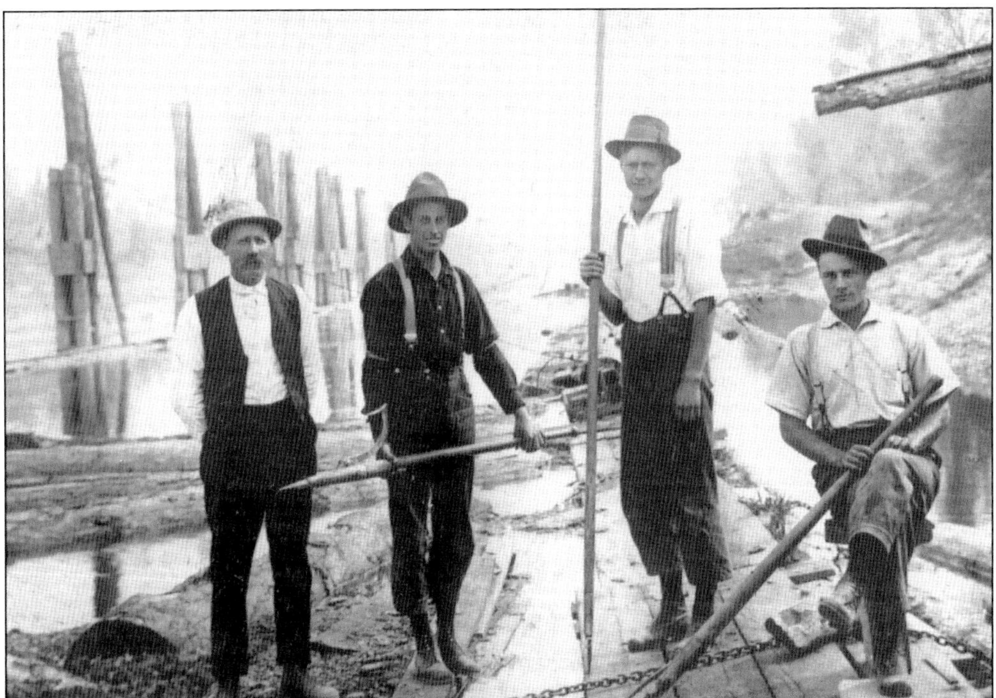

"Sunday River Crew." River loggers take a break from working the logs on the Pend Oreille River in 1916. They are, from left to right, John Johnson, Harold Shull, Harold Hoisington, and Hale Burnham. They are sorting logs by species for the different sawmills. The logs were either notched or branded with branding irons to indicate the different sawmills. The irons are similar to the ones used to brand cattle.

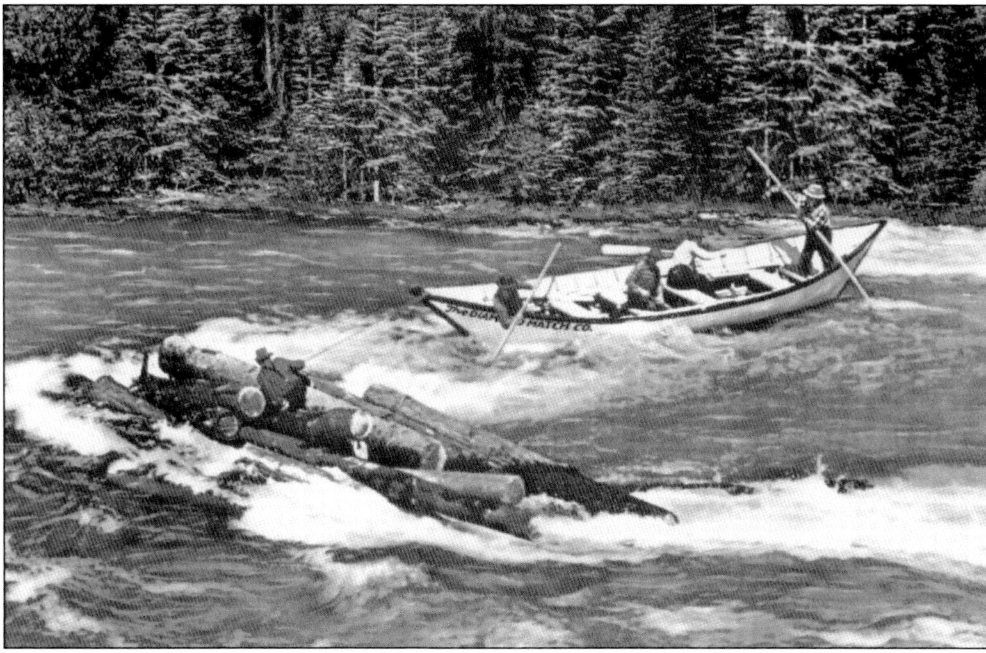

BATTEAUS. Shallow, flat-bottom boats called bateaus were used by the river pigs to keep the logs running in the river. During log drives in the spring, logs were washed down in flumes into the river. Loggers had to keep the logs running so they would not bunch up along the river and cause log jams.

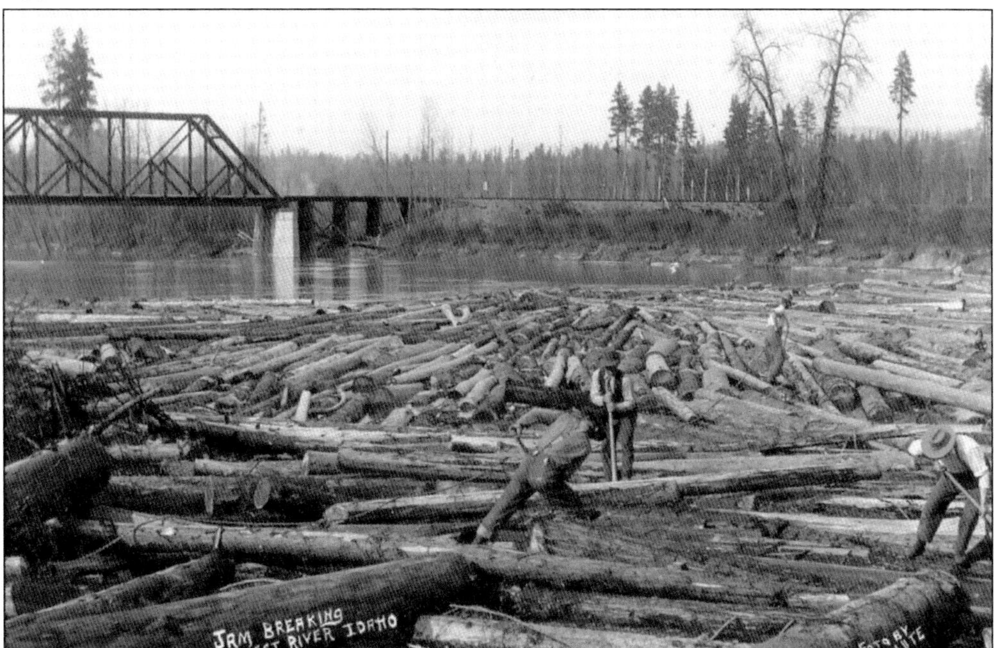

LOG JAM. When the logs rushed down the river, they often piled up and became locked in, causing a log jam. The river pigs looked for key logs and attempted to pull or push them out to allow the logs to float free. It was very dangerous work; every year, loggers were hurt or killed.

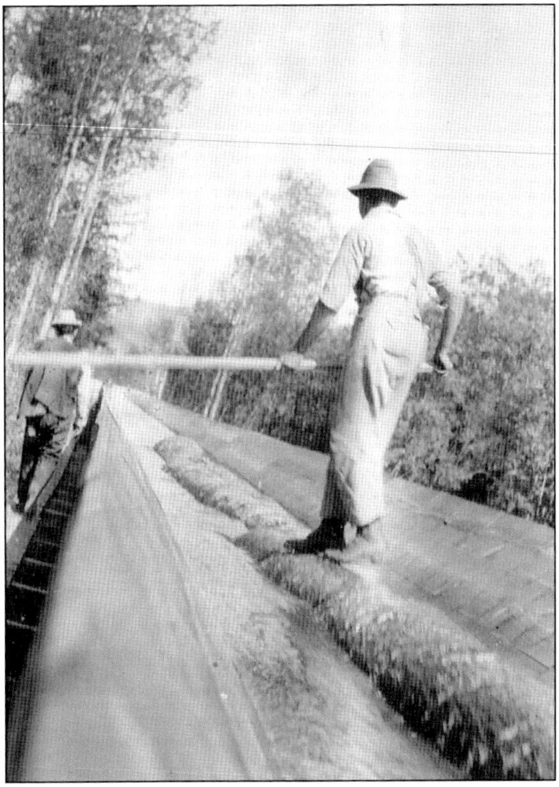

Log Flume. The V-shaped lumber flume is filled with rushing water and is used to transport logs down the mountainous terrain to the river or to a log landing. Here, the logger, called a flume walker, is checking the flume and watching the logs as they go down. The big sawmills in Pend Oreille County used miles of flumes to get logs out of the mountains to either the river or a mill.

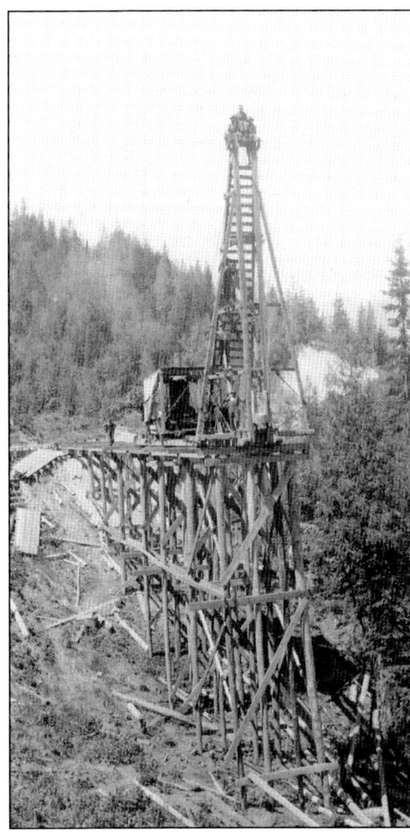

Pile Driver. Flumes had to be surveyed and engineered in order to work efficiently. Pile drivers were used to drive in the poles or posts, creating the foundations for the flumes. In the early days, small, portable sawmills were often set up nearby to produce the lumber for the flumes.

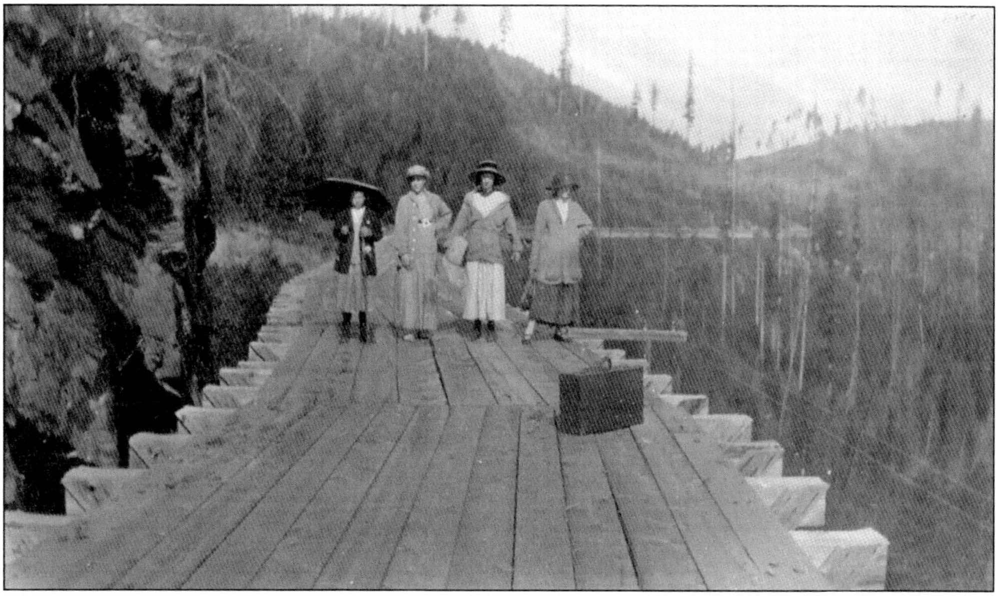

Lehigh Flume. The Lehigh water flume was built in a box form. The top was covered. People would walk, ride bicycles, or even drive motorcycles on top of the flume. Shown here are, from left to right, Bernice and Hazel Love, Mrs. Hamrick, and Mrs. Ward taking a walk on the flume.

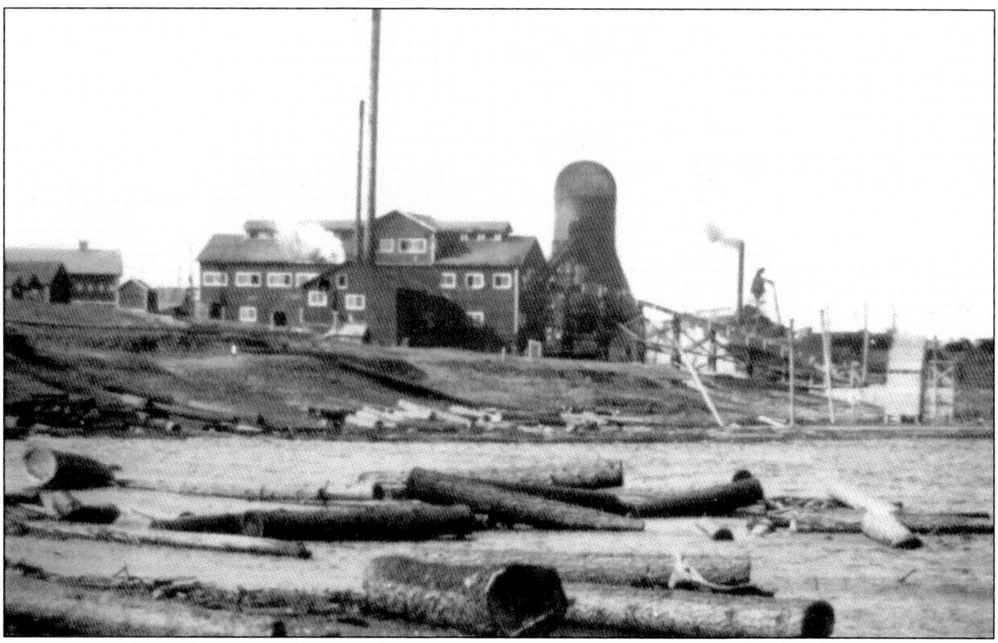

Dalkena Lumber Company. The original community went by the name of Glenco. Henry Dalton and Hugh Kennedy constructed a large sawmill around 1903. They combined their names and called the community Dalkena. During the big 1910 forest fire, part of the mill and the Dalkena community was destroyed. The mill was rebuilt and continued to operate until 1936.

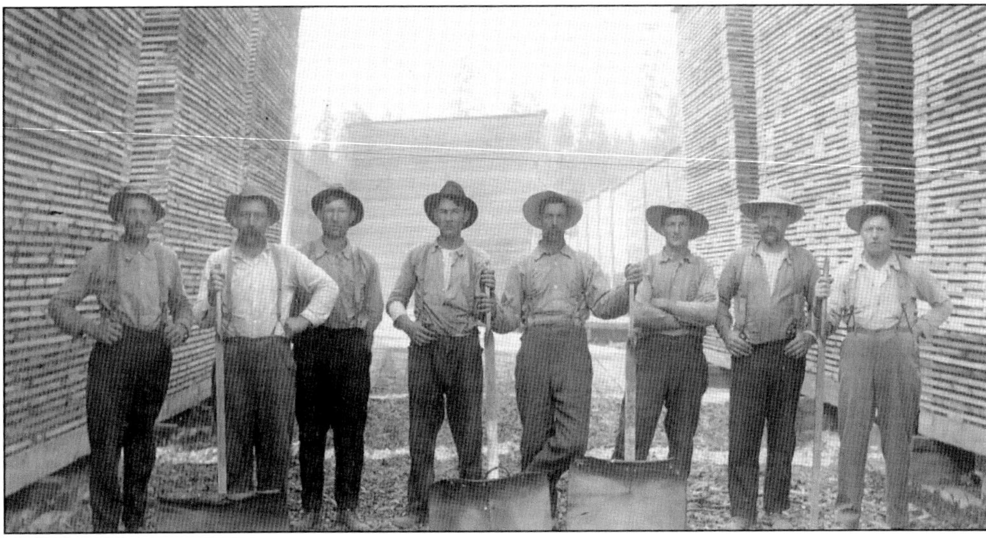

Piles of Lumber in Dalkena. Piles of lumber are air-drying at the Dalkena Lumber Company. It took skilled men to build the high stacks of lumber. Once the lumber was dry, it was either shipped out as raw lumber or sent to the planing mill. The Dalkena Lumber Company employed hundreds of men, rented small houses, and had a company store for the workers. It supported the local school and community.

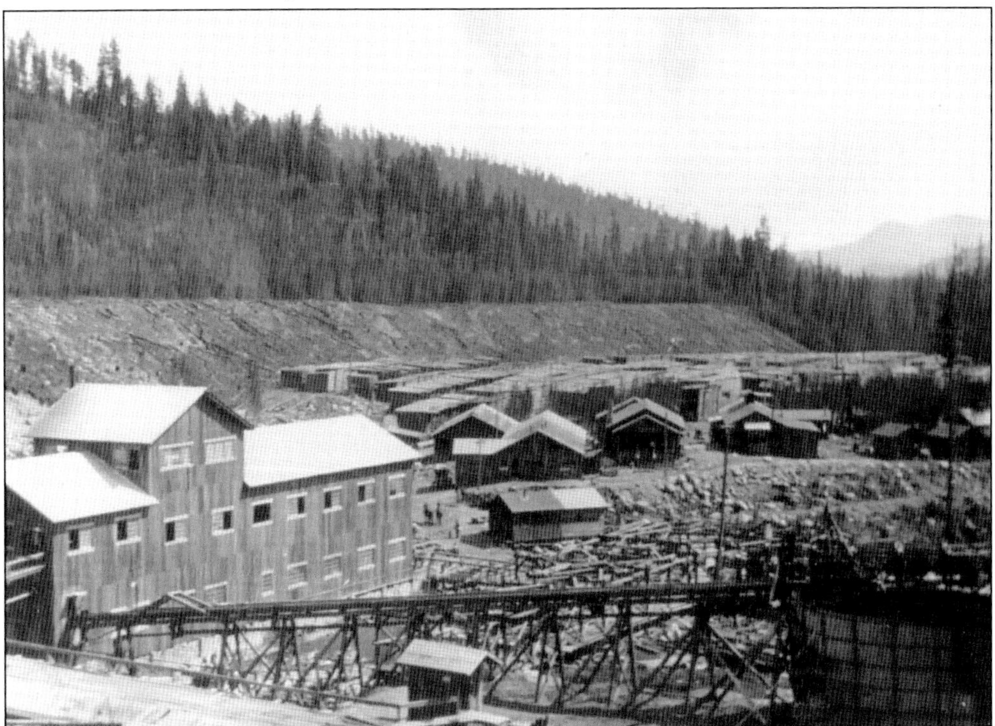

Diamond City, Washington. The large Diamond Match Lumber Company constructed Diamond City, a small company town in the LeClerc basins for about 200 workers. It had a community center, a school, and a baseball team. The Diamond sawmills cut white pine stock for matches. At that time, everyone used matches for wood stoves and other uses.

Aerial Lumber Sling. Diamond City millworkers would load match lumber stock onto a carrier sling. The thick one-and-one-eighth-inch cables on high towers carried the slings over Dry Canyon, forests, and then over the Pend Oreille River to Lost Creek. Supplies and mail would be returned to the mill and to the residents of Diamond City via the carrier sling.

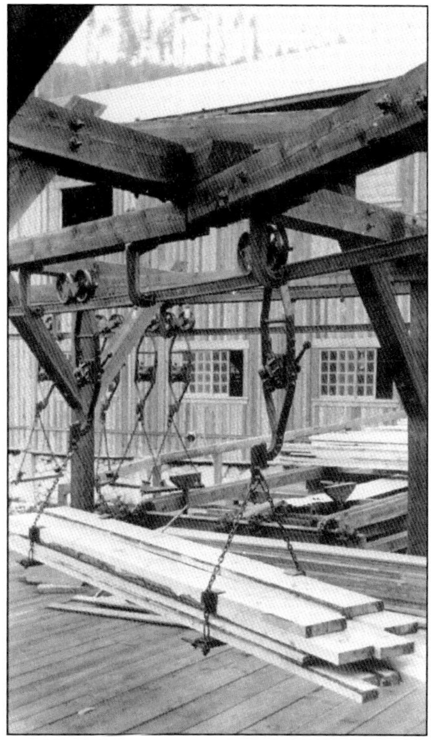

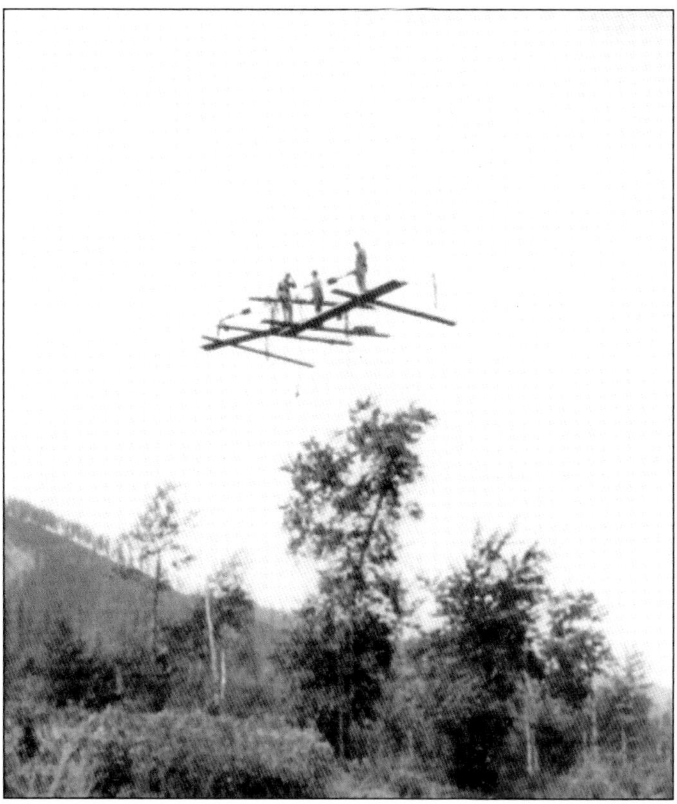

Aerial Tram. The three-and-a-half-mile aerial tram carried match lumber stock across the Pend Oreille River at Diamond City. Riding the tram across the river was not encouraged, but it was done occasionally by millworkers and repair workers. The tram took the lumber across the river to Lost Creek, where it was loaded on railroad cars and shipped to Spokane.

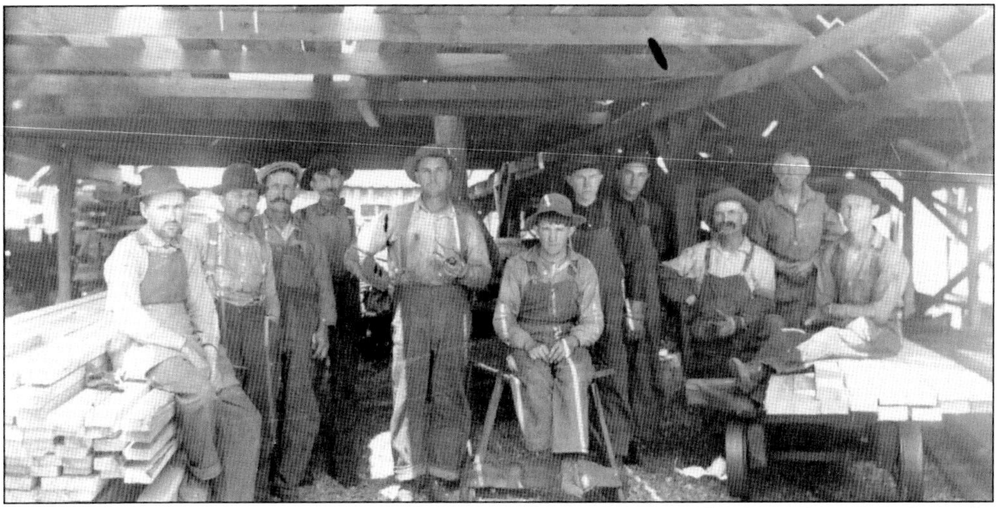

GRAHAM SAWMILL, SCOTIA. There were hundreds of small sawmills throughout Pend Oreille County. Some were portable mills that could be moved from one place to another, but most were in makeshift buildings. Posing here are, from left to right, Dam Dennis, Charles Graham, Walter Smith, Happy ?, Sam Saduke, Carl Graham, Charles Graham Jr., Alvin Graham, Tommy James, John Lenmon, and Alonzo McGuown.

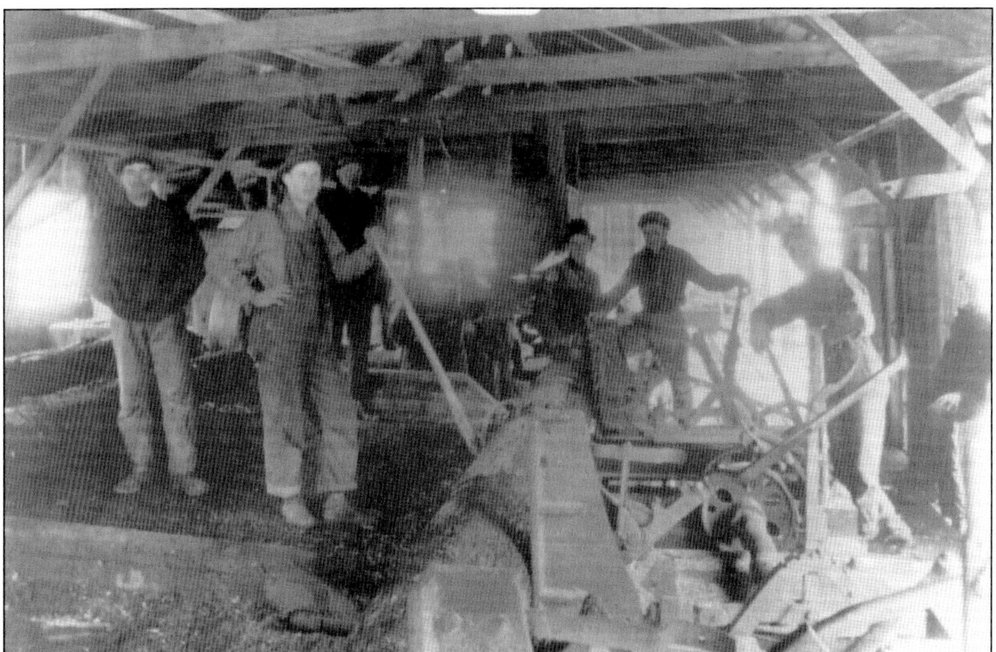

ELLERSICK FAMILY SAWMILL. The Ellersick family ran a number of sawmills for many years. Shown here is the interior of one of their sawmills. The identified men are Frank Ellersick Sr. (second from left) and Uncle Jack. Frank has the cant hook and is turning the log for Uncle Jack at the Little Muddy Lumber Company at Ione in 1921.

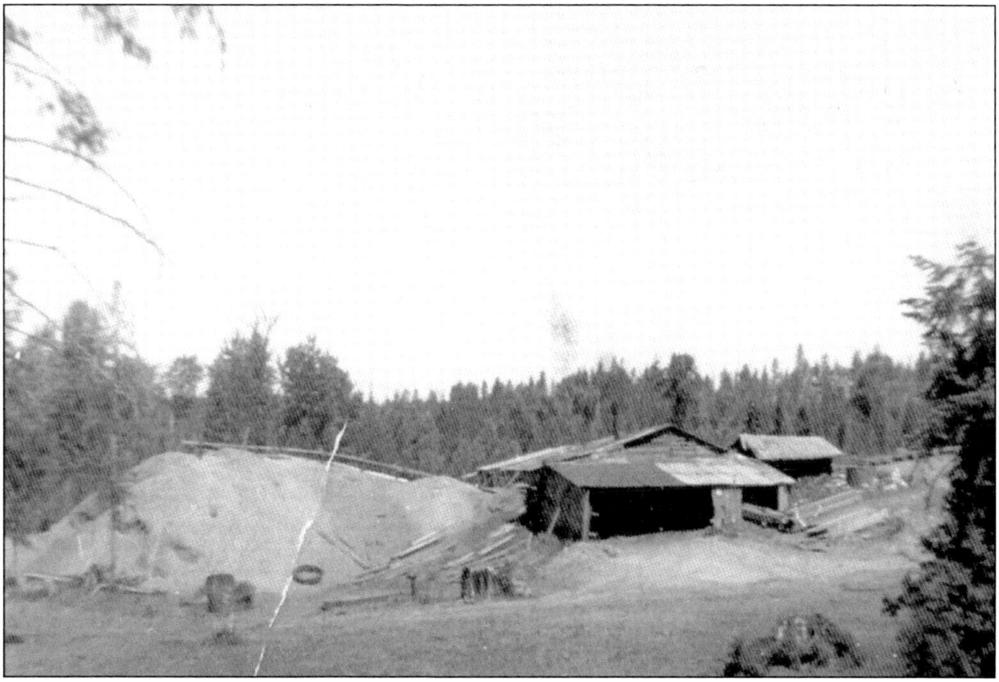

C.C. Clark Sawmill, Clark Valley. The Clark family owned and operated a sawmill from 1932 until 2010. It was an example of the hundreds of small mills located in isolated valleys in the county. It was the longest-running and last family-owned mill in the county. The Clarks produced lumber for hundreds of buildings in the Newport area and for developers in Spokane. The sawmill machinery was donated to the Pend Oreille County Historical Society.

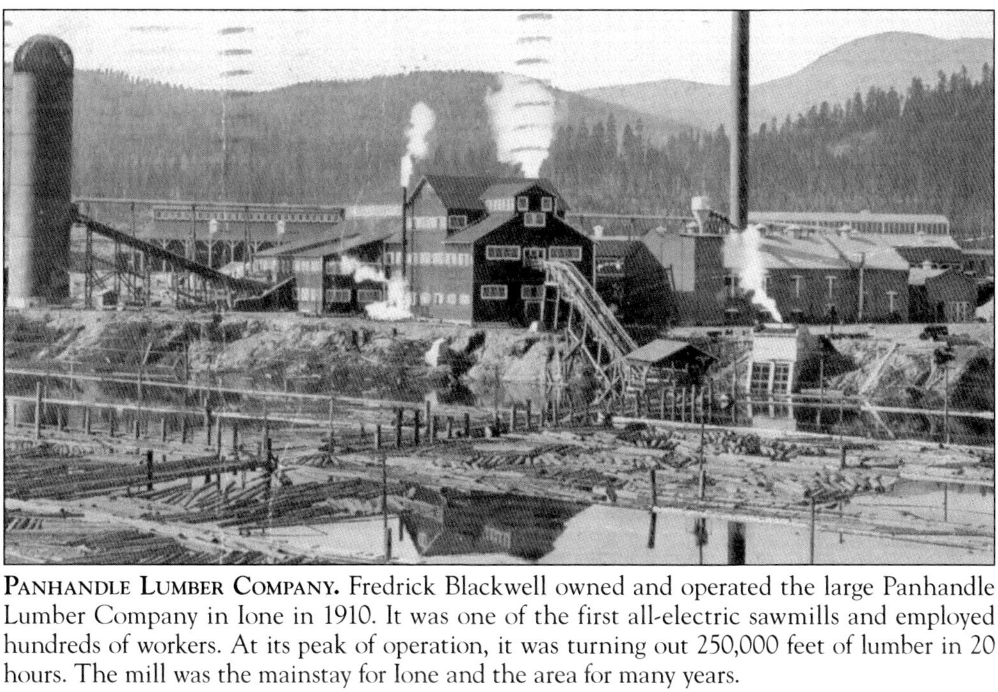

Panhandle Lumber Company. Fredrick Blackwell owned and operated the large Panhandle Lumber Company in Ione in 1910. It was one of the first all-electric sawmills and employed hundreds of workers. At its peak of operation, it was turning out 250,000 feet of lumber in 20 hours. The mill was the mainstay for Ione and the area for many years.

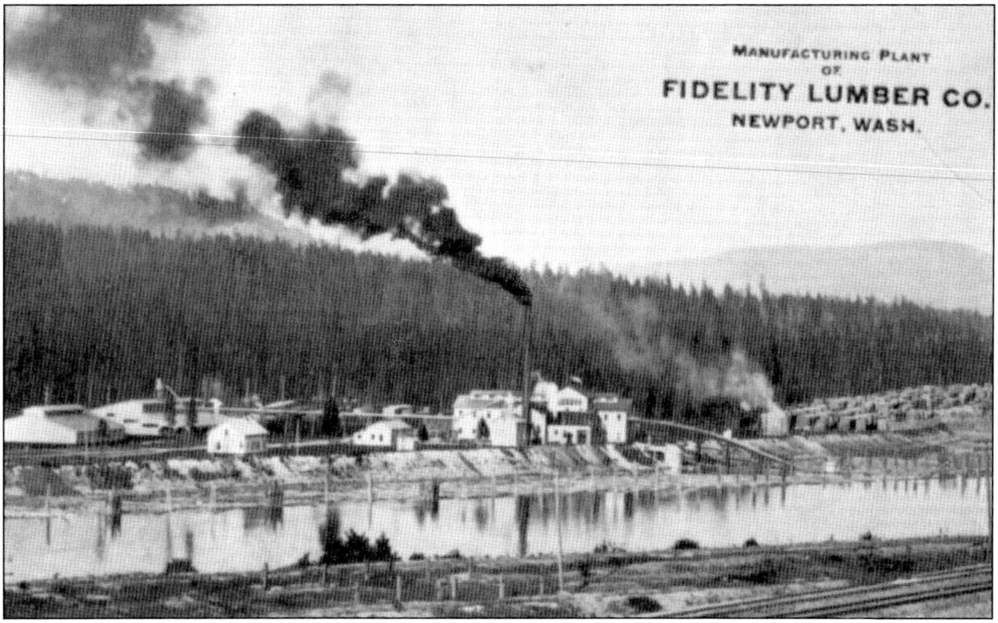

FIDELITY SAWMILL. The Fidelity mill was one of the large sawmills across the river from Newport. In later years, the Diamond Match Lumber Company and other companies were situated on the same site. The mills employed hundreds of workers and produced thousands of board feet of lumber. The mills supported the Newport area.

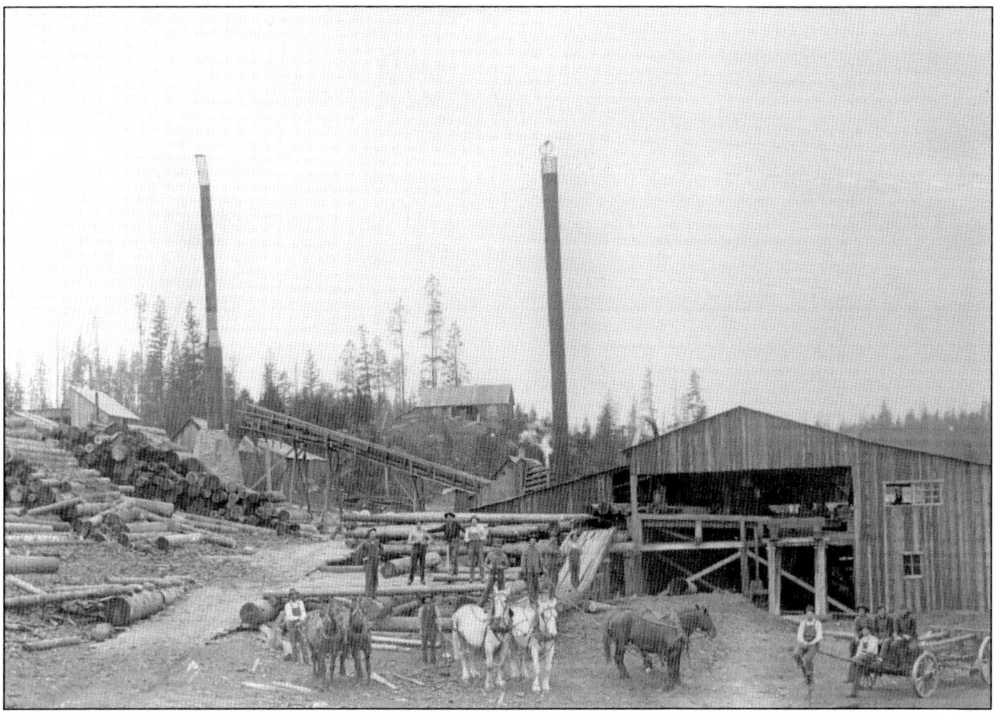

PENRITH SAWMILL. This sawmill was located in the small community of Penrith, on the southern end of Pend Oreille County. It flourished for years, until all the useable timber was cut. The mill and community then disappeared. Note the piles of logs, the horses, and the primitive equipment.

Six

Communities and Social Life

Throughout the years, there have been a number of communities in Pend Oreille County. Some of them were mere dreams, such as Crescent, Sullivan, and Tacoma Creek. Others were centered around sawmills, such as Diamond City, Scotia, Penrith, Blueslide, and Dalkena. Those towns experienced boom times while the timber lasted. Today, only a few foundations and old buildings remain, and those communities are ghost towns. Others, like Usk, Ruby, Jared, and Tiger, cling to life as unincorporated villages. Jared, once a boat landing with a handful of buildings, is now home to the large Riverview Bible Camp.

Today, there are five incorporated towns in the county. Newport serves as the gateway to the Pend Oreille Valley and was incorporated in 1903. It is the county seat, with schools, a hospital complex, churches, and staple businesses. The population is over 2,000. Diamond Lake, near Newport, is a thriving resort community of summer and permanent homes. Cusick, in the central part of the county, was founded by Joe Cusick in 1902 and was incorporated in 1927. Sawmills supported the town until the 1960s. It is the home of the Pend Oreille County Fair.

Ione, Metaline, and Metaline Falls, in the mountainous northern part of the county, have populations of fewer than 500. Ione was settled in 1894 and was incorporated in 1910. For many years, the large Panhandle Lumber Company sustained the town. Metaline is the oldest community in the county, with a history of prospecting and mining. It was incorporated in 1948. Metaline Falls, incorporated in 1911, was founded by Lewis Larsen in the early 1900s. The Cutter Theatre is a popular present-day attraction.

Historically, barn-raising, wood-cutting bees, sports, picnics, parades, bands, social organizations, and celebrations played a role in the social life of all the communities. Today, the arts, social events, and a variety of outdoor activities lure tourists and others to the area.

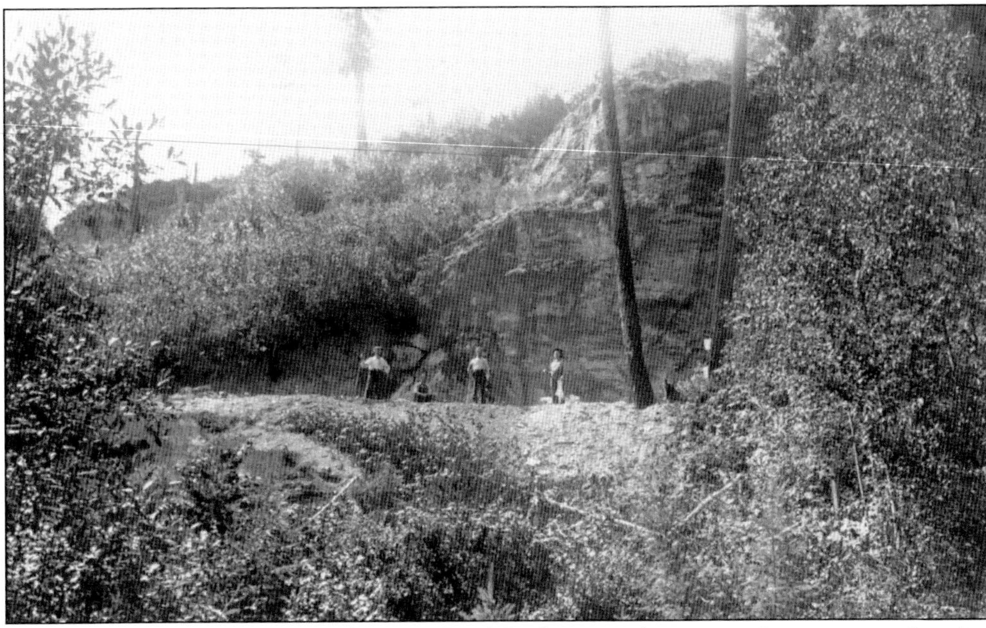

Cement, Washington. In the early 1900s, Frank Jordan, a civil engineer who grew up and studied in England, discovered a mountain of raw materials for making cement. He contacted investors and had machinery brought in by steamboat and started a cement-manufacturing plant. The little community of Cement developed around the plant. However, Jordan ran into legal and financial problems; in a few years, the plant and town disappeared.

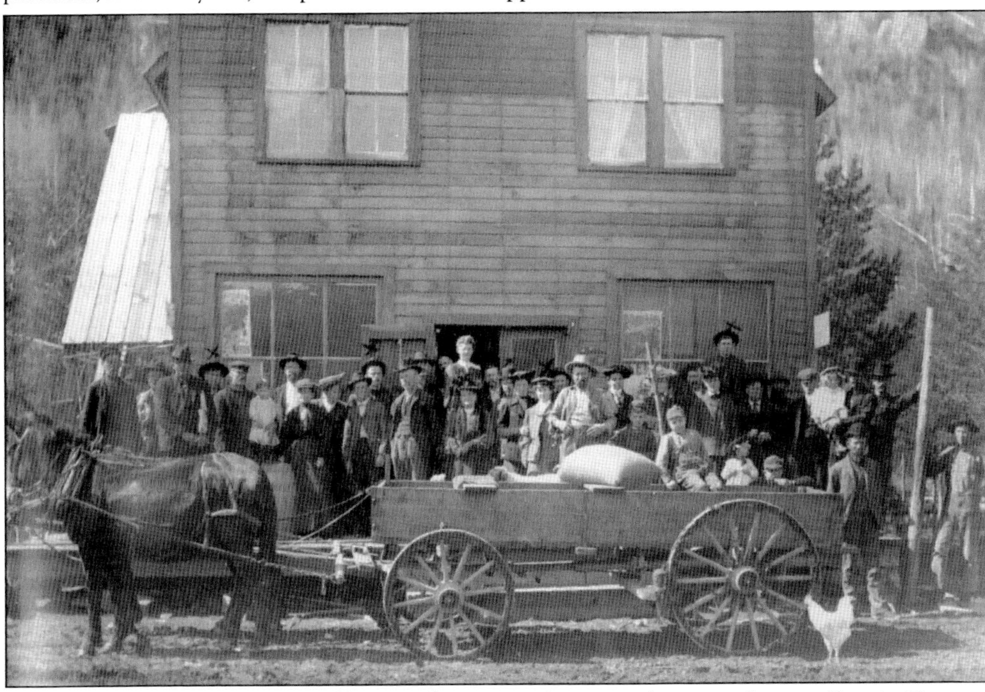

General Store in Cement. William Weltzine ran the general store and post office in Cement. His store was the central gathering place for area homesteaders and settlers. Here, people have gathered and are watching the delivery of goods on a wagon drawn by horses.

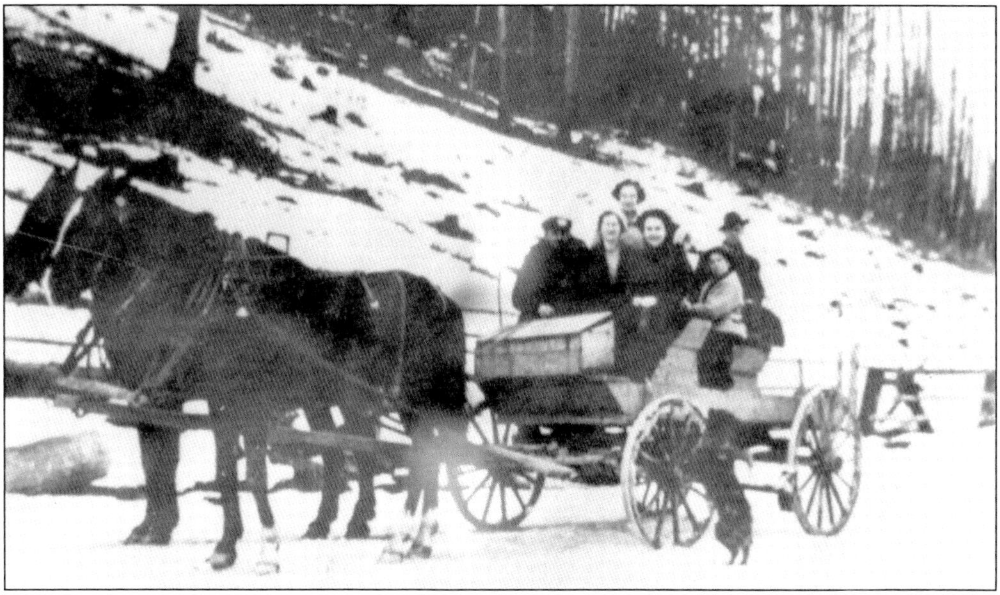

WINTER TRIP TO ALADDIN/CRONIN. Aladdin/Cronin is located in the northern part of the county. This photograph shows a typical family traveling during the winter in an open wagon, on their way through the wilderness area. There were dozens of small trading-post communities only a few miles apart in the region in the early years.

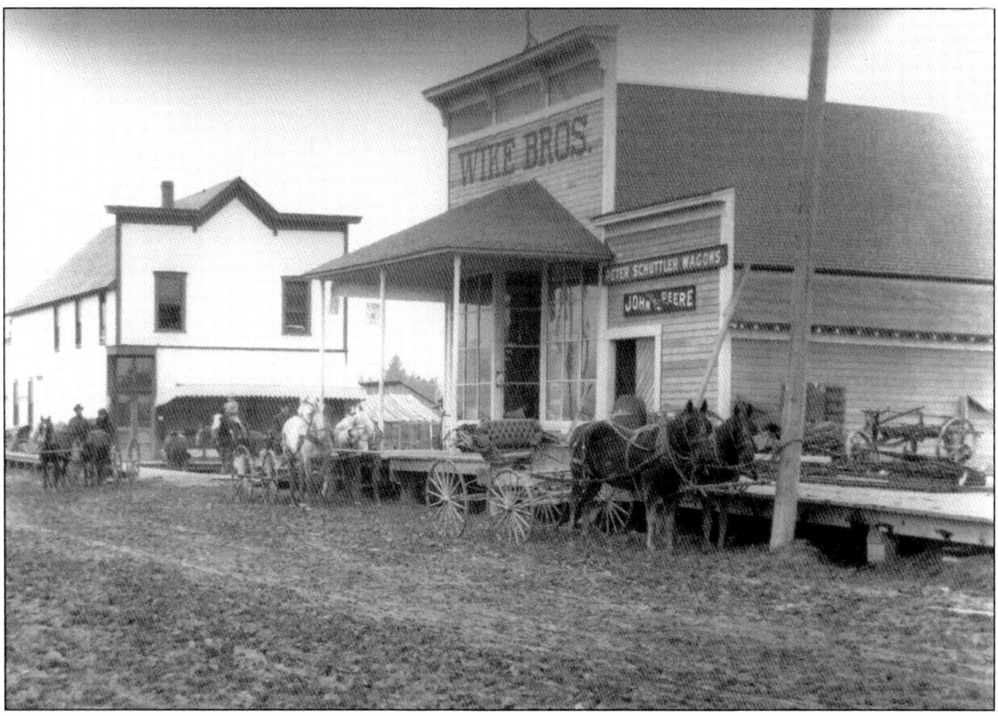

WIKE STORE. Adam Wike owned and operated the Wike Store in Cusick. The farmers in their open wagons and horses often came to the community on Saturdays for shopping. Large sawmills supported the town until all the timber was cut. Today, it is a pleasant community, with schools, a library, a skating park, and stores.

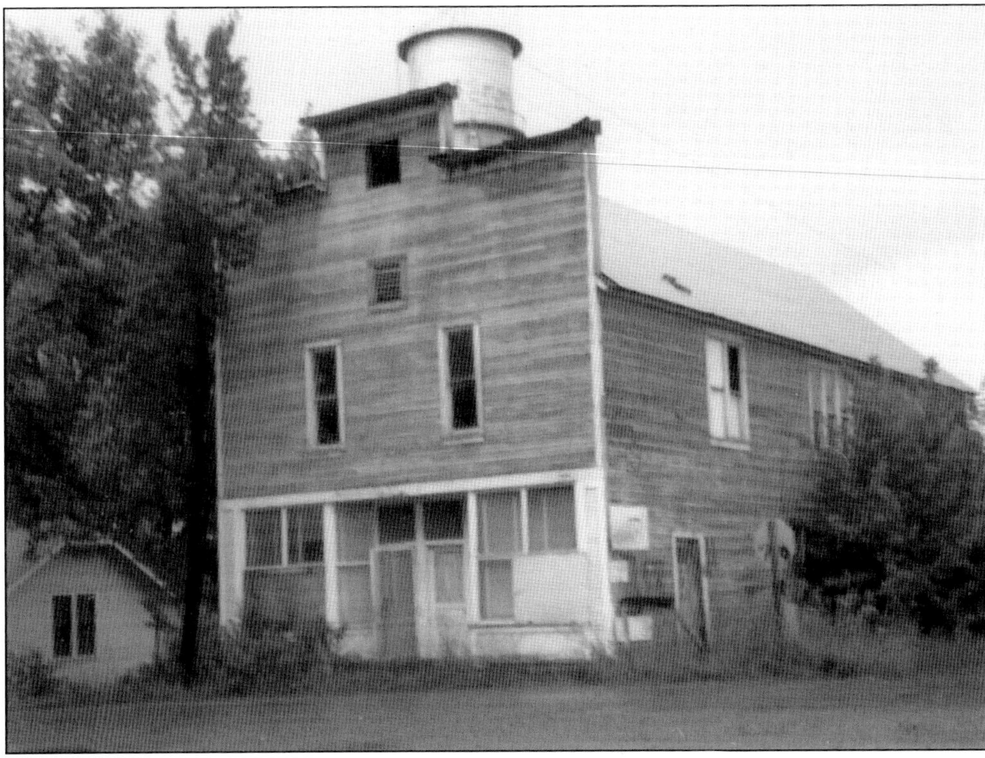

WIKE HALL. The two-story Wike Hall was built in 1911 in Cusick and served as the social center. Residents remember sitting on benches, eating bags of 5¢ popcorn, and watching black-and-white movies. The heating system was not the best, and smoke would often fill the room. In that case, the audience would walk down a narrow outside stairway and wait until the room was clear. It was all part of an evening's excitement. It burned down in the late 1980s.

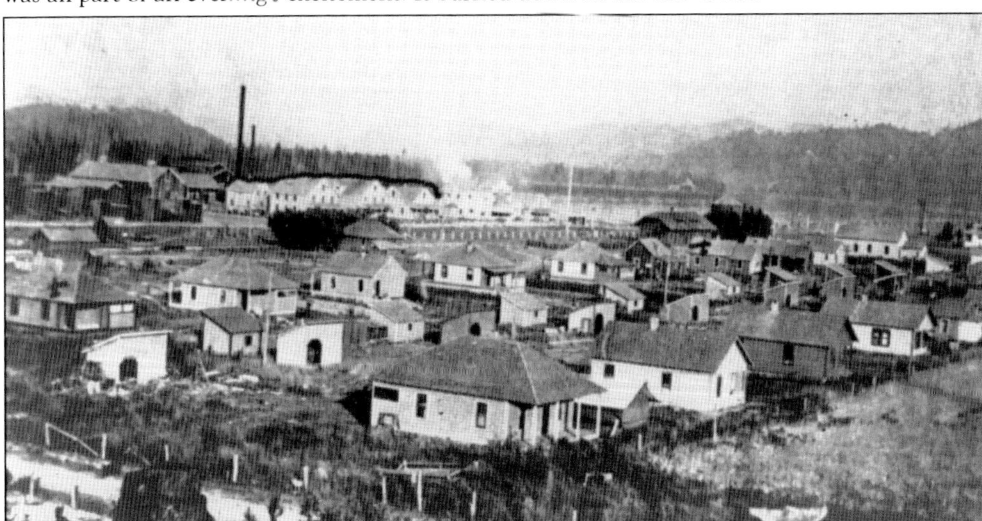

DALKENA, WASHINGTON. This c. 1912 photograph shows Dalkena. In 1903, Henry Dalton and Hugh Kennedy erected and operated a large sawmill, which was the backbone of the community and nearby area until 1936, when the mill burned. Today, it is a sleepy farming and resort community.

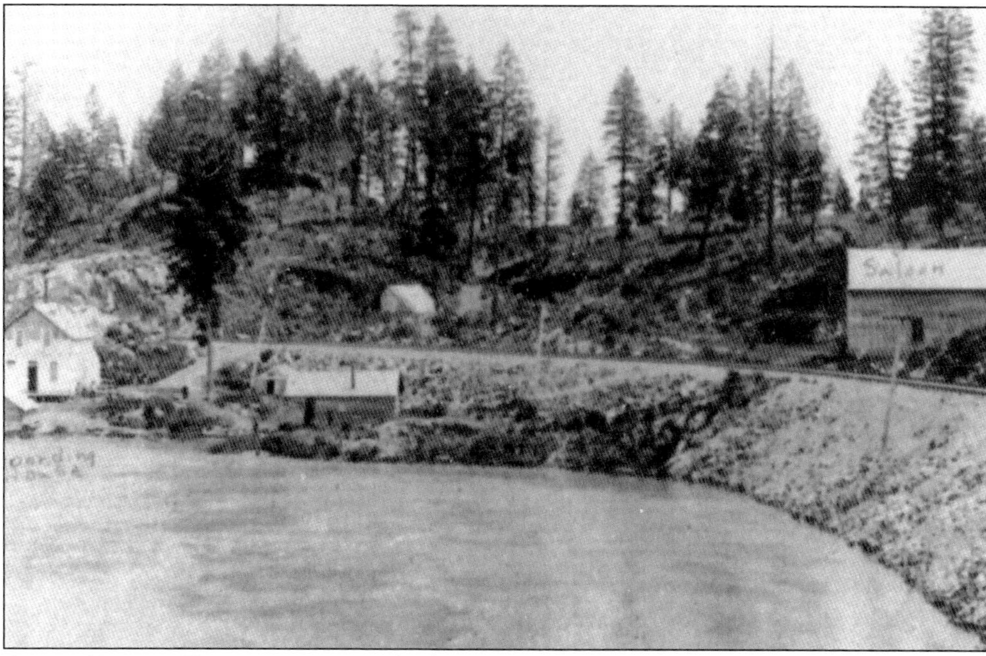

ALBENI POIRIER TRADING POST. In the late 1800s, homesteader Albeni Poirier's trading post consisted of a boardinghouse, a saloon, and a small school for the Great Northern Railroad construction workers and families. The early steamboats stopped at the trading post. Nearby, a small community developed and became a new port for the steamboats. It took the name of Newport, Idaho.

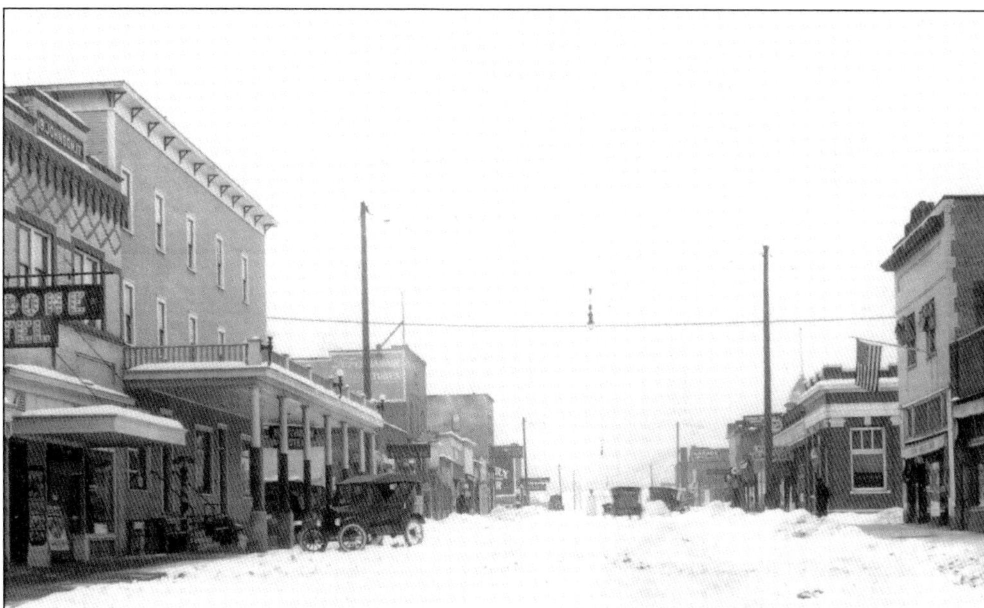

NEWPORT, C. 1920. Warren and Charles Talmadge purchased 40 acres of land across the Washington State line, close to the Great Northern Railroad depot in 1895. Businesspeople in Newport slowly moved into the new location. In 1901, the post office was moved from Idaho, and the community took the name of Newport. Later, the Idaho community became known as Oldtown.

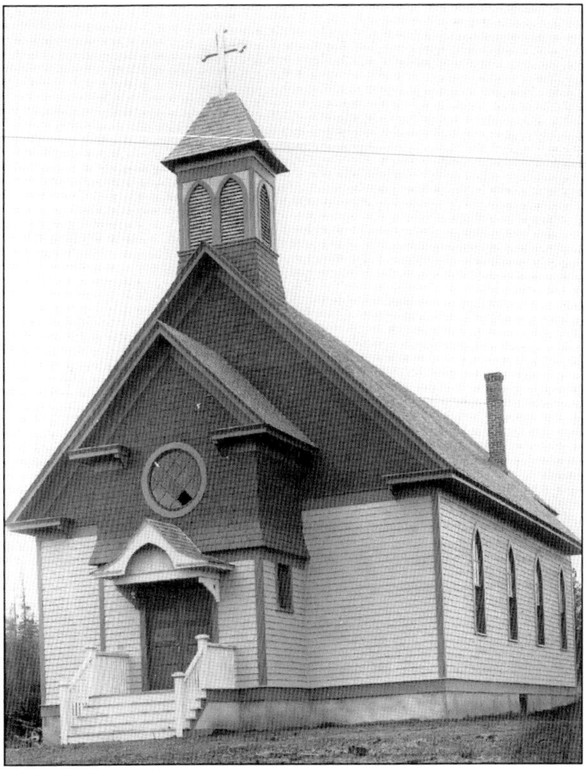

St. Anthony Catholic Church. The land for St. Anthony Catholic Church in Newport was donated by Fredrick Blackwell in 1908. The church was built in 1909. The congregation was visited by the "Church on Wheels" in May 1923. In 1979, construction on a new church building was completed. In 1981, when the United Church of Christ burned down, the Catholic congregation invited its members to share their building until a new church could be erected.

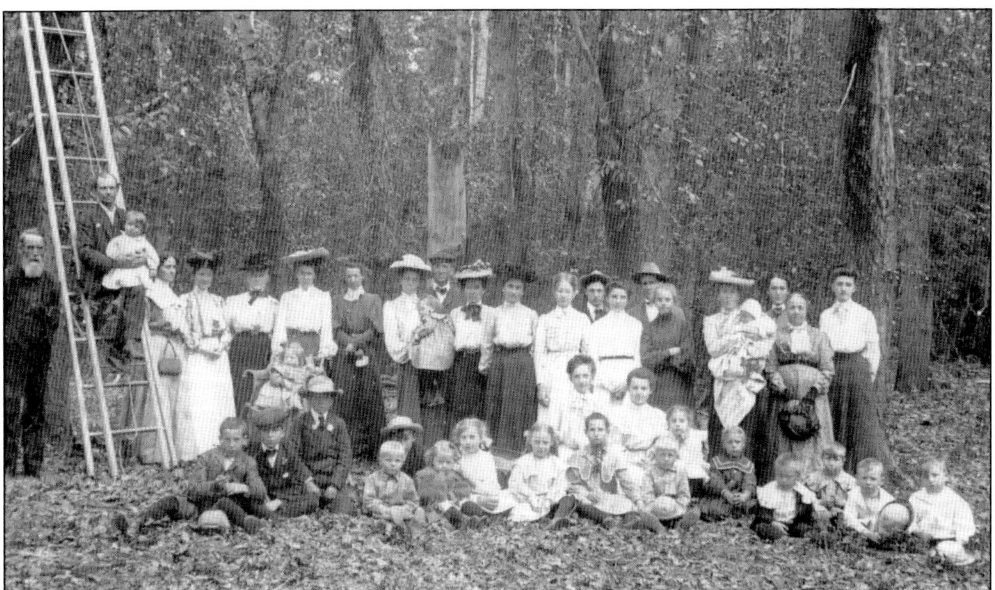

Church Picnic. Hope Congregational Church held picnics in the early years. It was one of the first protestant churches in Newport. Over the years, the congregation added Methodist residents when their church burned down. Today, it is the United Church of Christ. Since 1981, the congregation has joined with the Catholic and Mennonite congregations for Lenten suppers and services each year.

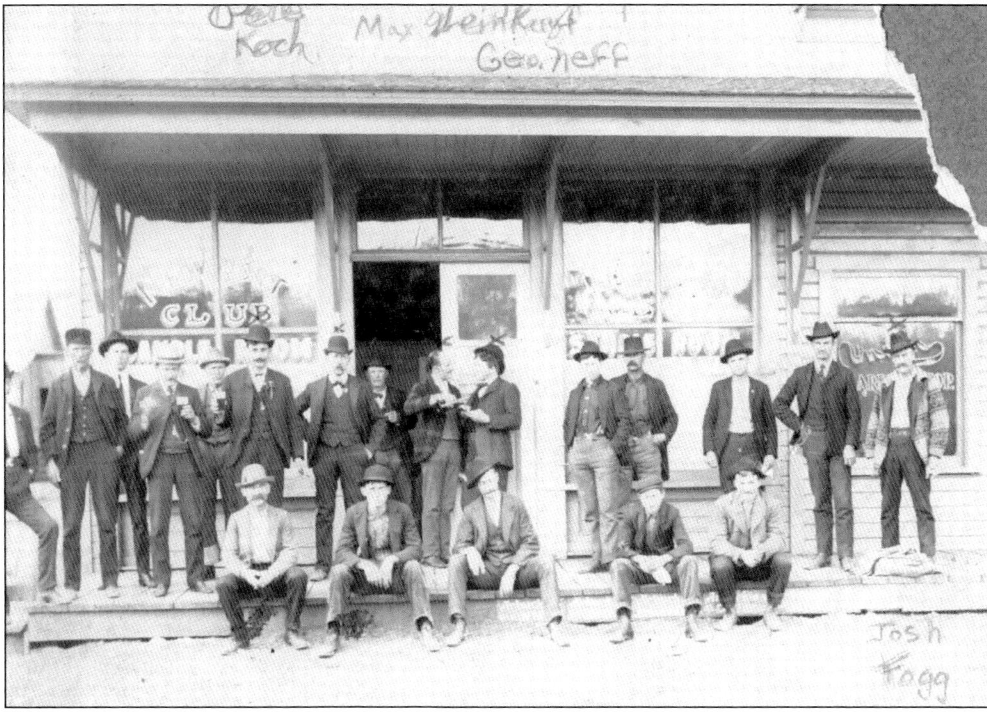

Kelly's Bar. Kelly's in Newport is one of the oldest saloons in the State of Washington. It opened in 1894. The beautiful backbar was shipped by boat around South America and then by rail from San Francisco. The establishment has changed names and been remodeled several times over the years. In the busy days in the 1900s, John Koch kept a tame bear in the back of the bar.

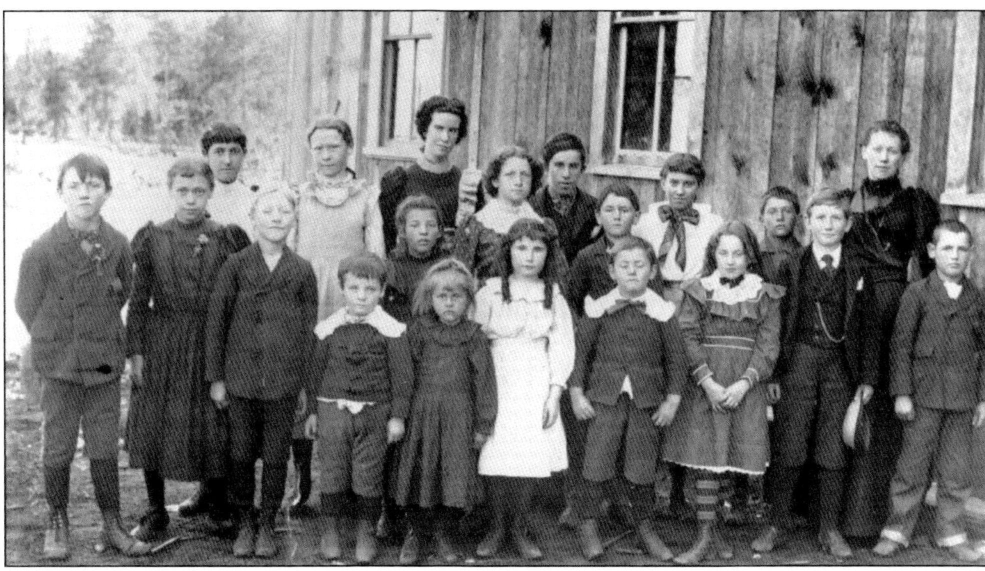

Newport Cemetery School. The Cemetery School was a typical one-room schoolhouse located at the edge of Newport near the local cemetery. It represents one of hundreds of one-room schools in the county. The young teacher taught students of all ages and all grades. In the late 1920s, districts and schools were consolidated. Now, there are only a few large schools in the county.

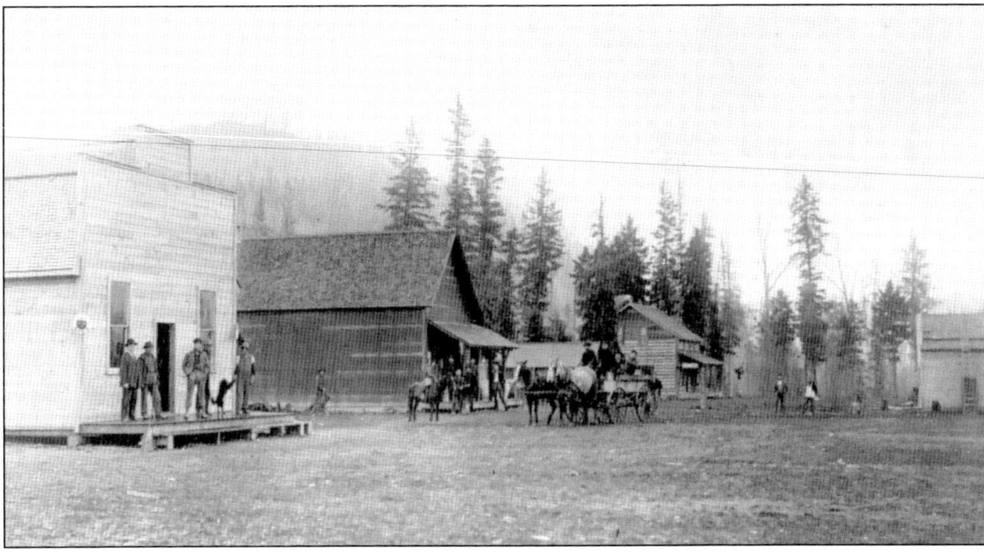

Ione. James Morrison and Elmer Hall staked claims for the townsite of Ione in 1894. Elmer Hall had the first post office in his cabin in 1896. With the arrival of the Idaho & Washington Northern Railroad and Panhandle Lumber Company in 1910, the community started to boom. The large all-electric sawmill was the backbone industry of the community and area for many years. The town was incorporated in 1909.

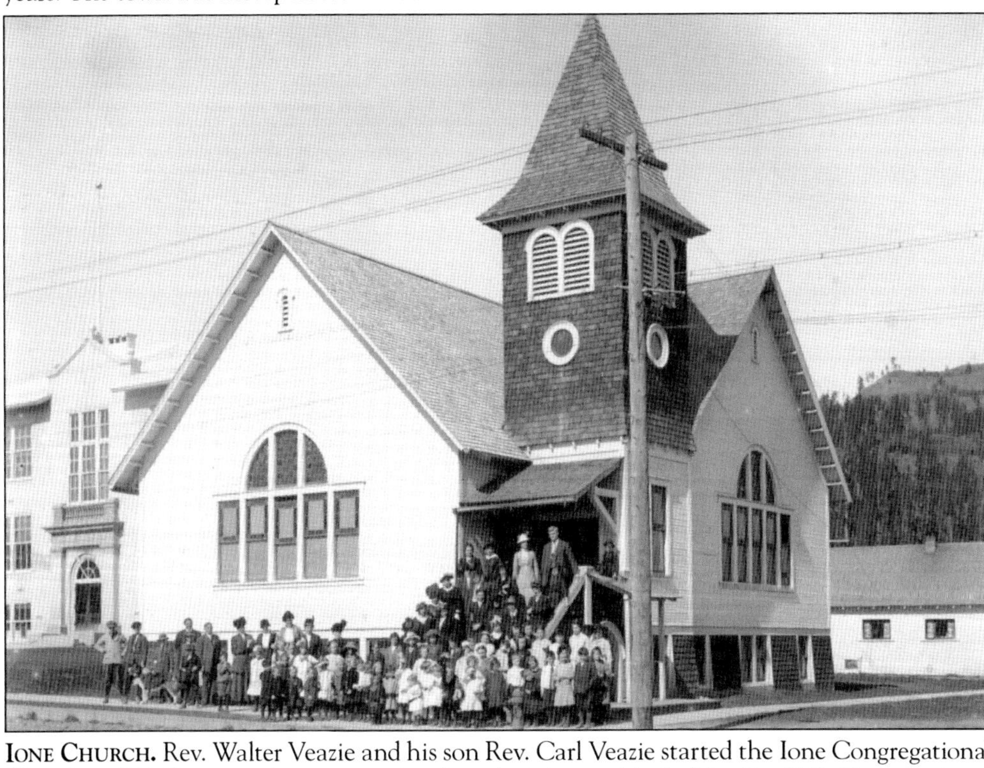

Ione Church. Rev. Walter Veazie and his son Rev. Carl Veazie started the Ione Congregational Church in 1910. For years, the congregation shared ministers with the Metaline Falls Congregational Church. The church and community flourished during the years that the Panhandle Lumber Company was running.

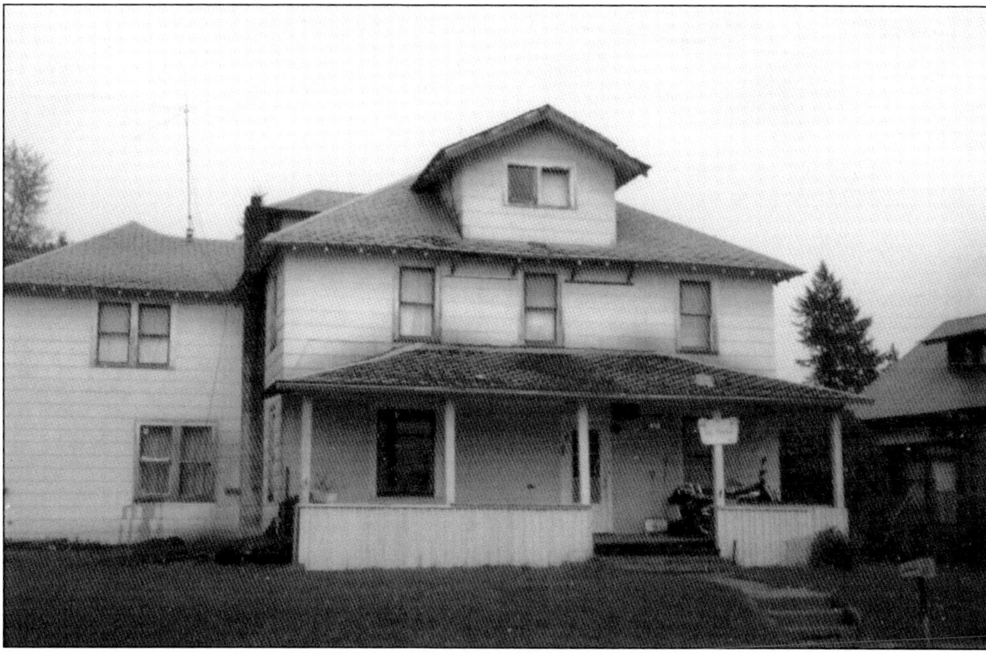

Ione Hospital. This hospital was built as a large residence. It was converted into a hospital, which served Dr. Conner and other doctors and the community for many years. Recently, it burned down.

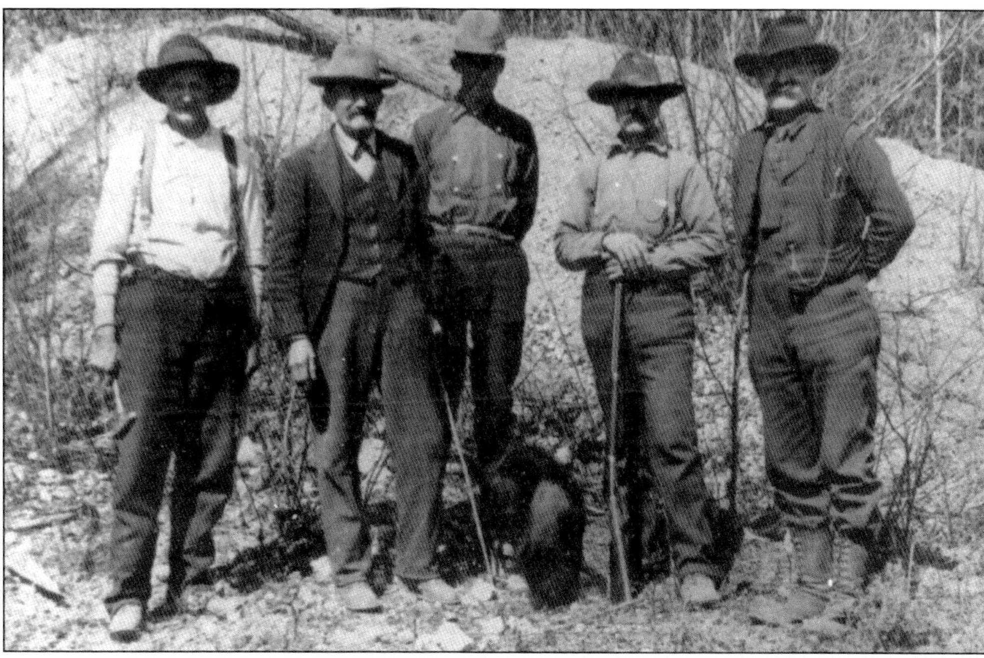

Platting Metaline. In 1859, gold was discovered, and a ragtag community sprang up. It was flooded in 1894 and then moved to higher ground. Around 1909, the men pictured here in unknown order, ? Smock, Doc Doane, Art Dehuff, George Samms, and civil engineer W.W. Warner, platted the town of Metaline. During World War II, "soldier-miners" for the cement plant in Metaline Falls were housed in the community.

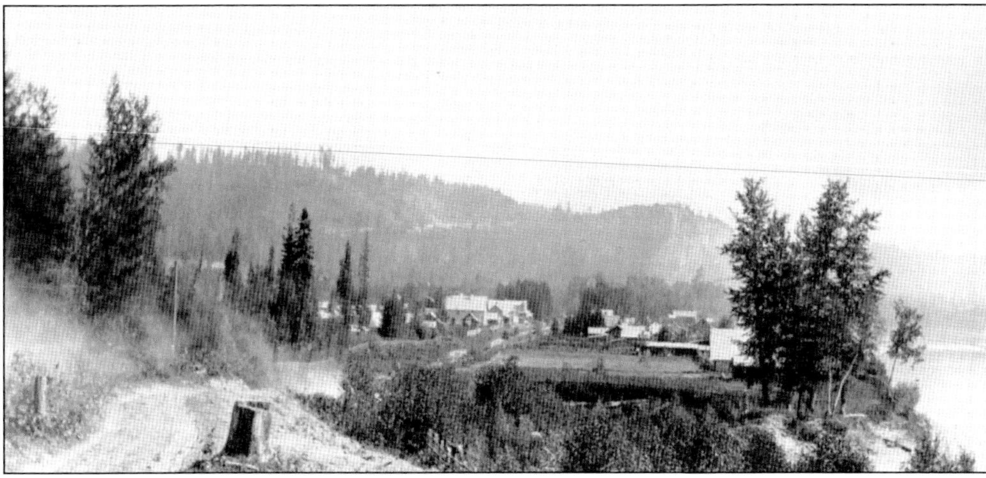

METALINE. The community of Metaline is located across the Pend Oreille River from Metaline Falls, in the north end of Pend Oreille County. It has a long history as a mining town. Gardner Caves is just a few miles from Metaline. Today, it is a quiet community attracting those interested in the rural life.

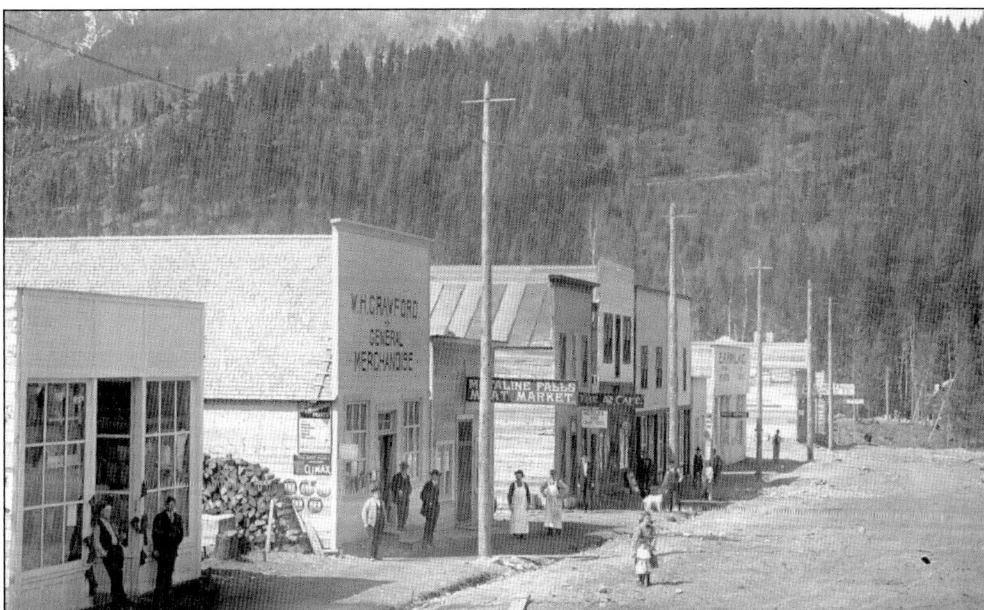

METALINE FALLS. The town of Metaline Falls is located in the beautiful mountainous north end of the county. Enoch Carr had the first mining claims in the area. Around 1904, Lewis Larsen, a mining engineer, discovered a mountain of raw materials for making cement. He acquired Carr's claims and those of others and, by 1910, founded the town of Metaline Falls. Seen here are some of the first businesses that were built in the town.

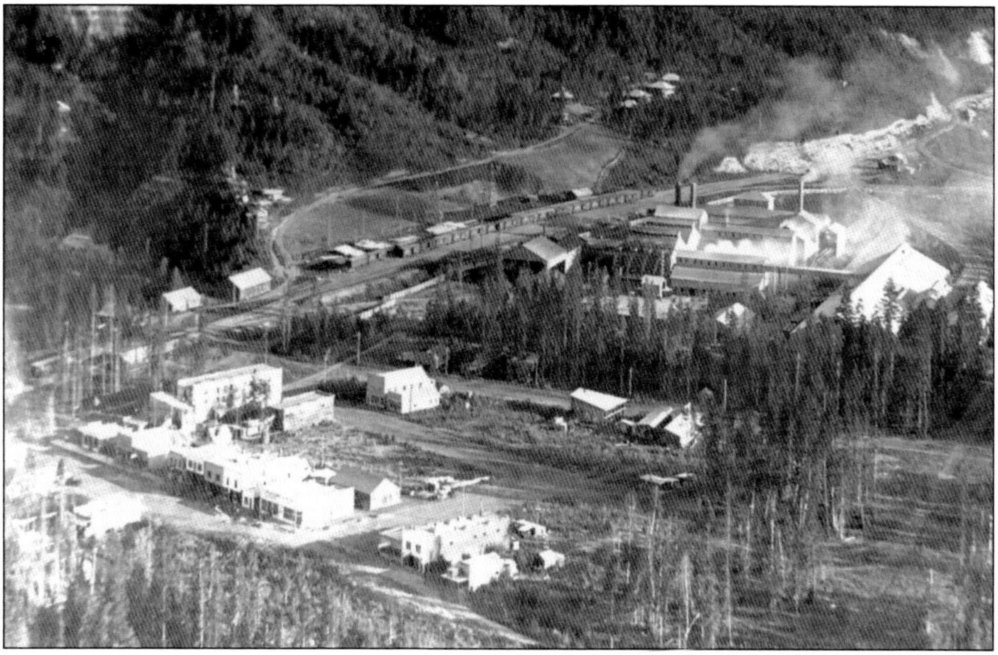

METALINE FALLS AREA. The photograph shows some of the zinc and lead mining areas near Metaline Falls, the large Lehigh Portland Cement Company, and the town. Hundreds of people were employed in both industries in the early years. After the Idaho & Washington Northern Railroad reached Metaline Falls in 1910, carloads of ore were shipped out each day.

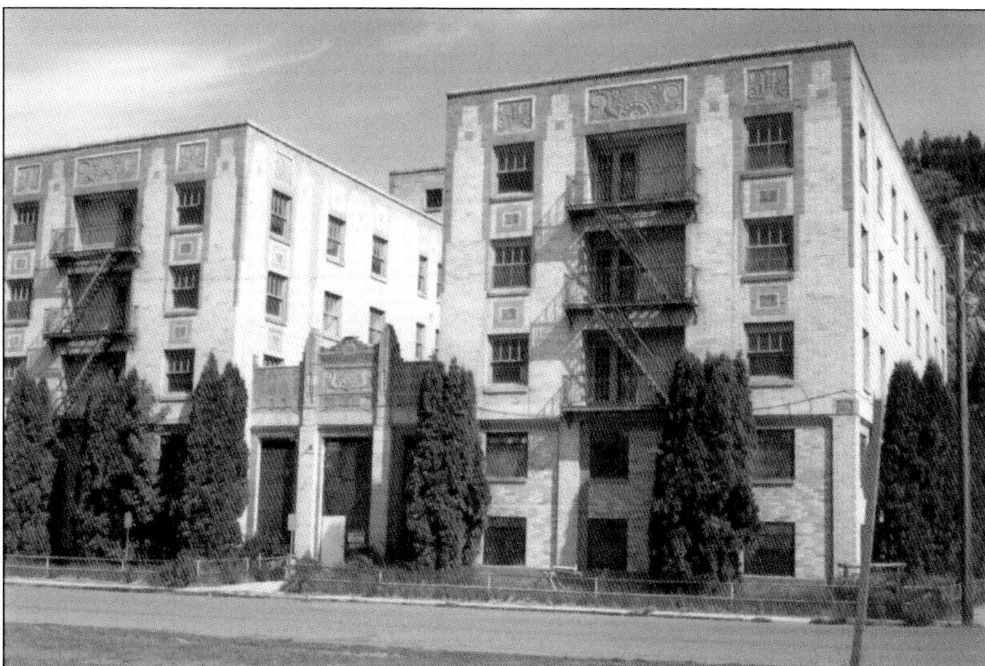

PEND OREILLE APARTMENTS. In 1929, Lewis Larsen started construction on an apartment building for miners and cement workers. Note the beautiful Art Deco exterior. The building has gone through several changes, and today is a deluxe apartment house.

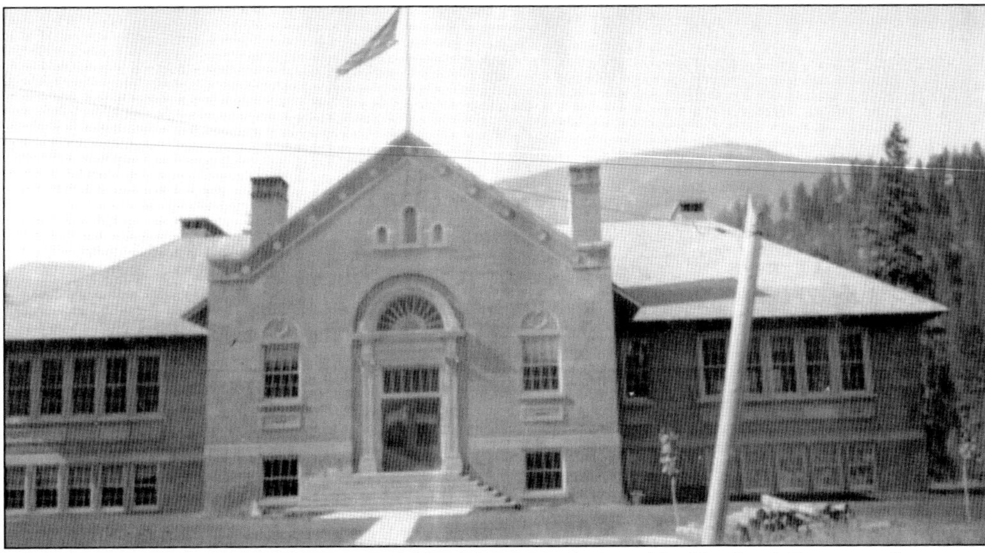

Metaline Falls School. This beautiful building was designed by Kirtland Cutter and was used as a school until 1972. Later, it was used as offices for the Selkirk School District. In 1990, after years of neglect, Eva Gaye, Alan Six, and a committee remodeled and restored the building. The Cutter Theatre has become an outstanding center for various arts and entertainment for Metaline Falls and the greater community.

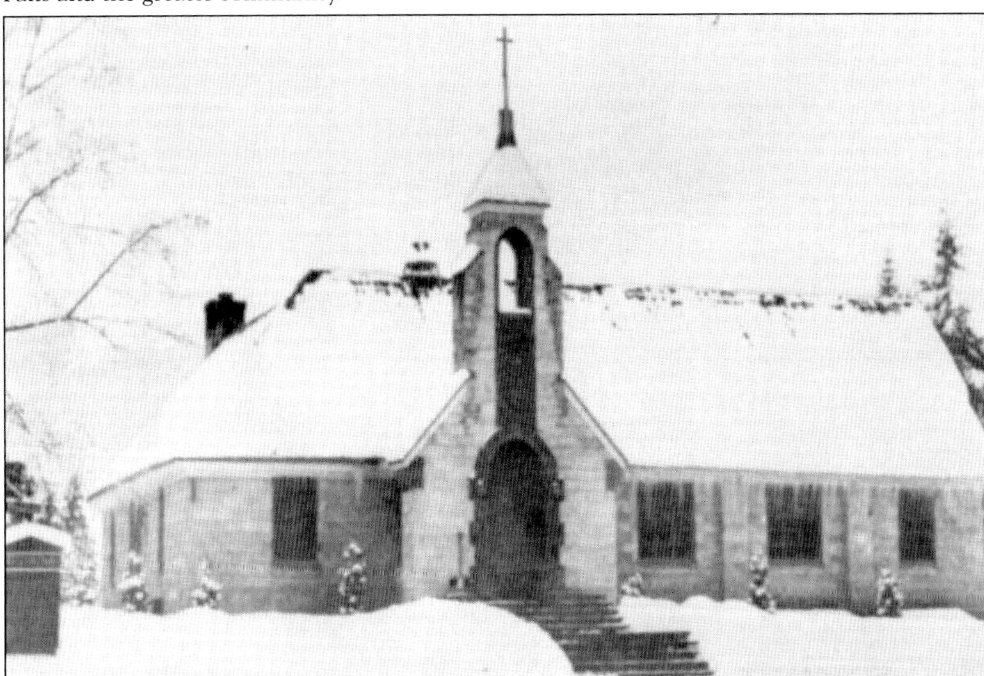

Metaline Falls Congregational Church. The Congregational church in Metaline Falls has had a long history of a loving ministry in the community. In 1910, Sunday school was held above a saloon. A year later, the Congregational church was organized. In 1951, the first services were held in a new church building. It became the United Church of Christ in 1963. A number of dedicated ministers have served the congregation.

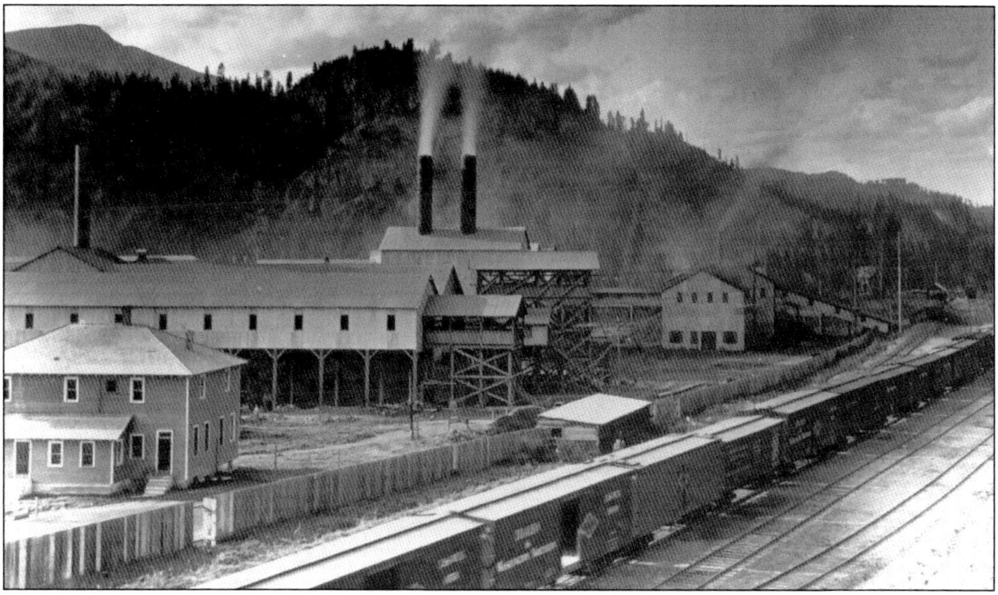

Lehigh Portland Cement Company. Lewis Larsen started the Inland Portland Cement Company in 1911. The plant put out 2,000 barrels of cement a day and had over 400 employees. In 1914, the Lehigh Portland Cement Company took over the plant, operating it until 1956. Cement from the plant was used in building Grand Coulee Dam. The plant went through several owners and closed in 1989.

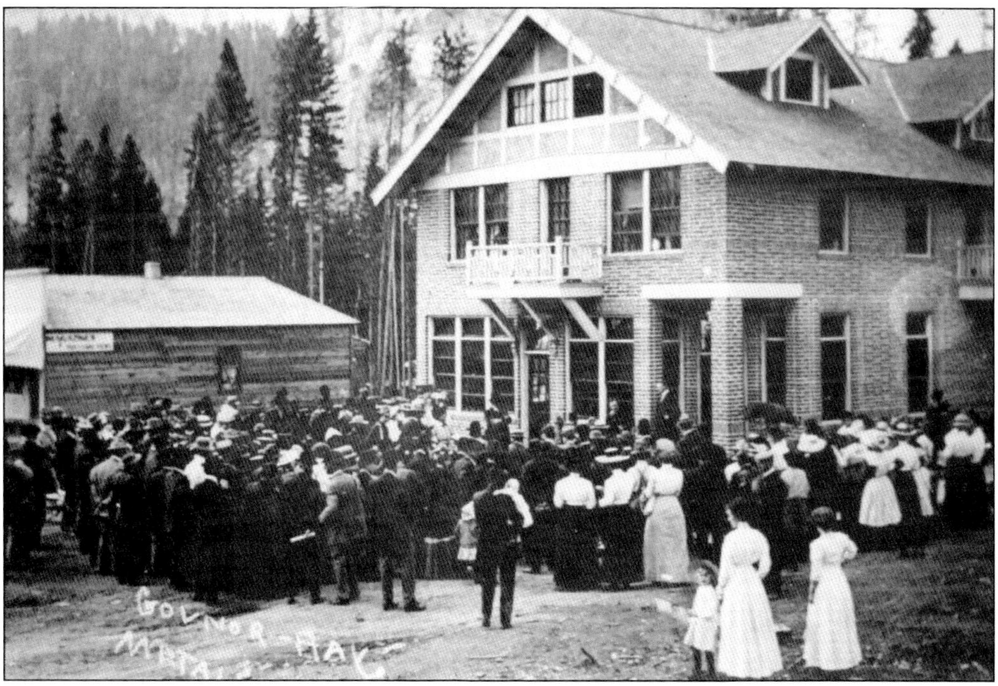

Washington Hotel, Metaline Falls. The beautiful brick, three-story hotel has gone through many changes over the years. This photograph shows people welcoming Gov. Marion Hay when he visited the county in 1911 after the creation of Pend Oreille County. The hotel was listed in the National Register of Historic Places in 1979.

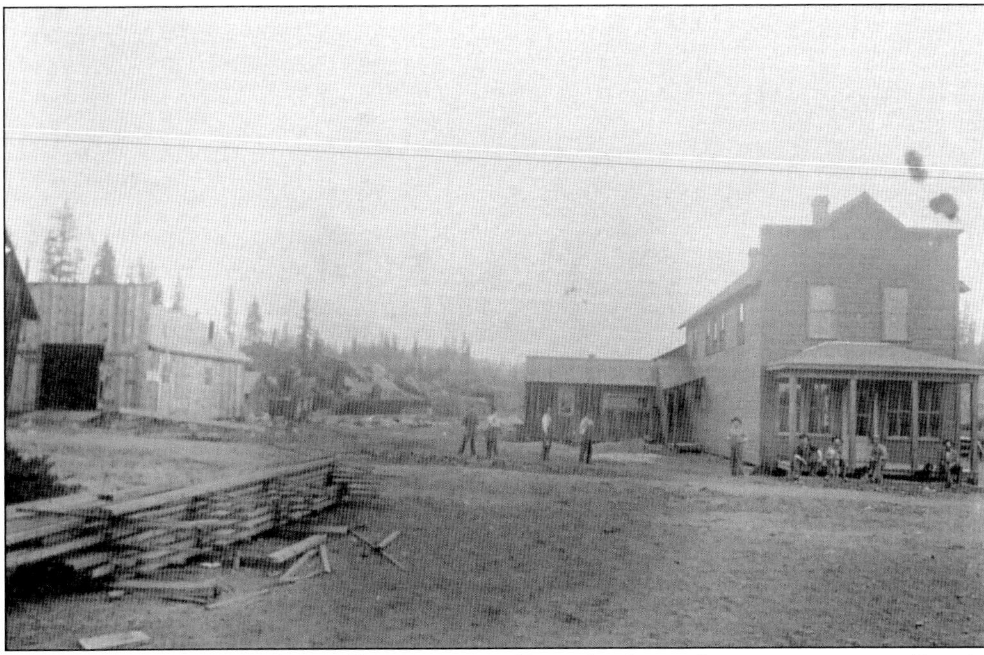

PENRITH, WASHINGTON. The small community of Penrith is located near an artesian well in the southern end of the county. It is believed the well is part of an underground river. In earlier years, Penrith was a busy sawmill town; however, after the forest land was cut over, the mill and town disappeared. It is a gentle rural area today.

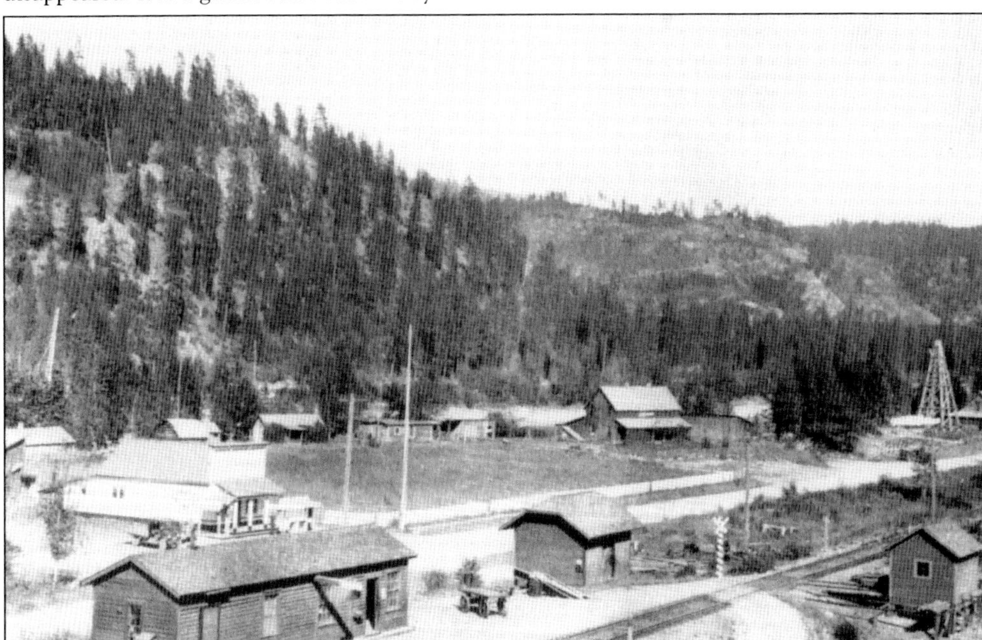

RUBY, WASHINGTON. Ruby was a small community with several businesses, a one-room school, and the Ruby Ferry. Nearby sawmills kept the town alive. The ferry was very busy in the 1920s, when the Diamond Match Lumber Company and Diamond City was running. Today, it is a quiet rural area beside the Pend Oreille River.

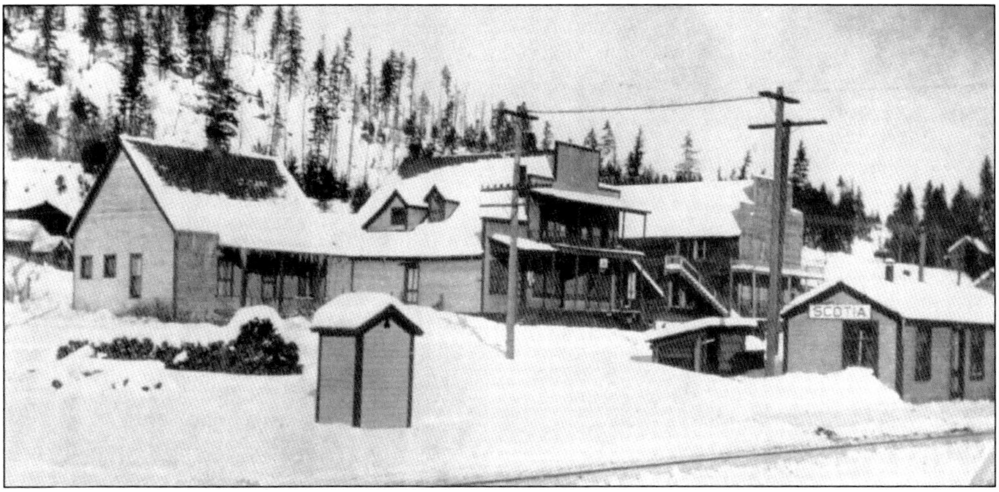

SCOTIA, WASHINGTON. In the late 1800s, the Scotia area was covered with thick forests. The Great Northern Railroad was built through the Scotia Valley, and the little community developed. The Graham family and others had several sawmills nearby. The town was booming. Once the forests were logged, the area declined. In recent years, Whitworth College received a donation of the land and is now using it for research studies.

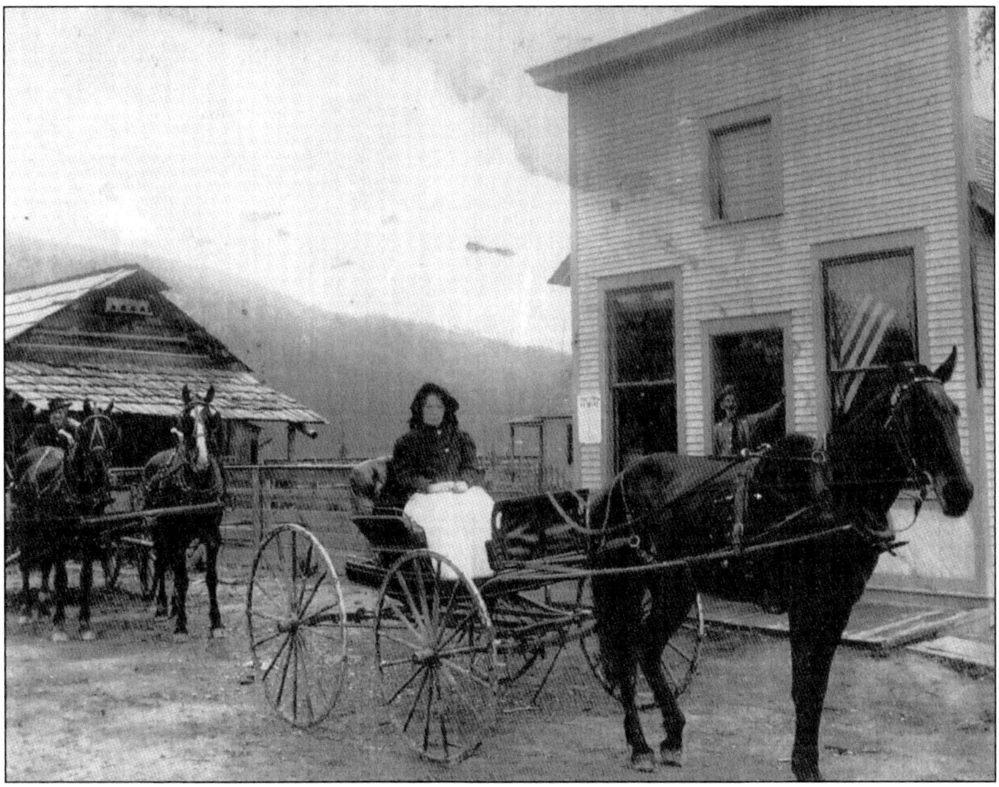

TIGER, WASHINGTON. Tiger is located in the middle of the county and is at the junction of all north, south, and west traffic. In 1884, Joseph Parker was the first settler in the area. George Tiger arrived in 1899, and the community and a creek bear his name. Jennie Wooding played an important role in developing schools and the Tiger community. Today, the area has the Tiger Museum.

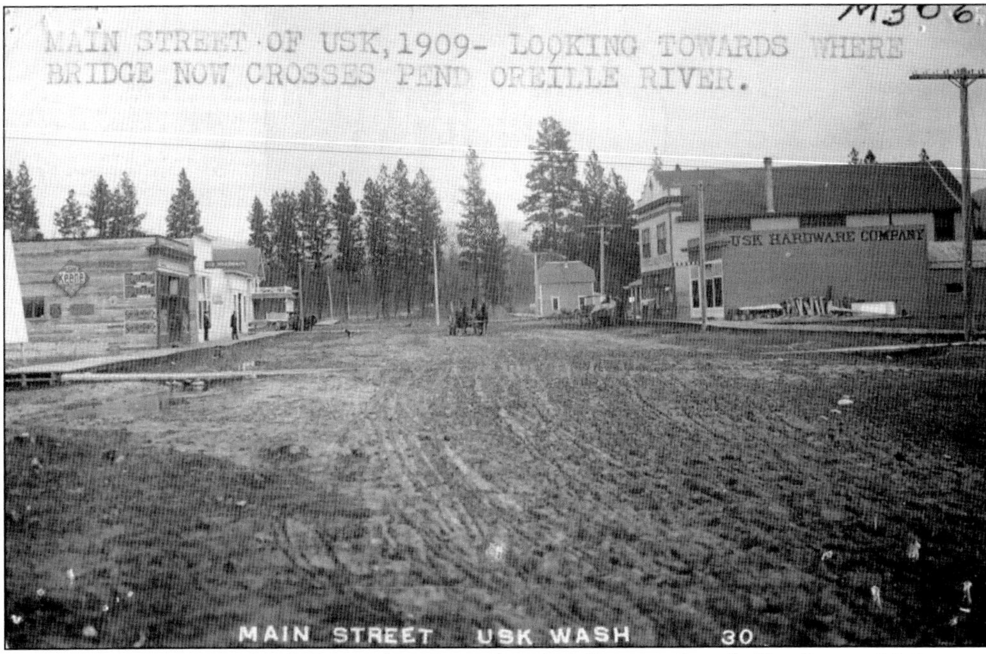

USK. The community of Usk, located in the Calispel Valley, was founded by George H. Jones in 1886. He named the community after his hometown in Wales. He started one of the first trading posts in the area and was involved in the steamboat business. Today, Usk is a busy little town with several businesses and nearby Ponderay Newsprint Company.

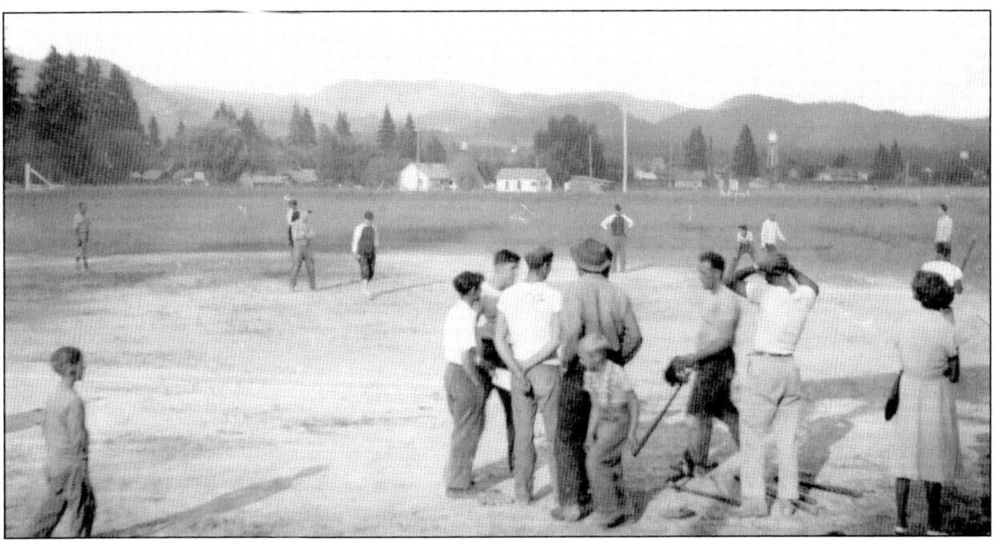

BASEBALL GAME. Sports played an important part in the social life of the residents of the county. Almost every little town and school had baseball teams, and they were very competitive. The story is told that, if a husky man was a good ballplayer, he could easily get a job as a lumberjack or logger.

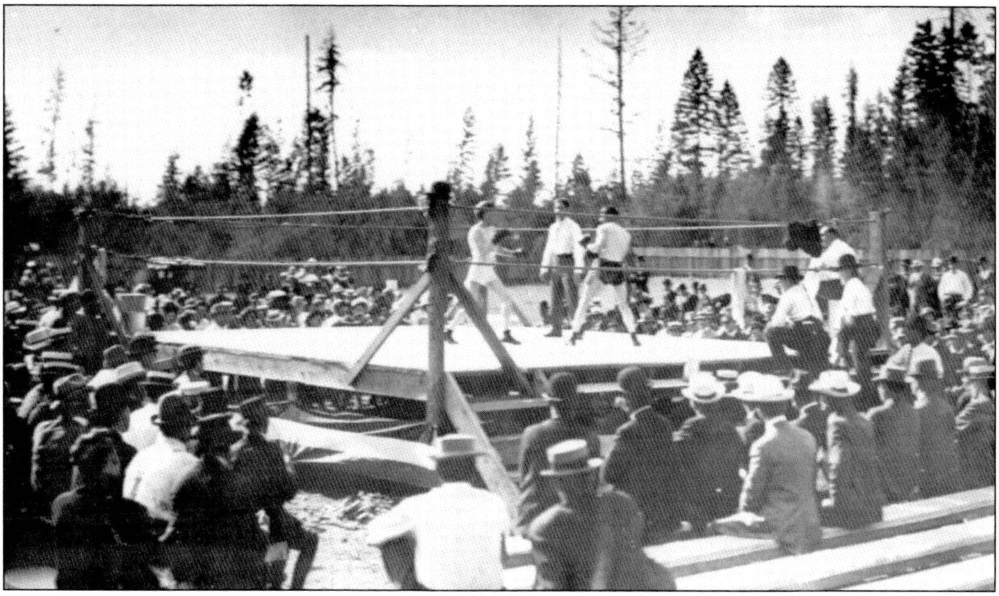

Boxing Match. Boxing was a favorite sport for the strong, sturdy loggers, millworkers, and others. Fred Lenhart from the Elk area was a light heavyweight contender and fought for several years in the Spokane area. He also had a match at Madison Square Garden. The contests were eagerly anticipated and well attended.

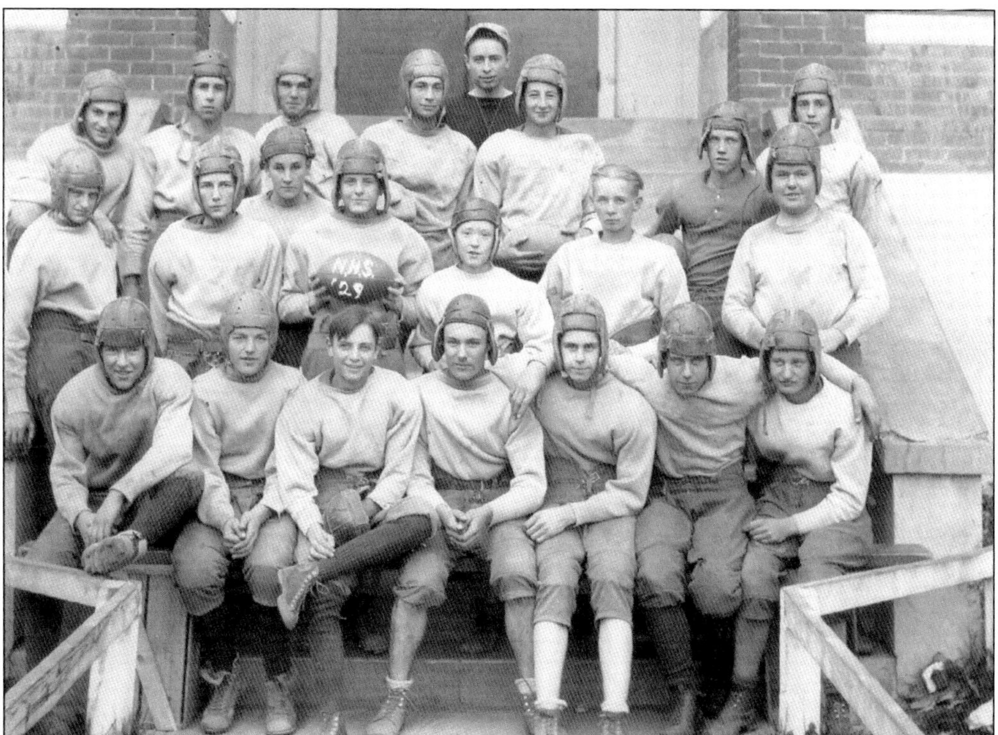

Football Team. A number of schools had football teams, and games drew large crowds. Note the era's uniforms worn by this team's members.

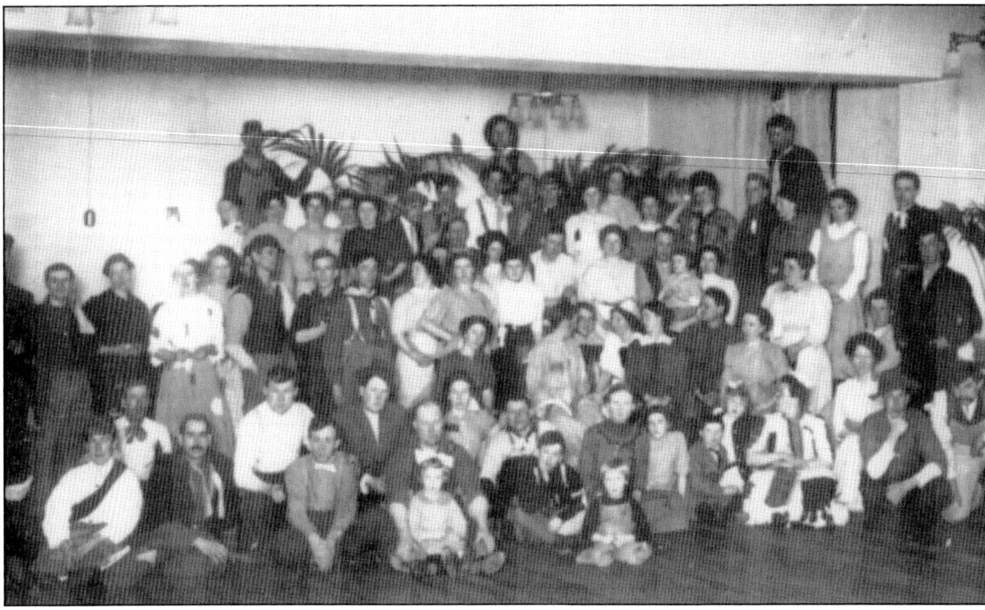

Community Dance. All kinds of dances were held almost every weekend in schools, barns, or any place that had a good floor. Often, dances started in the evenings and did not end until past midnight. Families would bed down small children on the floor in empty rooms. This group was preparing to spend the night dancing at Metaline Falls School. (Courtesy of Mary Gilmore.)

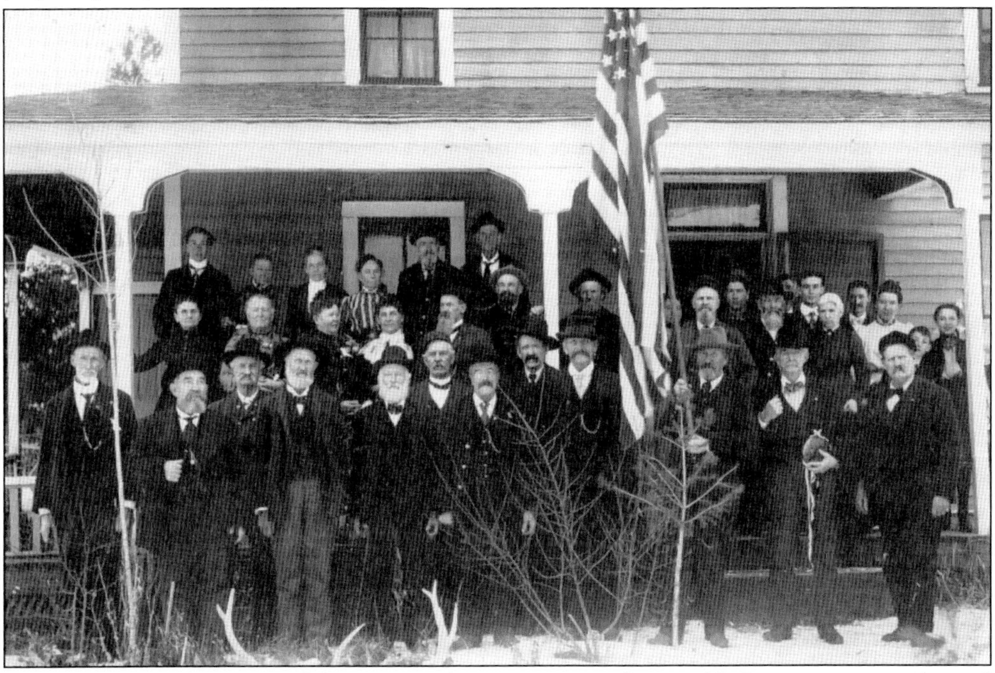

Lodge. In the earlier years of the county, there were many fraternal lodges—service and social clubs for both men and women that played an important role in the social life of communities. There were Grandmothers Clubs, Newcomers, card parties, the Elks, Moose, Job's Daughters, and many others. They were responsible for creating the friendly culture of the day. The Grange movement was very strong in the county as well.

RODEO. Throughout the history of the county, rodeos and horse races have attracted large crowds. Metaline Falls had a rodeo, and, for years, a rodeo was part of the county fair in Cusick. Today, an annual rodeo parade and rodeo are held at Newport.

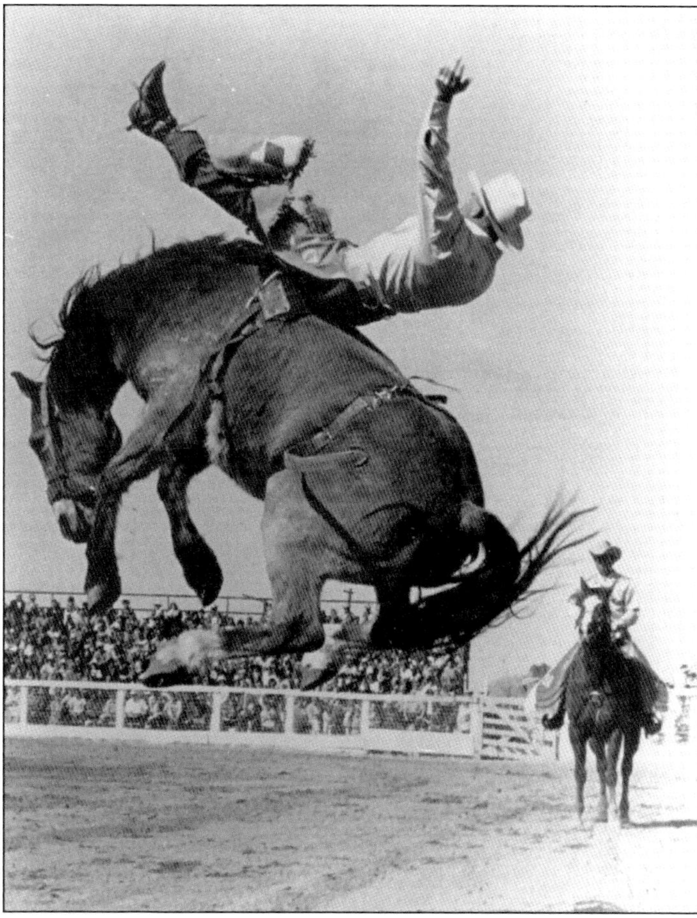

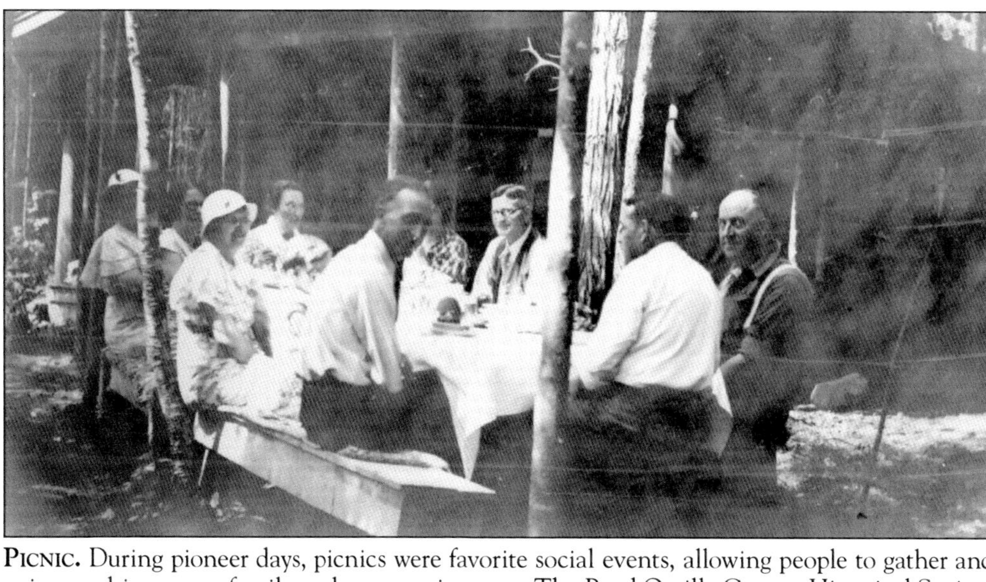

PICNIC. During pioneer days, picnics were favorite social events, allowing people to gather and enjoy catching up on family and community news. The Pend Oreille County Historical Society hosts an annual picnic at a favorite homestead in the middle of the county.

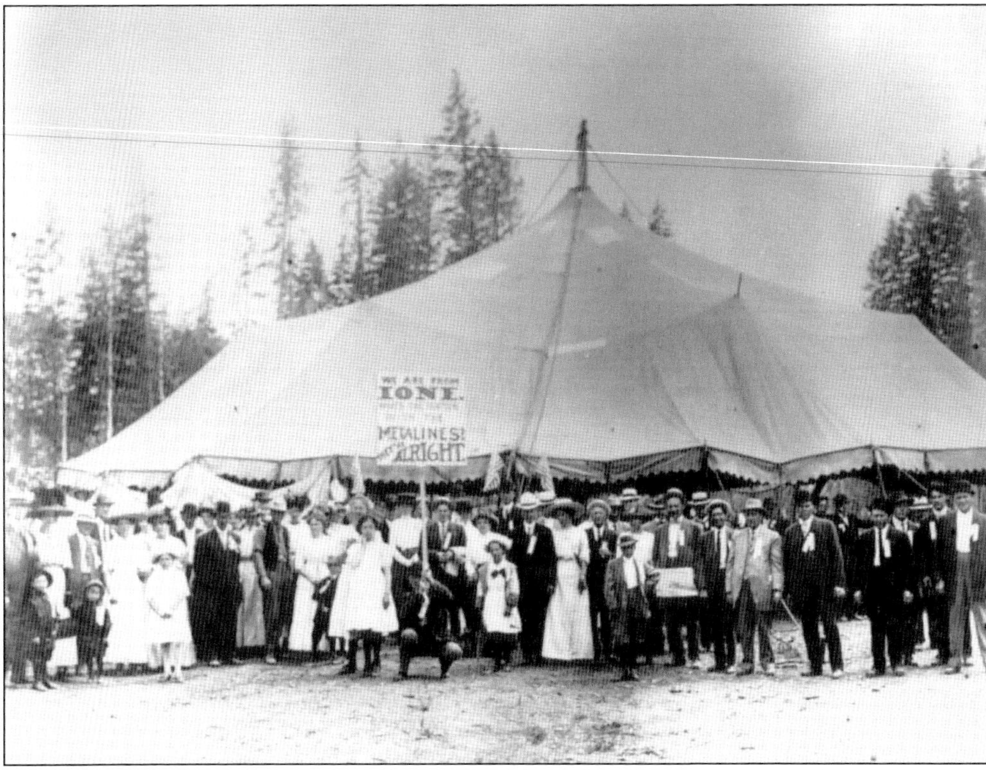

IONE CELEBRATION. Here, Ione residents gather to celebrate a promotion of their area around 1910. Hundreds of homesteaders and settlers welcomed such events, offering the chance to see and take part in races and games and to catch up with world and community news.

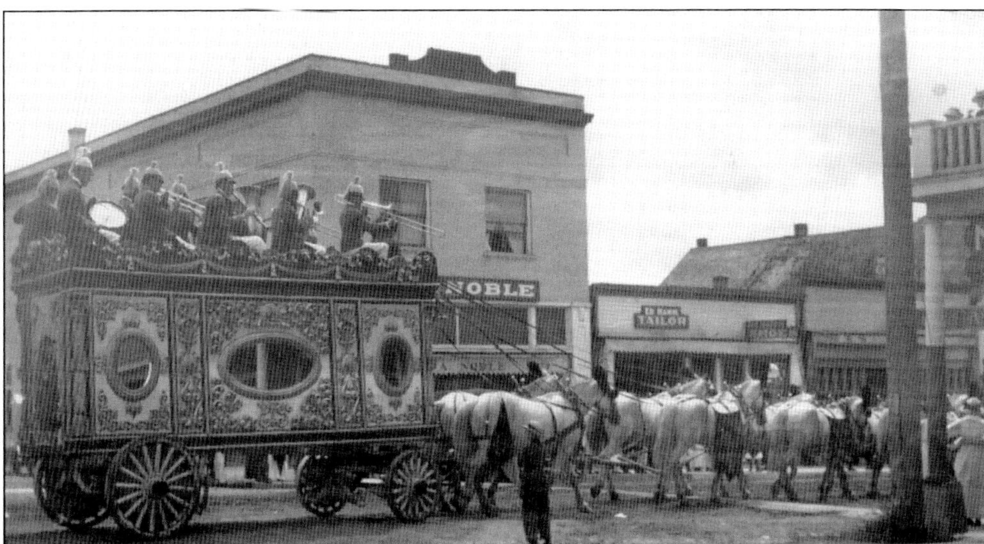

CIRCUS COMES TO NEWPORT. During pioneer days, the arrival of a small circus to Newport was an exciting summer event. For weeks, people looked forward to seeing the animals and enjoying a parade and the circus activities.

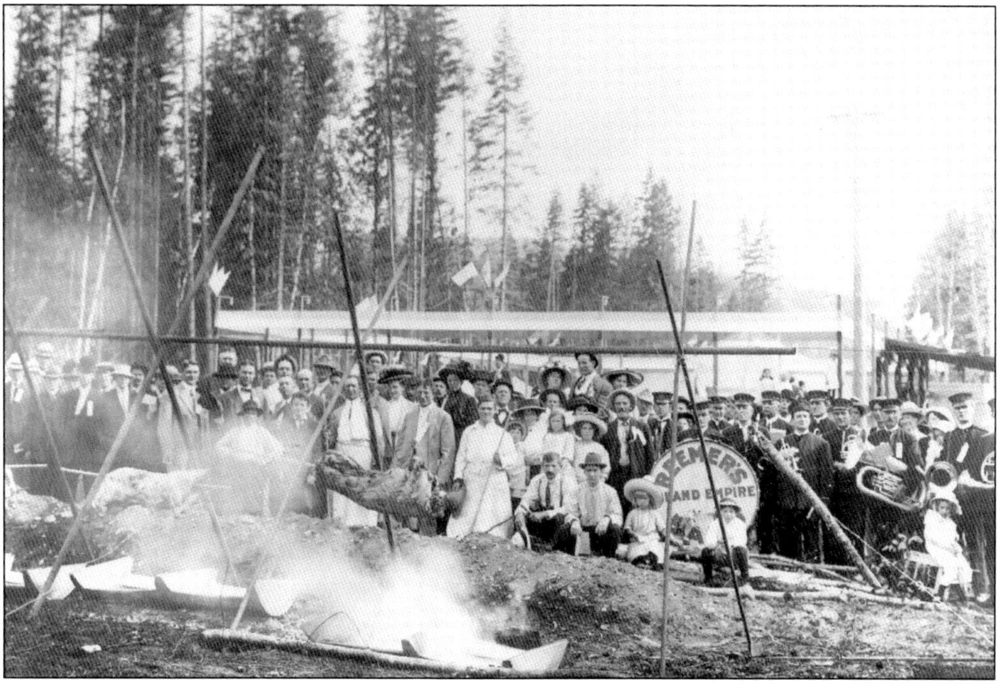

BARBECUE, METALINE FALLS. In 1910, a special bear barbecue was held to celebrate the arrival of the Idaho & Washington Northern Railroad to town. The Prouty brothers were paid $25 for each bear for the event. The large band at right was from Spokane.

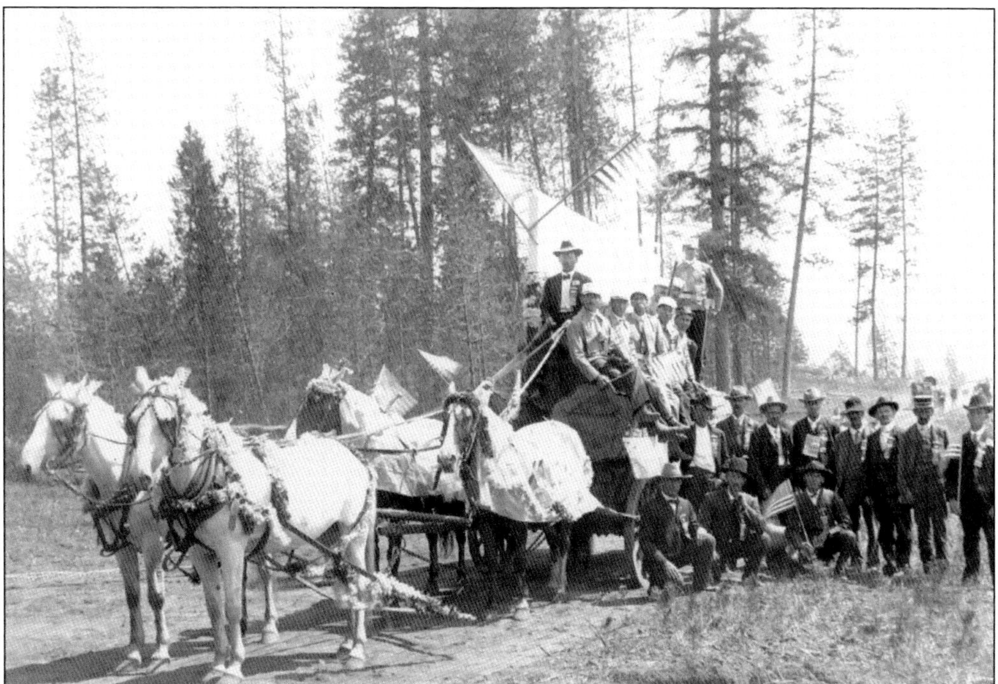

FOURTH OF JULY PARADE, NEWPORT. George Graupner rides on the Fourth of July parade float in Newport. The horses are decorated, and a group of men are ready to march behind the float.

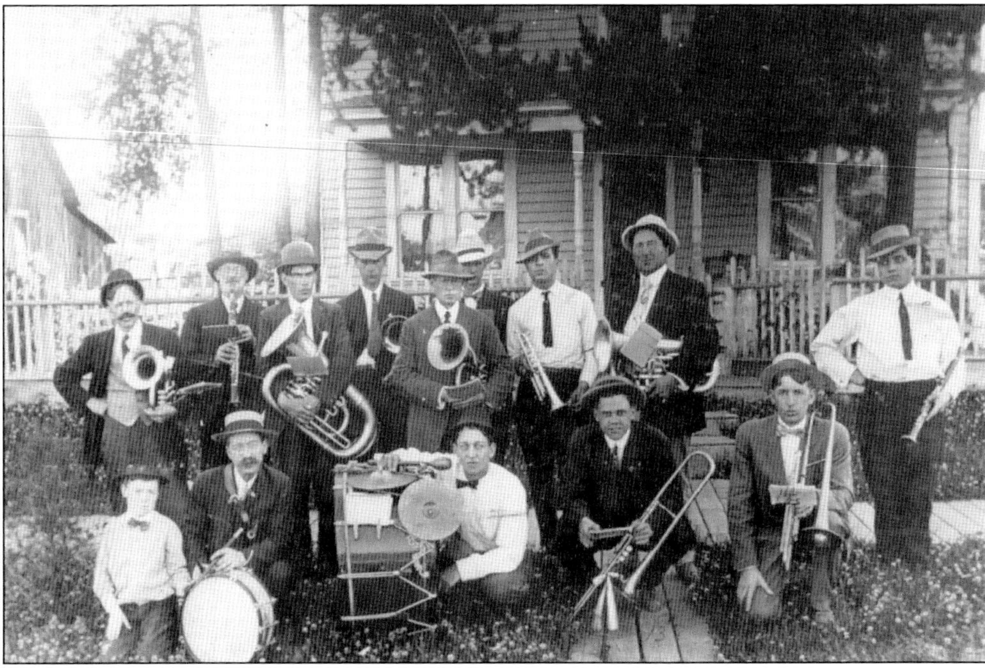

CITY BAND. Almost every community had a band that played for marches and special programs. In pioneer days, anyone who could play a musical instrument added to the social life of communities by playing at dances and parades.

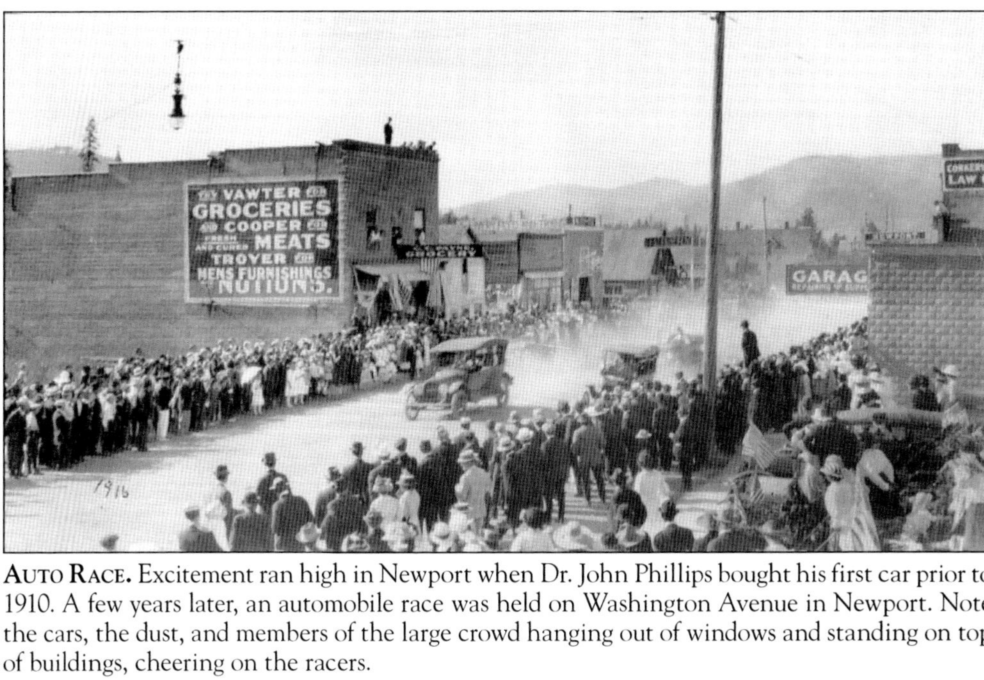

AUTO RACE. Excitement ran high in Newport when Dr. John Phillips bought his first car prior to 1910. A few years later, an automobile race was held on Washington Avenue in Newport. Note the cars, the dust, and members of the large crowd hanging out of windows and standing on top of buildings, cheering on the racers.

About the Organization

The Pend Oreille County Historical Society and Museum started in 1967. In 1978, it obtained the old Milwaukee depot. The Stuart Bradley Building was added in 1994. Dedicated presidents, especially Evelyn Reed, and hundreds of hardworking volunteers have maintained the museum and *The Big Smoke*, an annual publication containing pioneers' stories and history.

The museum has a well-stocked gift shop with books by local authors and hundreds of handcrafted items. Exhibits are displayed upstairs. In the Bradley Building, there are exhibits, an office, and a research department with digital resources for genealogical and research studies. Resources include scrapbooks, photographs, newspapers, and obituary information. Outside, there is a pioneer schoolhouse, church, hunting cabin, lookout fire tower, sawmill, print shop, caboose, and building with all kinds of tools.

The museum is a nonprofit organization, staffed by volunteers and funded by donations and a few small grants.

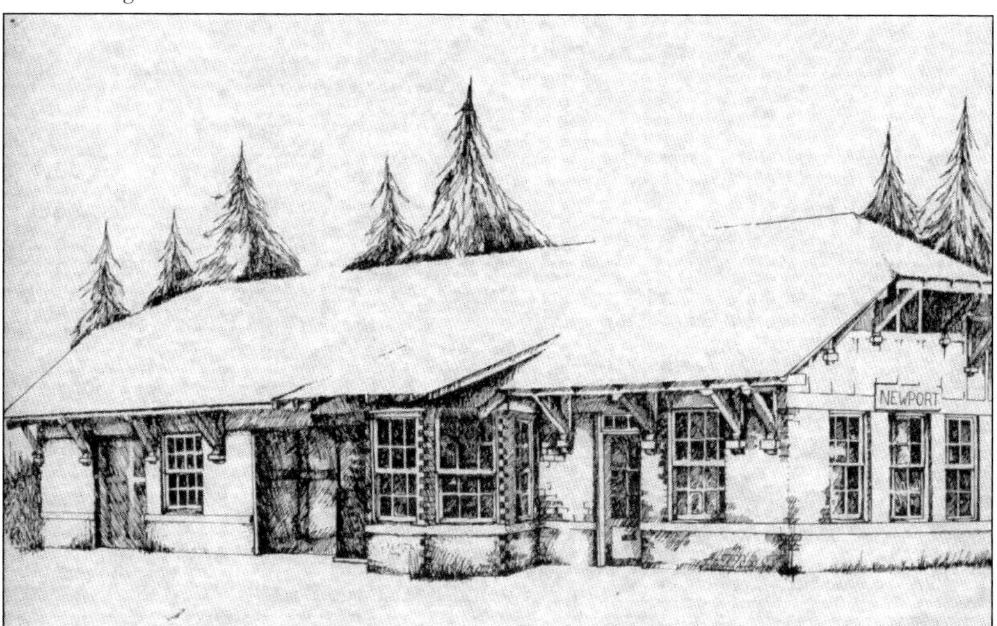